IMAGES
of America

CROSBY

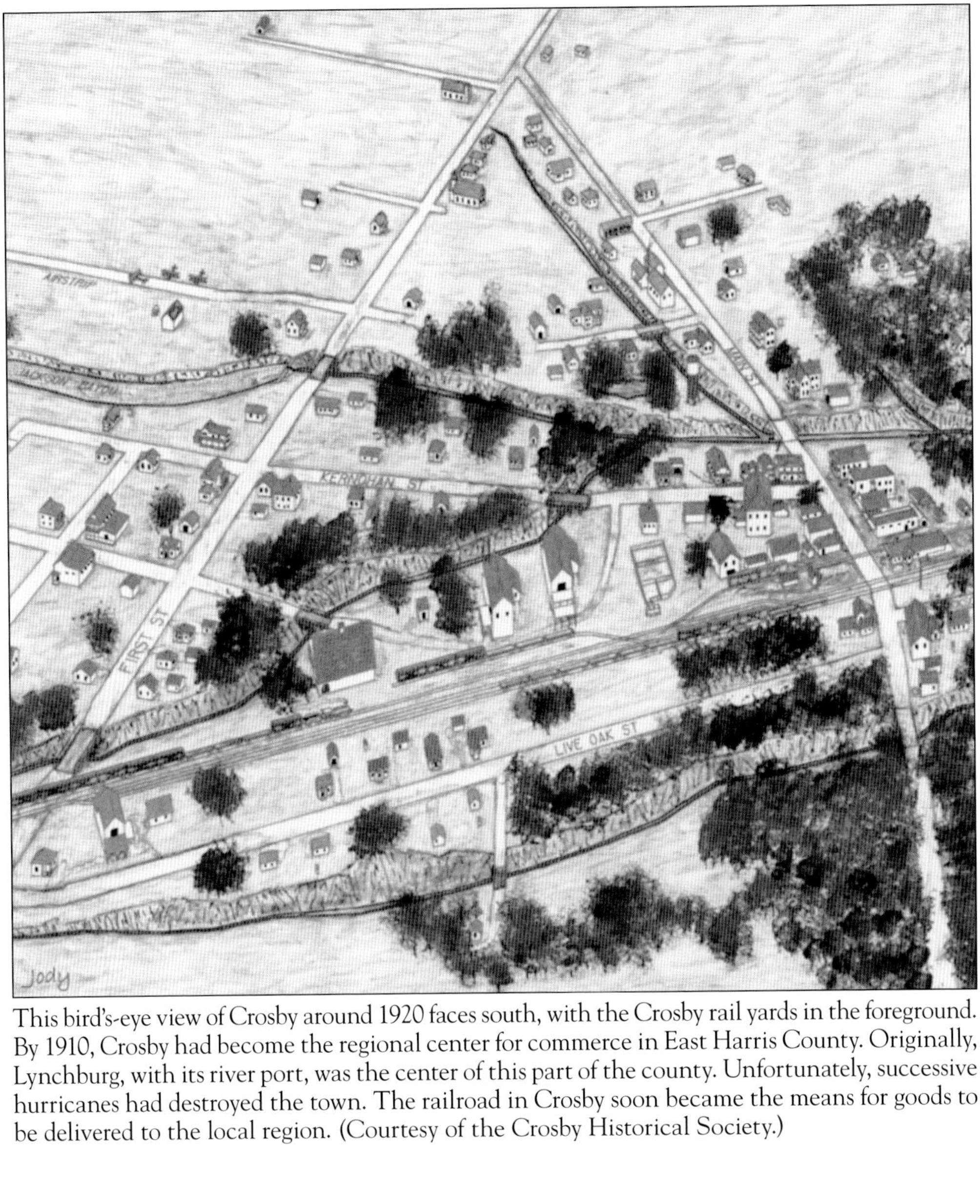

This bird's-eye view of Crosby around 1920 faces south, with the Crosby rail yards in the foreground. By 1910, Crosby had become the regional center for commerce in East Harris County. Originally, Lynchburg, with its river port, was the center of this part of the county. Unfortunately, successive hurricanes had destroyed the town. The railroad in Crosby soon became the means for goods to be delivered to the local region. (Courtesy of the Crosby Historical Society.)

On the Cover: On a busy Saturday in downtown Crosby in 1925, cars line Main Street. Prosperous cotton farmers and early refinery workers flocked to town on Saturday afternoon to shop, visit, take in a movie, or get an ice cream at F.W. Larson & Sons drugstore. Other residents took the one-and-a-half-hour train ride into downtown Houston to spend the day. (Courtesy of Lisa Duncan.)

IMAGES
of America

CROSBY

Jody Fuchs

ARCADIA
PUBLISHING

ISBN 978-1-4671-0617-7

Published by Arcadia Publishing
Charleston, South Carolina

Printed in the United States of America

Library of Congress Control Number: 2020944376

For all general information, please contact Arcadia Publishing:
Telephone 843-853-2070
Fax 843-853-0044
E-mail sales@arcadiapublishing.com
For customer service and orders:
Toll-Free 1-888-313-2665

Visit us on the Internet at www.arcadiapublishing.com

This volume is dedicated to my parents, June and E.G. Fuchs; wife, Debby; daughters Kelsey and Kailey; and all the wonderful people from Crosby who graciously shared their family photos with me and the community as a whole.

Contents

ACKNOWLEDGMENTS

I want to thank my wife, Debby, and my daughters Kelsey and Kailey for their help in researching the material for this book.

I want to especially offer my thanks to Donna Swanson Davenport, Al McAnespy, Klaus Duda, Ron Shanks, Susan Armstrong, and Dee Ann Rook for their incredible help and guidance, along with the many Crosby families that have shared their photographs.

Also, thanks go to the following organizations for sharing photographs from their collections to help shed some light on the history of our community: Chambers County Historical Commission, Chambers County Museum at Wallisville, Crosby Chamber of Commerce, Crosby Historical Society, Dayton Old School House Museum, El Paso Masonic Lodge No. 130, Harris County Historical Commission, Harris County Public Library (Crosby Branch), Highlands Historical Society, Houston Metropolitan Research Center, Museum of the Gulf Coast, Pasadena Historical Museum, Sam Houston Regional Library Research Center, Sampson Masonic Lodge No. 231, San Jacinto Monument Museum of History, and Wharton County Historical Museum.

Unless otherwise noted, all images appear courtesy of the Crosby Historical Society.

INTRODUCTION

The community that we call Crosby today began as an occasional encampment for the Karankawa Indians because of a free-flowing spring near Jackson Bayou and the Old Spanish Trail. The Karankawa were a highly mobile tribe that had a distinctive breed of small dogs. It is thought that the name Karankawa actually means "dog-raisers." They spent their summers along the coastal areas eating seafood and then traveled inland during the winters to hunt for deer and other game. They were reported to be among the tallest of the American Indians, averaging between six and seven feet. The Karankawa tribe was made up of five distinct groups: the Carancahuases, Cocos, Copanes, Cujanes, and the Guapites. Skirmishes between the early settlers and disease killed off the bulk of the tribe by the 1840s, but a small pocket supposedly survived near Banana Bend into the 1890s and occasionally traded with the early Crosby residents. The Karankawa Indians are thought to have lived in the coastal area between Galveston and Corpus Christi for at least 400 years before the first Anglo settlers arrived in 1823.

In 1823, Humphrey Jackson and his family purchased 4,605 acres from the Mexican government as part of Stephen F. Austin's original "Old Three Hundred" group of settlers in Austin's colony. These were the first land grants issued in Texas, making Crosby one of the oldest Anglo settlements in Texas. Humphrey was originally from a wealthy family in Ballybay, Ireland, where he had been studying to be a lawyer. A bloody rebellion led to a complete takeover of the Irish parliament by Great Britain in 1801. The Jackson family ended up on the losing side of the conflict, and he and several relatives fled to the United States to avoid the retribution that followed. He eventually ended up owning a cotton plantation in St. Martin Parish, Louisiana, after arriving there in 1808. After the death of his first wife, he married Sarah Meriman in 1814. The couple had four children between 1815 and 1822 (Leticia, Hugh, John, and James).

In September 1823, the Jackson family built a log cabin on their property near the mouth of the Jackson Bayou, where it joins the San Jacinto River. Unfortunately, Sarah died the following year. She is thought to be the first death of the new colonists, and her grave marker is considered to be the oldest gravestone in Harris County. It has been relocated by the Jackson family to the Chambers County Museum in Wallisville, Texas. Humphrey and his children remained on their land and continued to struggle to advance their settlement. He is thought to have later entered into a common-law marriage with the sister of the owner of the neighboring land grant, Mary Wilson. The Mexican government required that all marriages be performed by a Catholic priest, but there were not any priests anywhere in the colony. In 1833, Humphrey was killed by a tree he was cutting down when it fell on him. He was buried beside Sarah in what is today the original townsite of Crosby.

Mary Wilson died in October of the following year, presumably from malaria. She had moved, along with her brother and his family, to what is today Deer Park.

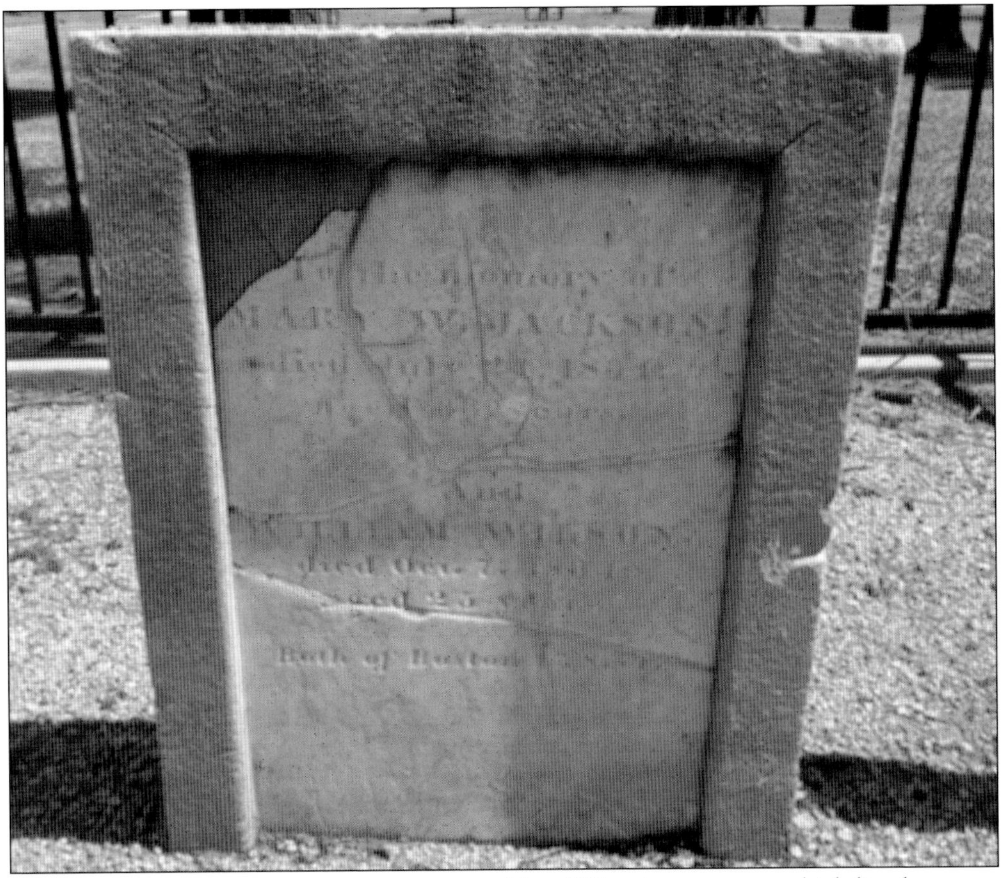

To the memory of
MARY W. JACKSON
died July 24, 1834
aged 33 years
And
WILLIAM WILSON
died Oct 7, 1834
aged 25 years
Both of Boston U.S.A.

Mary Wilson's gravestone, which lists her as Mary W. Jackson, is considered to be the second oldest gravestone in Harris County. Pictured above is the headstone, which lists both her and her brother William. It was originally located where the Shell refinery is today in Pasadena and was relocated to Deer Park. The gravestone is faded, but the inscription is seen at left

One

Early Pioneers and Infrastructure

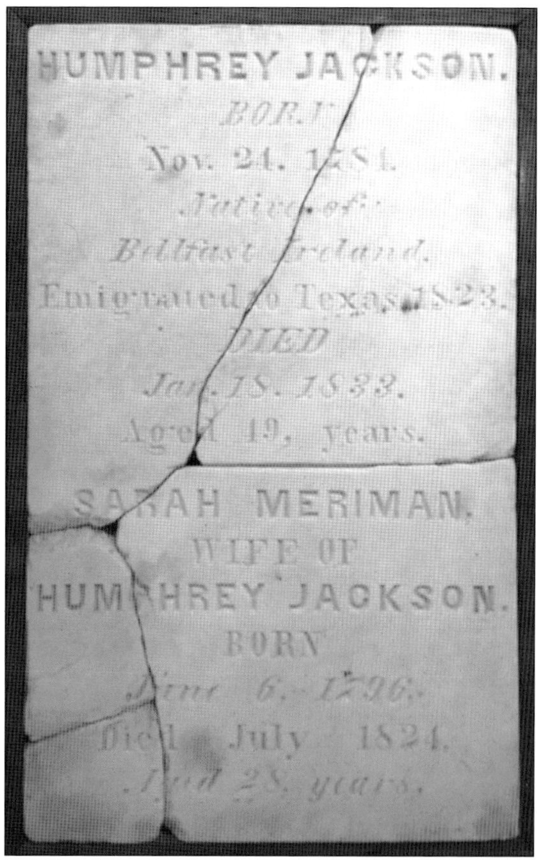

Pictured here is the original tombstone of Humphrey and Sarah Jackson. It sat on a brick base in the Crosby townsite for over 100 years. It is assumed that the Jackson family had relocated their home to a spot nearby. Their original homesite was near the mouth of Jackson Bayou, but it was flood-prone. The Jackson family is credited with establishing the location for the town of Crosby.

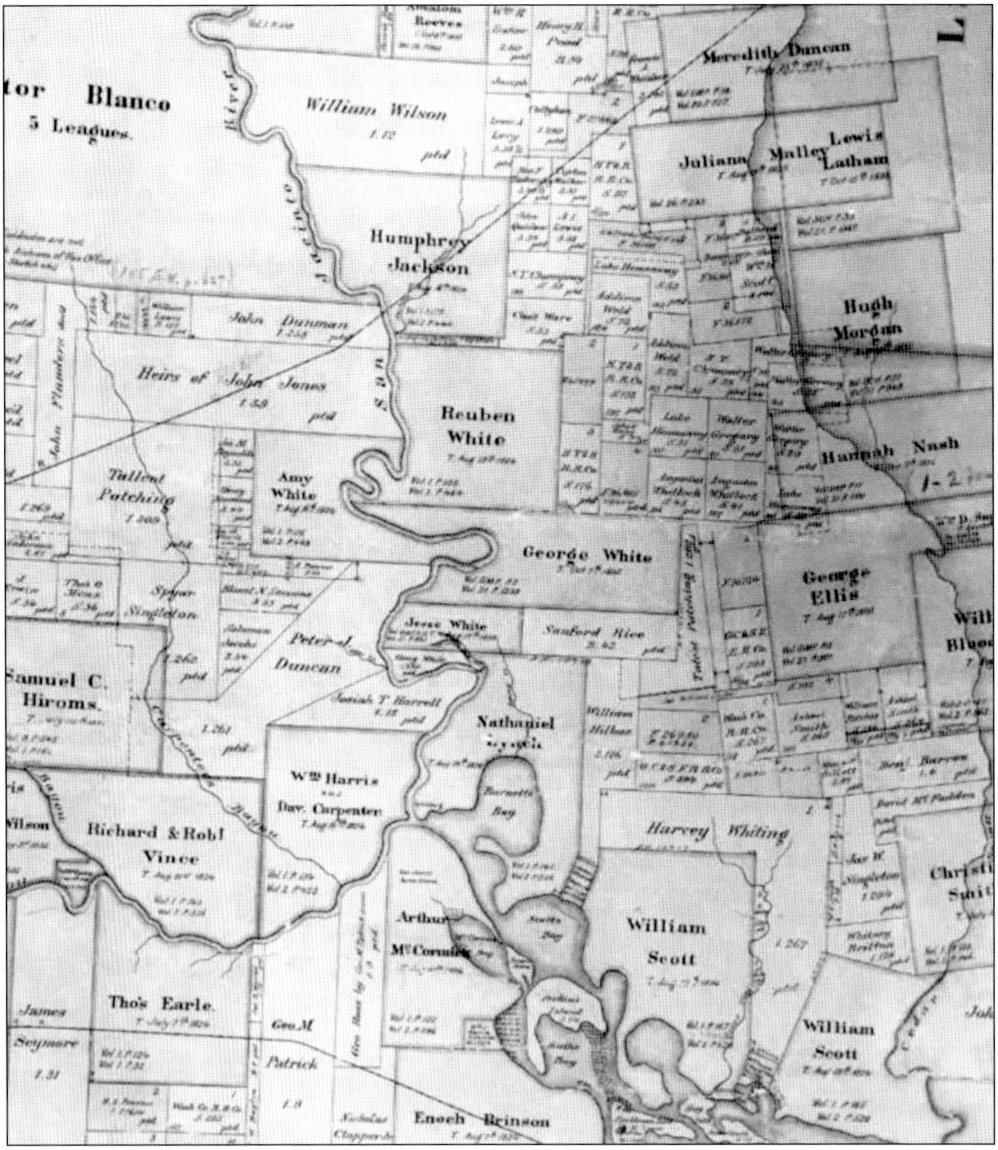

This 1886 survey map of eastern Harris County shows Humphrey Jackson's claim. It includes what would be the Crosby townsite in its far northeastern corner. It also shows his son-in-law Meredith Duncan's claim. Meredith had married Leticia Jackson in 1832. Humphrey died the following year. Texas won its independence from Mexico in 1836, three years after Humphrey died. The Jackson sons went to live with Leticia, and these events hampered Crosby's early growth. On May 7, 1857, the Jackson children completed the sale of their parents' property. By then, they had already relocated to Chambers County. Nevertheless, Crosby was located along the Old Spanish Trail that ran from the East Coast of the United States to the West Coast. It came right down FM 2100 (Main Street) and then turned up Crosby Dayton Road. The intersection of it and the railroad would eventually establish the town. (Courtesy of the Crosby Public Library.)

Pictured here is Humphrey's youngest child, James Merriman Jackson. He was the chief justice, county judge, sheriff, and notary public for Chambers County. He also worked as a doctor, dentist, druggist, scribe, commissioner, surveyor, assessor, postmaster, banker, and cotton ginner in Double Bayou. James Jackson also had amassed a 26,000-acre ranch, where he ran cattle. (Courtesy of the Jackson family.)

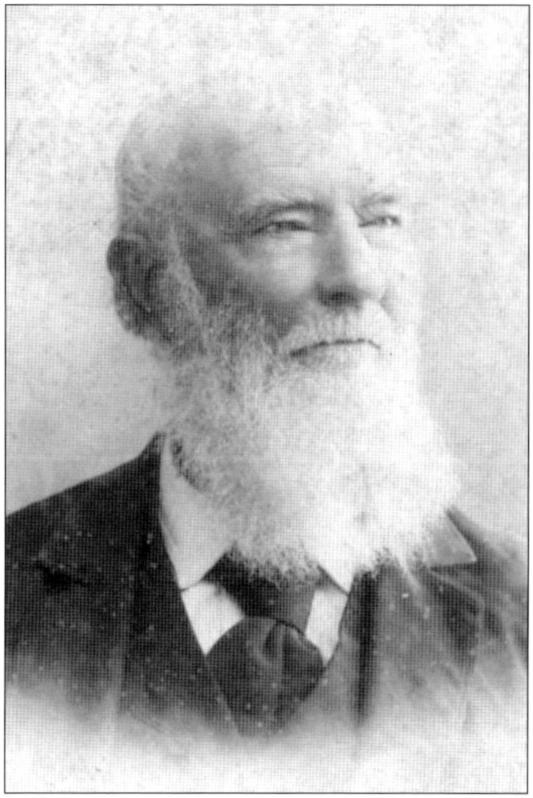

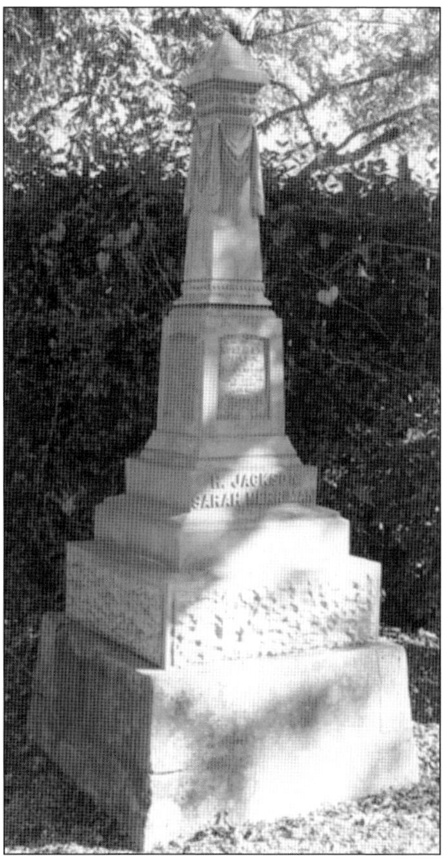

James Jackson purchased the $134 white zinc monument pictured here made by the Monumental Bronze Works Company in Bridgeport, Connecticut, in 1882. It was placed next to his parents' marble gravestone. It is fortunate that he left behind such an impressive monument for his parents because it tells the story of the early family and marks the location of their burial in the confines of the Crosby townsite.

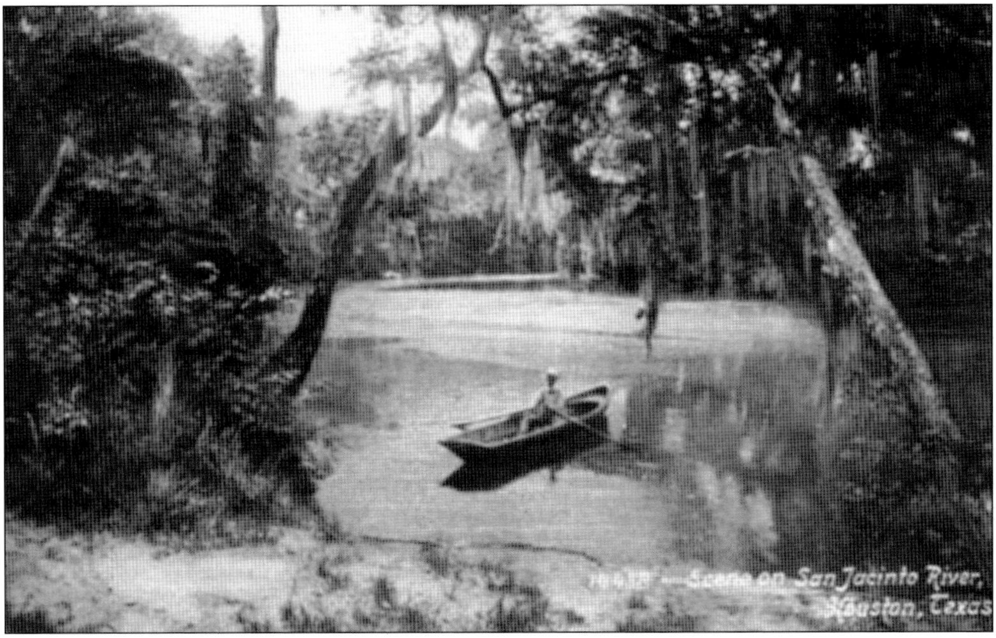

One of Humphrey Jackson's noted accomplishments was the scouting and recommended location for a ferry to cross the San Jacinto River in the Crosby area. One of the early names for Crosby is thought to be Jackson's Crossing. Pictured below is what is thought to be a pre-1908 ferry photograph. David Penn was the ferry operator. He was hired by Harris County to operate the ferry. In 1908, a bridge was constructed that replaced the ferry. It was next to the present-day bridge on Old Highway 90. Above is an early postcard near that crossing. (Both, courtesy of the Penn family.)

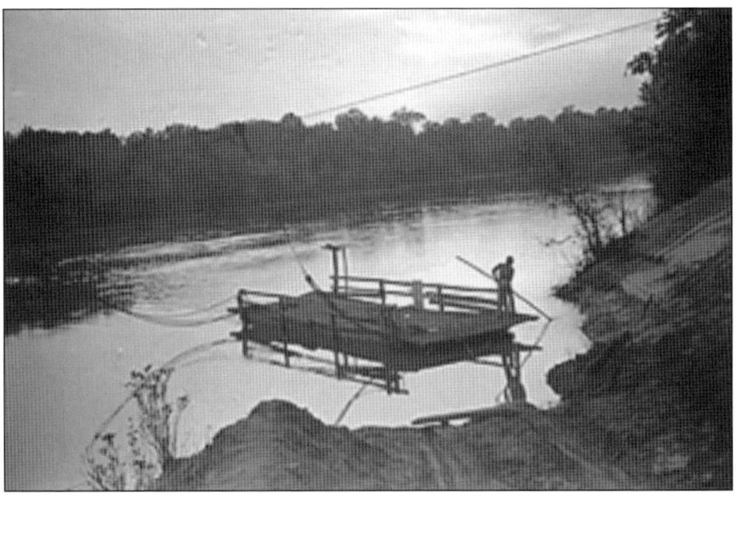

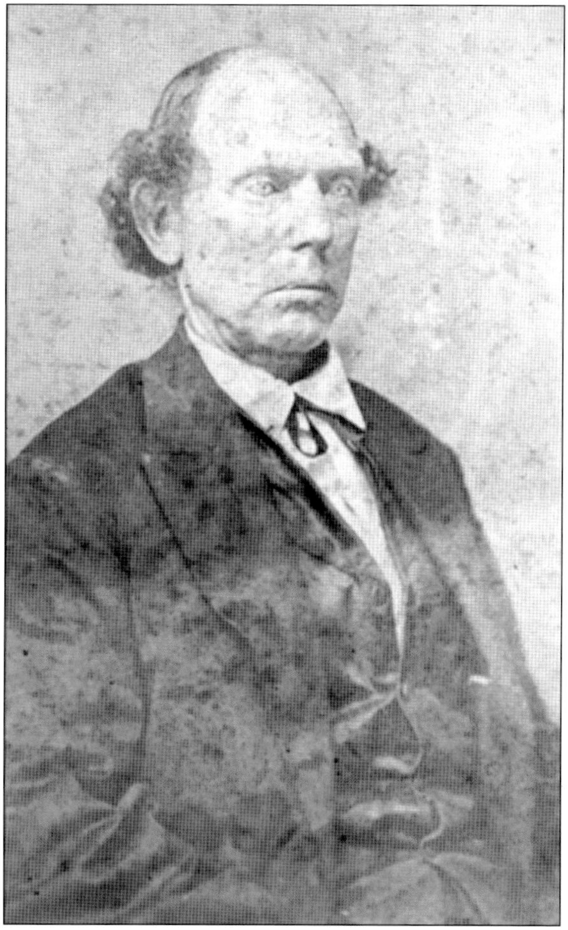

The Jackson family sold portions of their parents' land grant to investors during the 1840s and 1850s. These investors included the mayors of both Houston and Galveston. In 1851, John Milburn Simms (right) acquired 1,426 acres of the Humphrey Jackson grant for $500. The Simms family built a cotton plantation where the present-day Crosby High School is. He was soon followed by Mercer McKinney, who built the home pictured below. The McKinneys bought 566 acres next door. In 1857, construction began on a rail line from Houston to New Orleans, which passed through the Simms property. In 1860, the community acquired the name Gentry, having been named after the owner of the railroad. The rail line was mostly completed in 1862, just a few months prior to the start of the Civil War. (Both, courtesy of the McKinney family.)

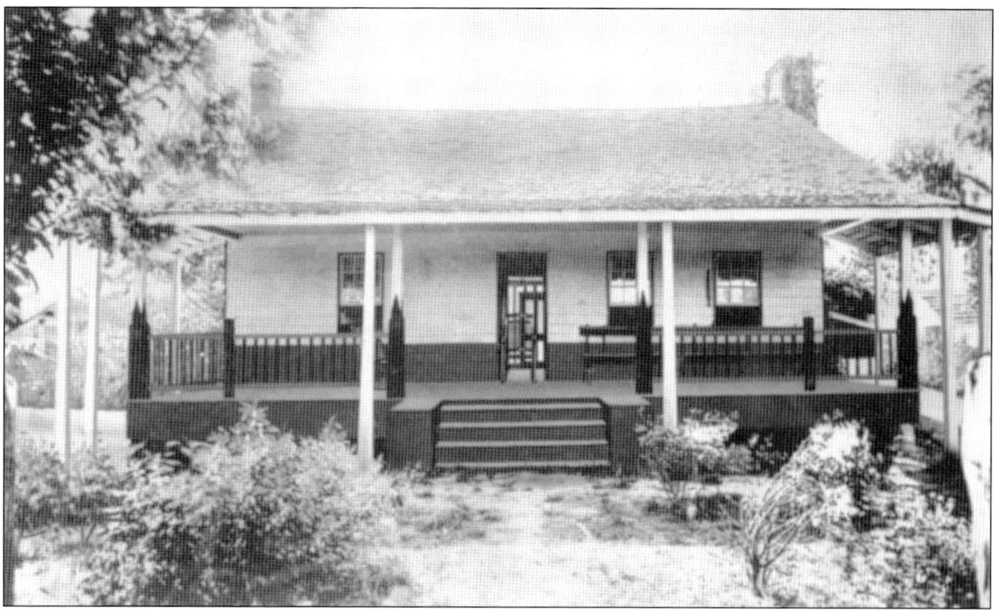

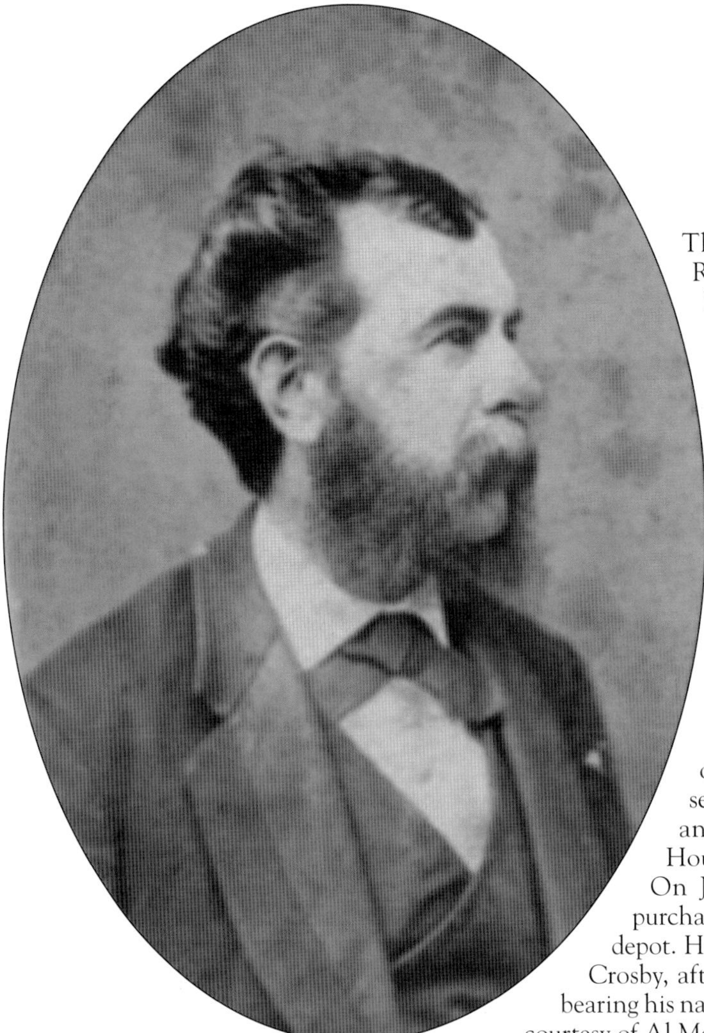

The Texas & New Orleans Railroad was a vital supply link for the South. It was used to transport soldiers and materials throughout the Civil War, but it was in terrible shape by the war's end. It was mostly abandoned until 1876, when a new company purchased the railroad. Josiah F. Crosby (left) was named vice president and took charge of local operations. Crosby was a Houston attorney before moving to El Paso due to a lung disease. He spent much of his life there, where he served as a state representative and a judge. He returned to Houston to run the railway. On January 15, 1877, Crosby purchased the land to construct a depot. He named the new train stop Crosby, after himself. A train engine bearing his name is pictured below. (Both, courtesy of Al McAnespy.)

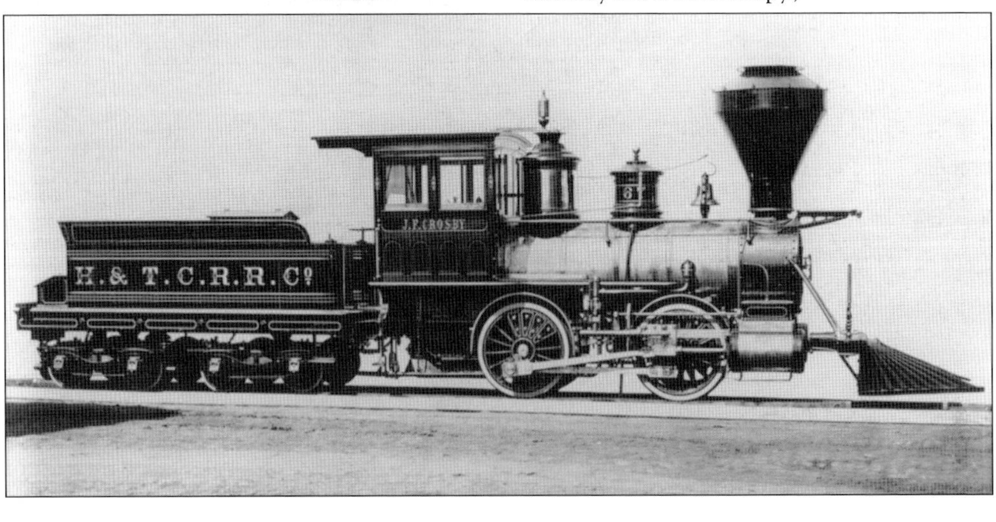

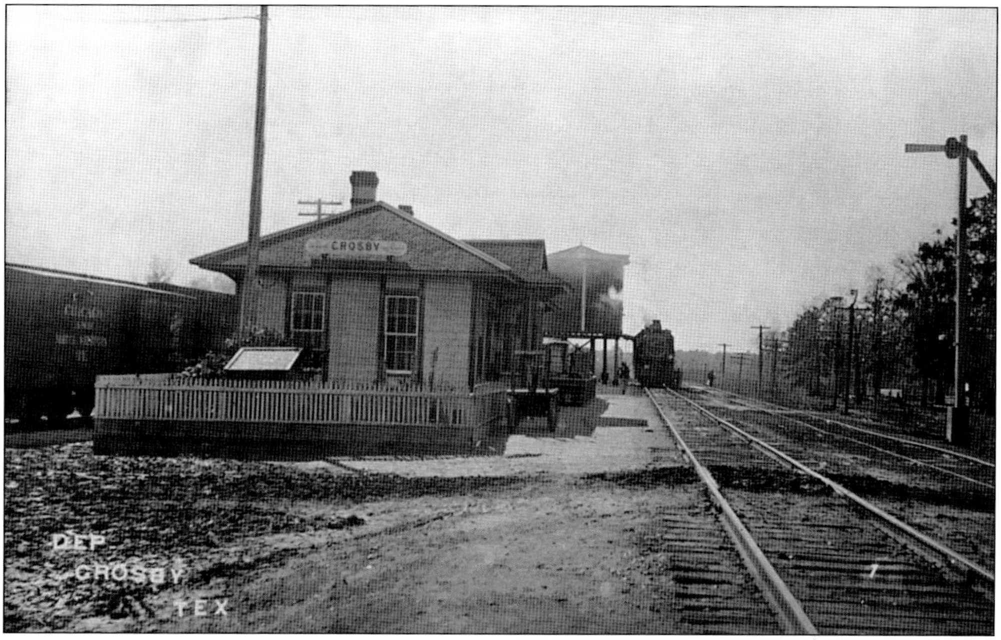

A large rock marked the train stop location before 1892. In 1895, the Crosby railroad depot was built. It was on the south side of the tracks at their intersection with Main Street. The railroad water tower is visible in the background filling the steam boiler on the train's engine. This 1910 photograph looks west. (Courtesy of Lisa Duncan.)

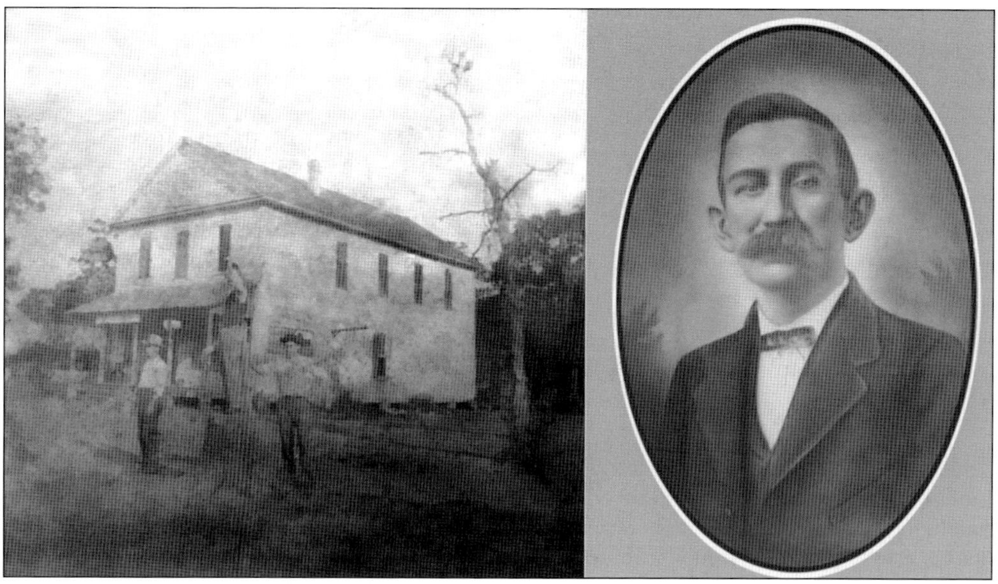

The first commercial building in Crosby was erected in 1865 by Charles P. Karcher. It was located north of the tracks and across from the eventual depot. The town grew from this location once the railroad went back into operation. The store was later sold to R.E. "Heinan" Dunks (pictured) and his older brother Jeff Dunks. Also pictured is the Dunks store around 1906. (Courtesy of Klaus Duda.)

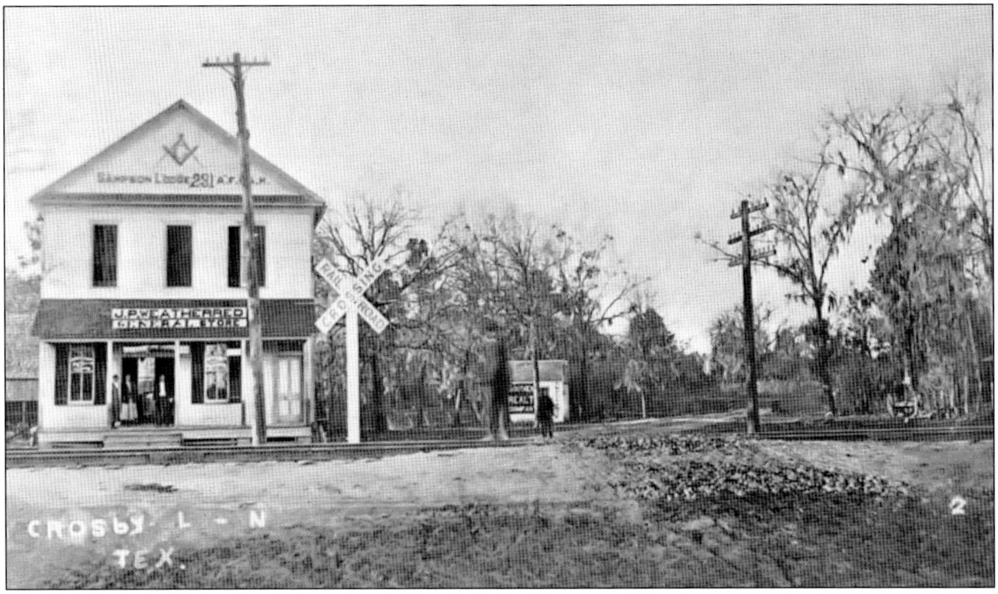

The Dunks general store building was destroyed in the fall of 1900 by a hurricane, and this new store was built in the same location in early 1901. Pictured above is a view looking north along what is today FM 2100 in 1910. At that time, the downstairs was being leased by J.P. Weatherred. Below is the Dunks general store interior in 1918, with R.E. "Heinan" Dunks and his nephew Archa Dale Smith. In 1900, R.E. was elected Harris County commissioner, which he served as until 1906. He then ran for Harris County treasurer but lost by a small margin. (Both, courtesy of the Barrett family.)

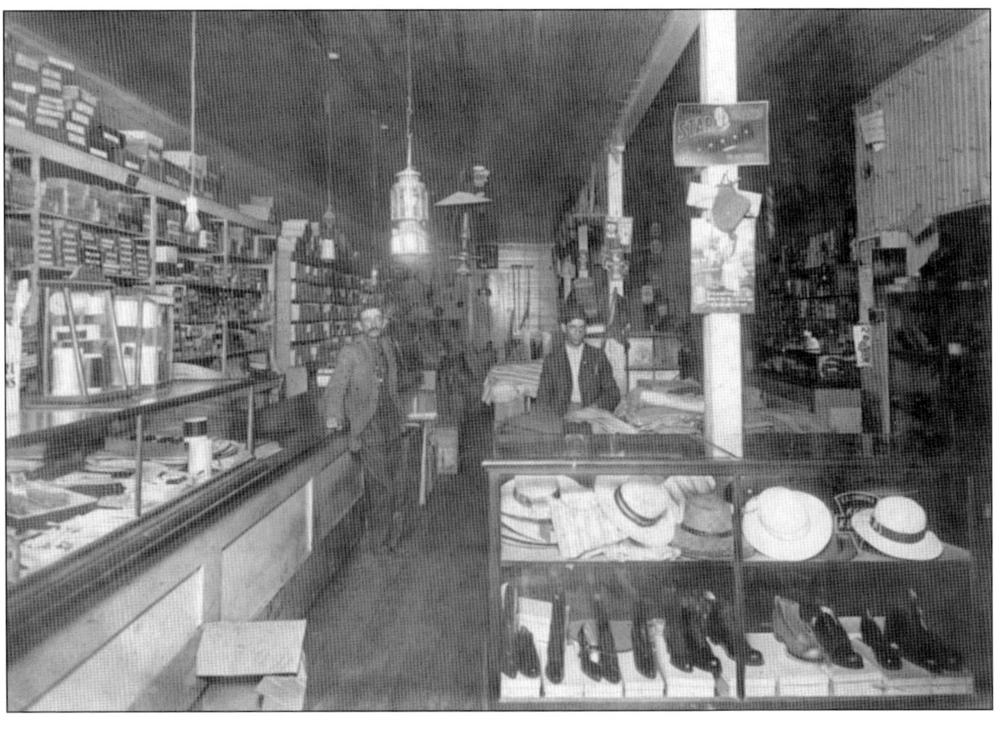

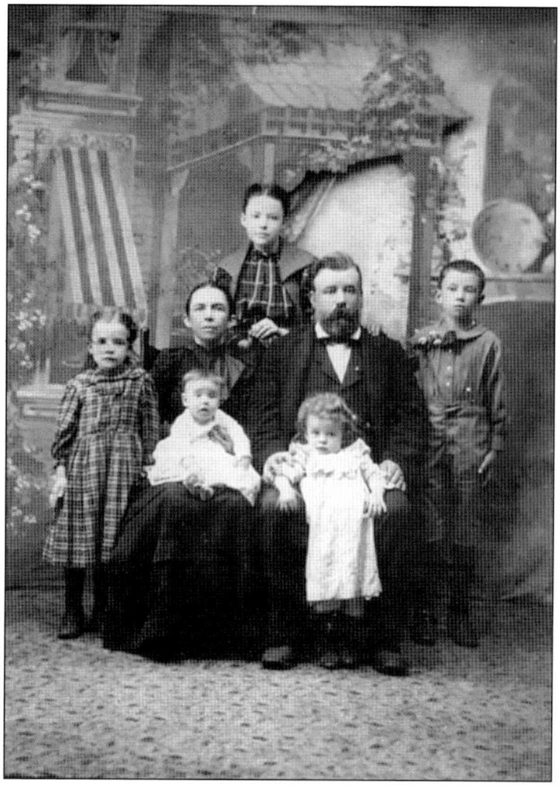

The population of Crosby began to surge after 1876, with cheap, fertile land available at the intersection of the Old Spanish Trail and a major rail line. The first doctor arrived in 1895. Dr. W.R. Hollingsworth and his family are pictured here. He was an employee of the railroad. (Courtesy of the Keller family.)

Two groups dominated the early settlers. Swedish families relocated from up north and arrived mostly by train. Czech families relocated mostly from Fayette County, and many of them came by wagon. Pictured here is Fredrick W. "Fritz" Jaeger on a horse with the Crosby prairie in the background.

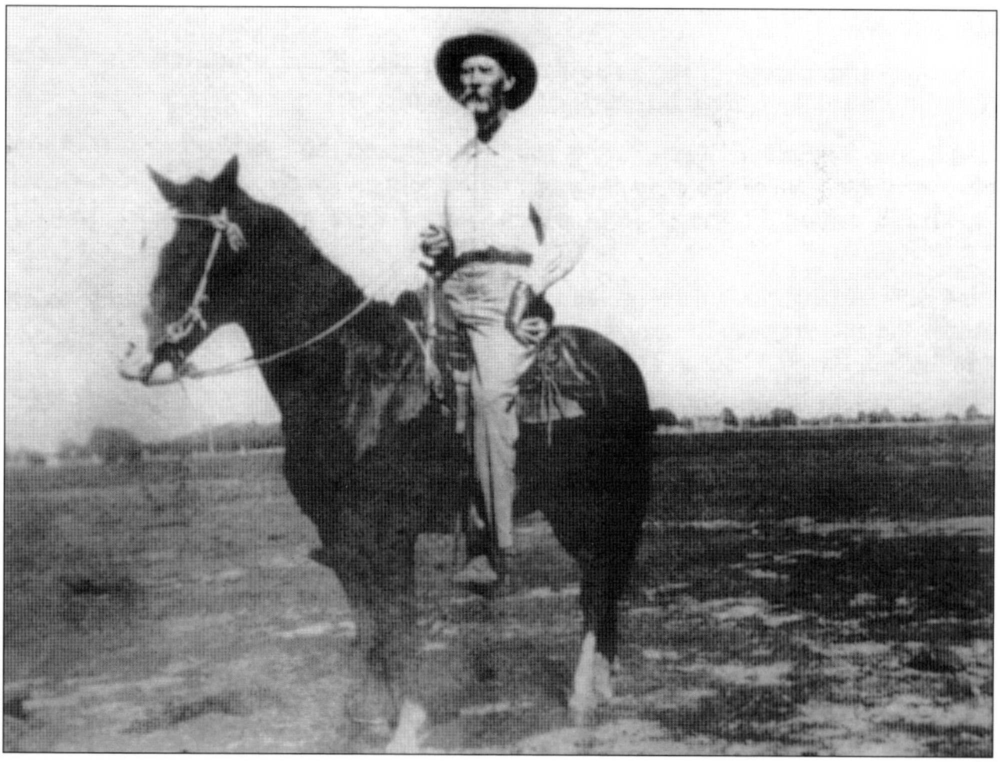

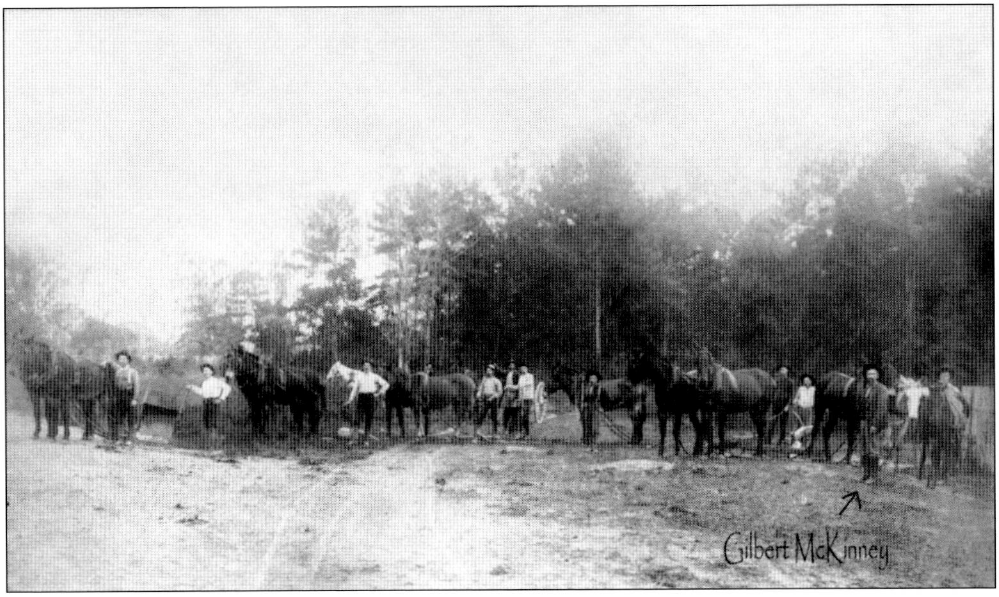

The town was platted by the railroad in 1903, but the first actual road was built in 1890. Today, that road is FM 2100, pictured above. Essentially, it was a raised section of dirt with a ditch carved out on both sides. Around 1903, oyster-shell toppings were added to some of the roads. Below, workers Joseph Clawson, George Ethington, and Jim Ewell are spreading oyster shells on FM 2100 (Main Street), near the railroad tracks around 1906. In the background, the R.E. Dunks general store and the railroad depot are visible. (Above, courtesy of Billy McKinney; below, courtesy of Cathy Harbour.)

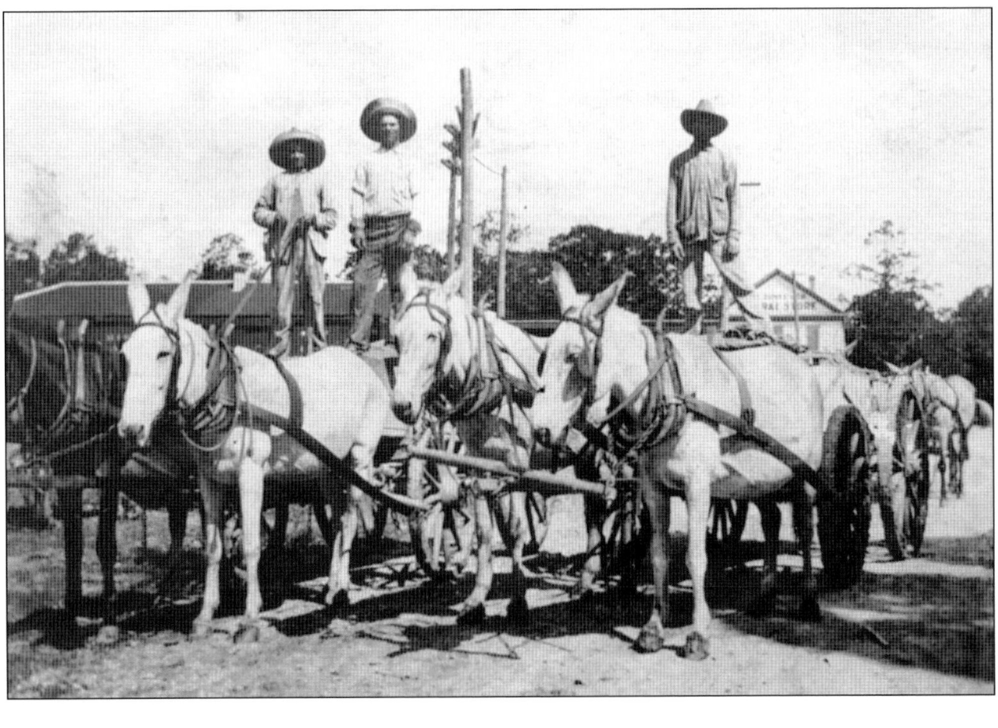

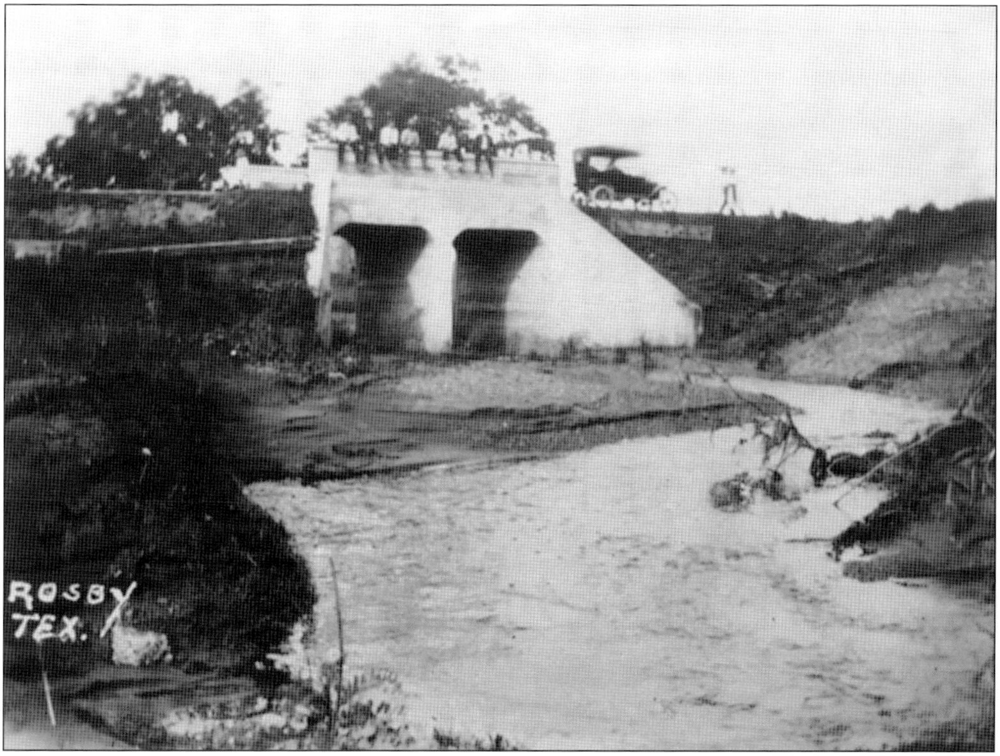

These c. 1912 photographs show a new prototype concrete bridge built over Jackson Bayou on Main Street just south of the railroad tracks. It was built by Crosby resident and Harris County commissioner John T. Hare. Below is a view of the bridge looking south along Main Street with the Gustafson Cotton Gin behind the buggy driven by Foster Curtiss. (Above, courtesy of the Swanson family; below, courtesy of the Trousdale family.)

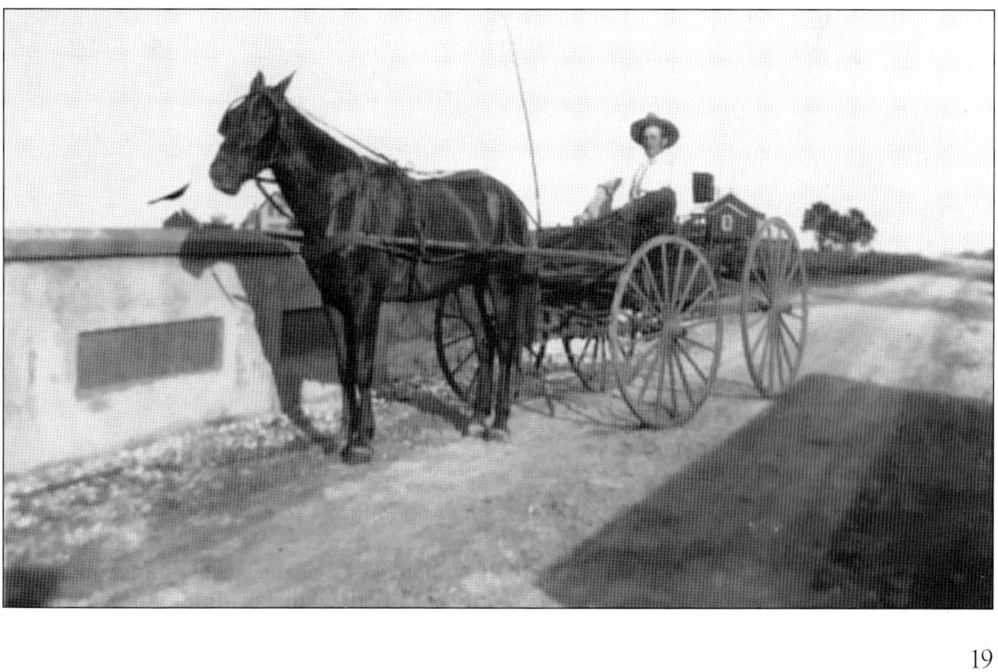

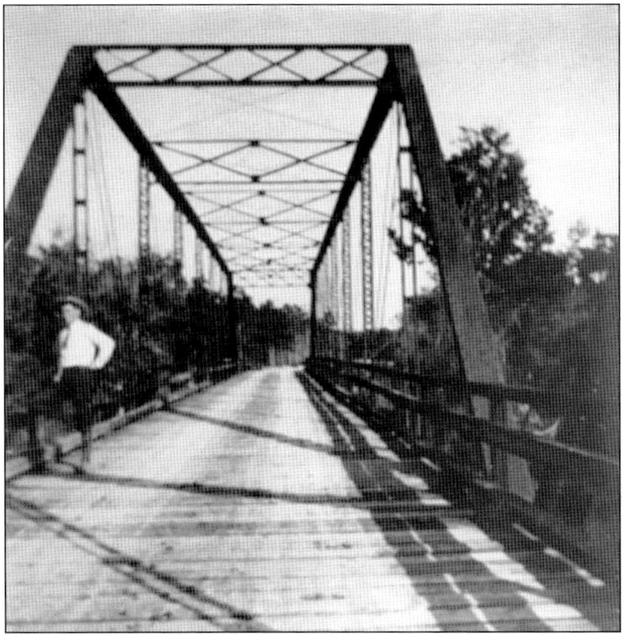

This bridge over the San Jacinto River was built in 1907–1909. Prior to its construction, travelers had to take a hand-drawn ferry at the same location to cross. Like the coming of the railroad, the bridge changed everything, making Houston a short drive away. These are some early views of the completed structure. This would later become US Highway 90. Pictured below is Alice Anderson standing on the San Jacinto River bridge around 1916. The bridge cost $22,000 in 1907. It was finally replaced in 1976 with a modern concrete bridge that still stands today. (Both, courtesy of the Anderson family.)

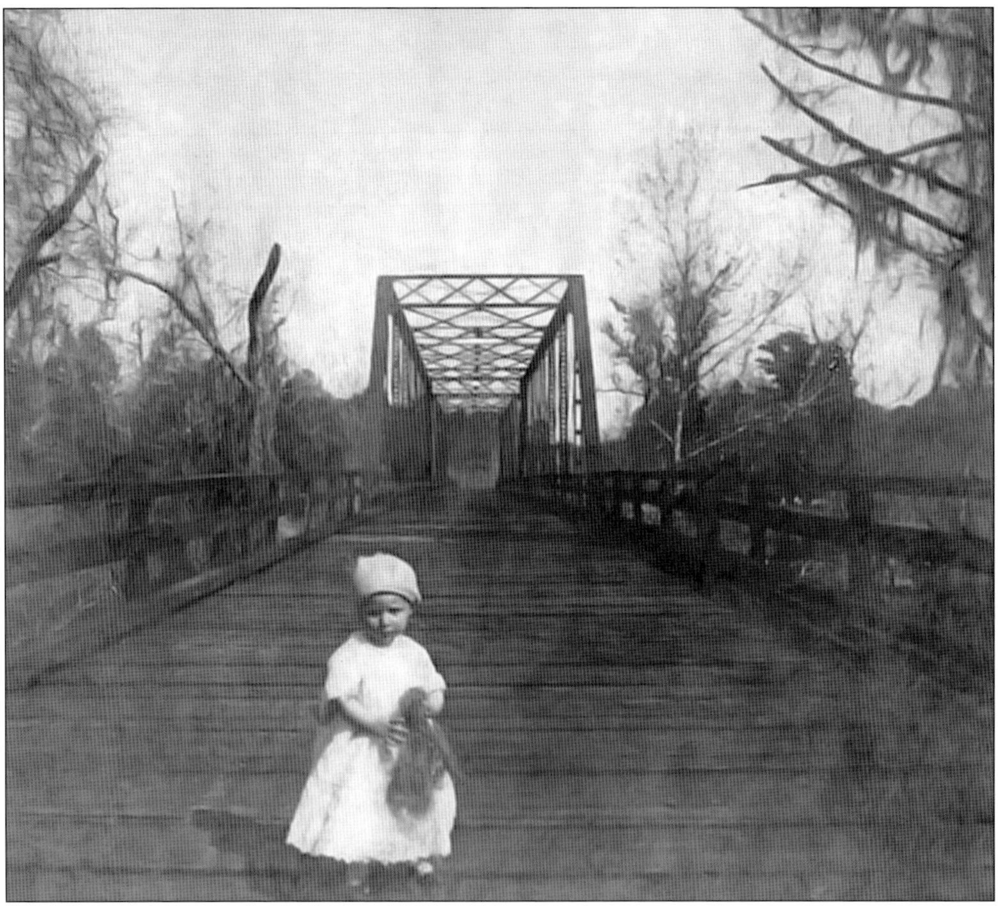

Two

EARLY BUSINESSES

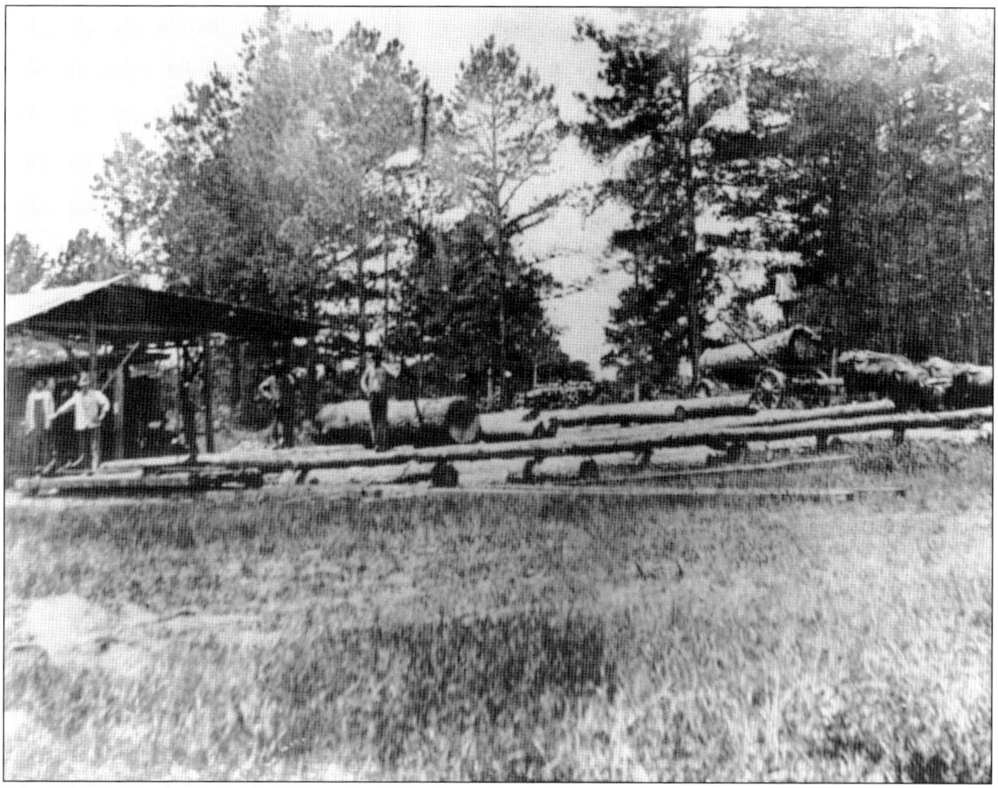

This photograph was taken in 1908 of Leonard Lord's sawmill with his brother's oxen at right. The sawmill was near Cedar Bayou on the Crosby-Baytown Road at the time of this photograph. The Lord brothers moved the sawmill from time to time to place it near the trees they were harvesting. (Courtesy of the Lord family.)

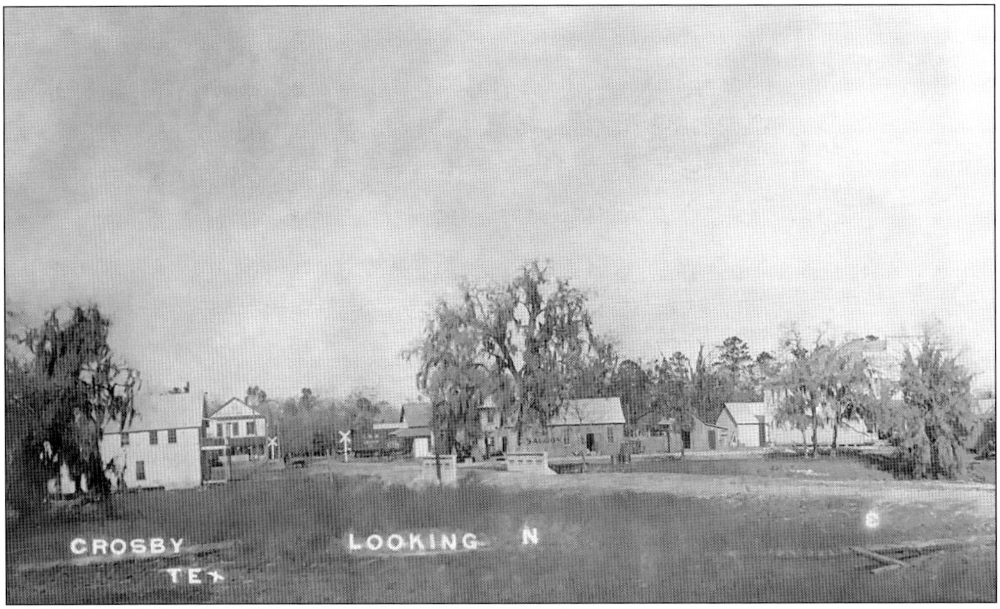

Pictured above is downtown Crosby in 1910, looking north toward the railroad tracks. Main Street (FM 2100) is seen in the foreground. Below is the Texas Mercantile Company, which was owned by William M. Truxaw. It was Crosby's fourth general store, and it was on Kernohan Street. It sold groceries, farm implements, lumber, grain, hay, and everything residents would need, from cornmeal to caskets. The post office was moved to this location in 1915, and Truxaw served as the postmaster. The store was sold to the owners of the Crosby Mercantile Company around 1930. (Both, courtesy of Lisa Duncan.)

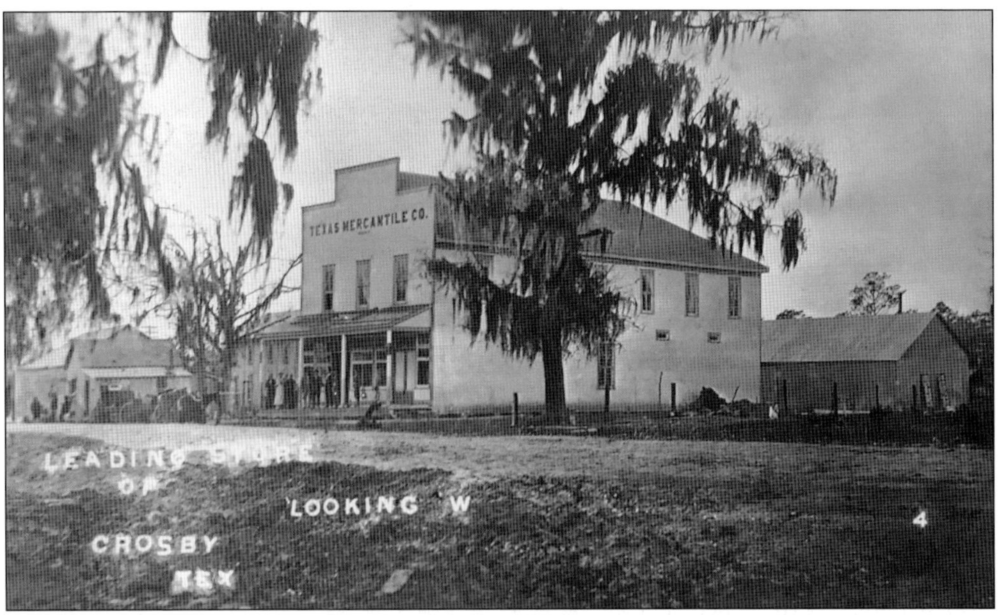

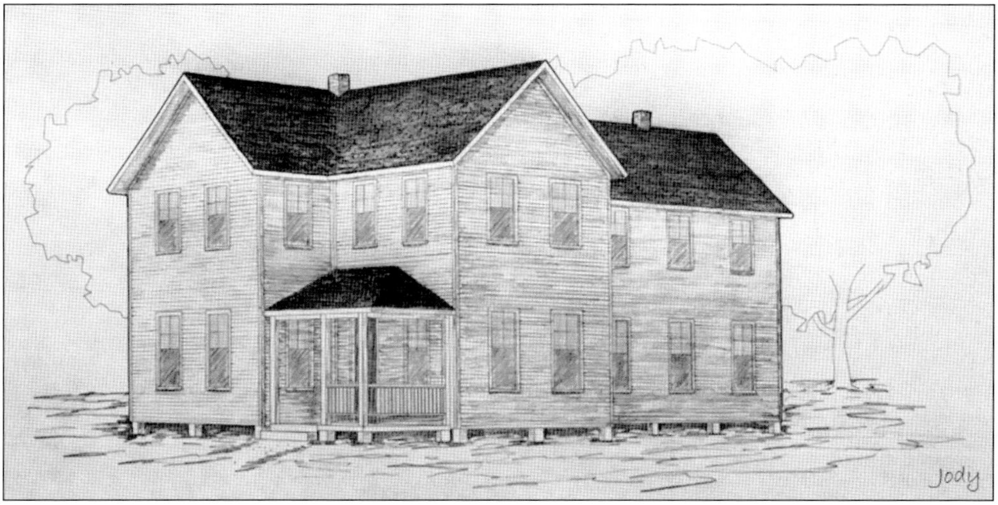

Pictured here is the Lynch Hotel & Boarding House. It was built in 1906 on the west side of Main Street near the corner of what is now Fourth Street. The boardinghouse was owned by William Lynch, who also ran a livery stable where he rented out horses and buggies to visitors to Crosby as well as picking people up from the depot and taking them wherever they wanted to go. Often, these were salesmen or prospective land buyers. Usually, they would need to stay overnight in his boardinghouse in order to catch the train the next day. (Author drawing.)

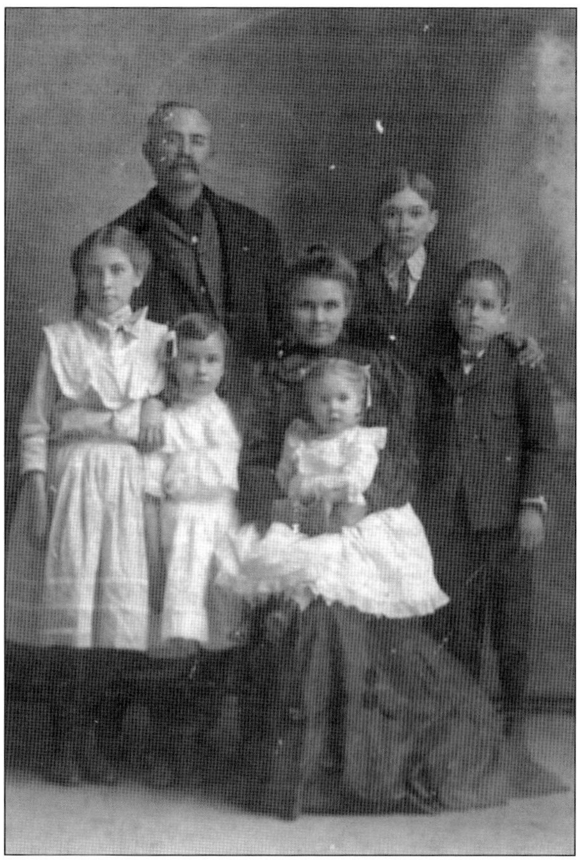

William Lynch and his family are pictured here. Rachel Lynch was the daughter of Adam Huffman. The town of Huffman was founded by Adam and his brother Josiah around 1840. (Courtesy of the Lynch family.)

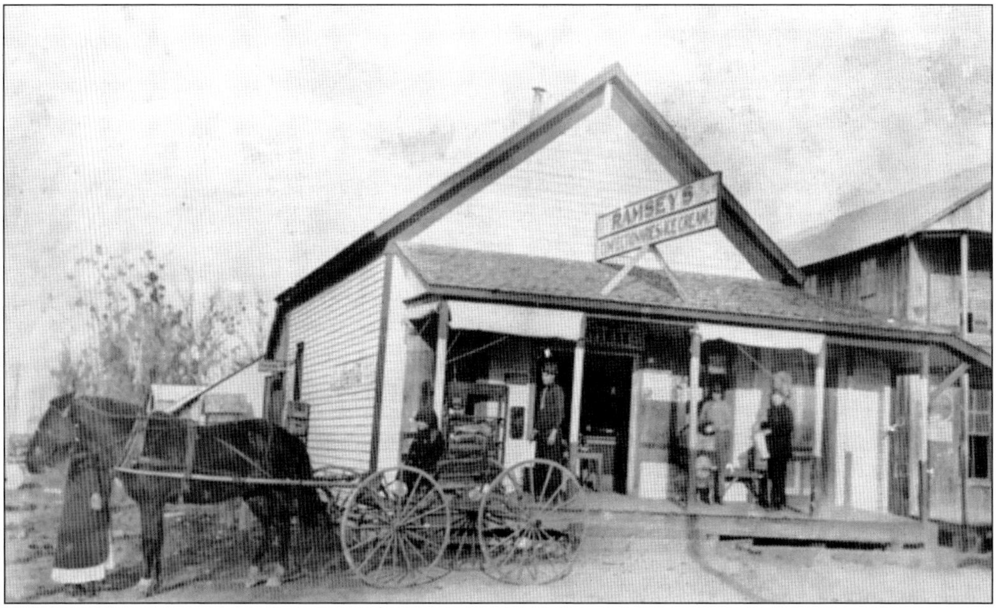

Ramsey's confectionery was on the east side of Main Street next to the railroad tracks. It was built in 1904 and owned by Charles Edward Ramsey. In 1914, he relocated his business across the street next to the train depot and changed the name to Ramsey's Drugs.

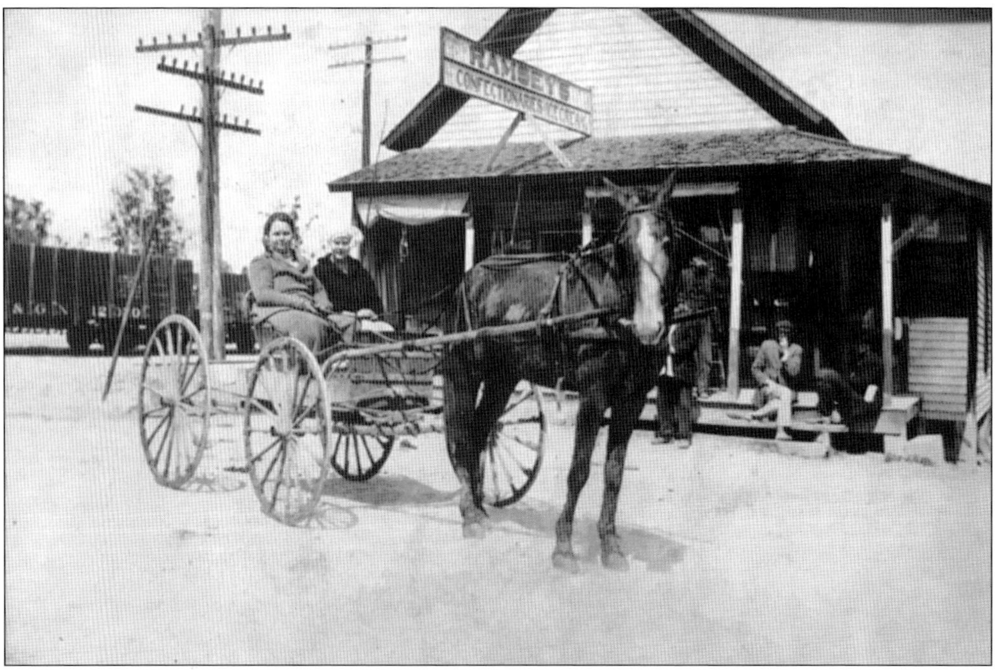

Charles Ramsey died in 1919 from the Spanish flu. His wife, Rose, worked in the drugstore with him but quickly sold the business to Frank Larson. This view of Ramsey's Drugs in 1918 looks northeast, with Alvie Anderson and Ester Dahlquist seated in the buggy. (Courtesy of the Johnson family.)

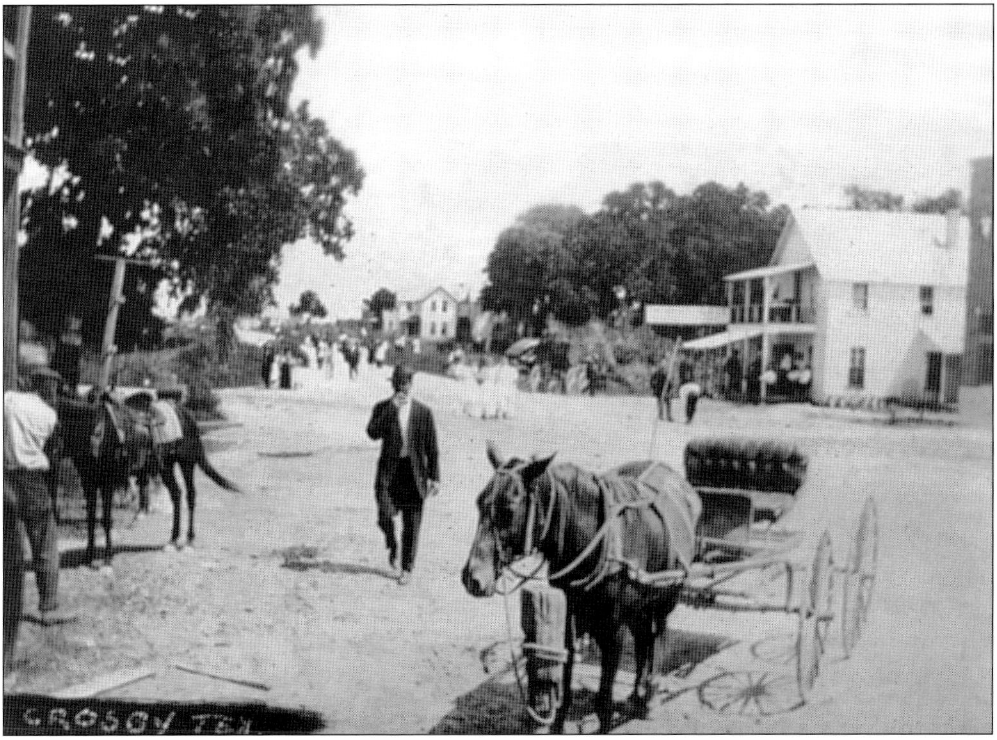

This 1914 view of Main Street looks south. The horses are tied up in front of the Sirocka Saloon. The white building in the foreground is the White Elephant Pool Hall. The large white building in the distance is the Lynch Boarding House. The large oak tree on the left is thought to be the hanging tree. (Courtesy of Cecil Newton.)

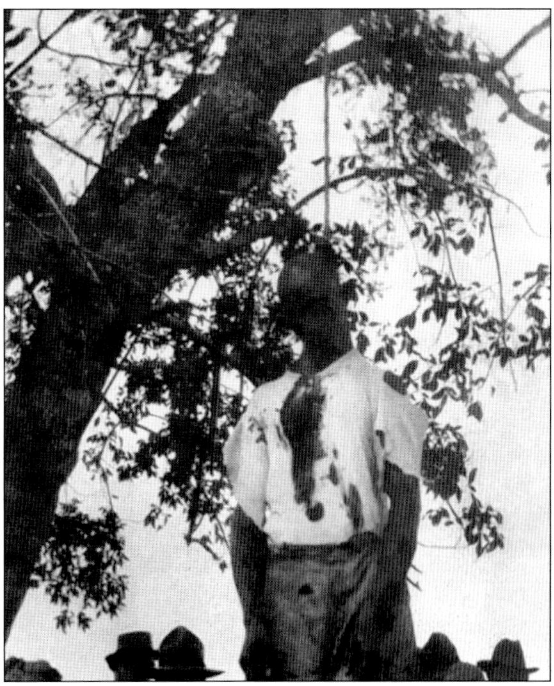

Before there was a jail in Crosby, the residents often dealt with local criminals themselves. The man being hanged here was a horse thief. Horse thieves were one of the more despised criminals because early settlers relied heavily on their horses and had a deep attachment to them. The last legal hanging in Texas by a county sheriff was in 1923. (Courtesy of the Lord family.)

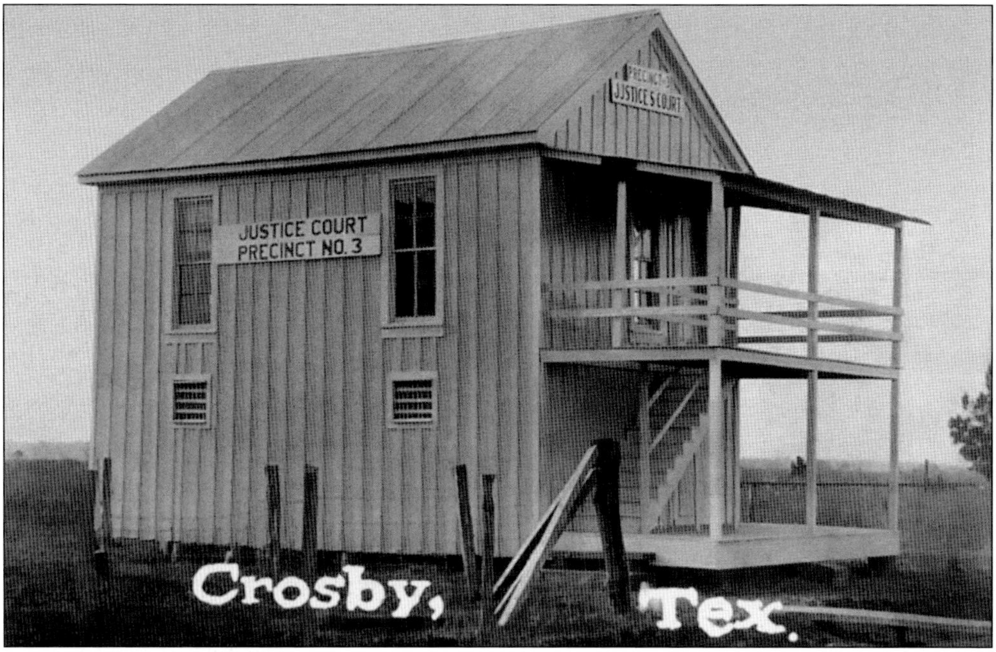

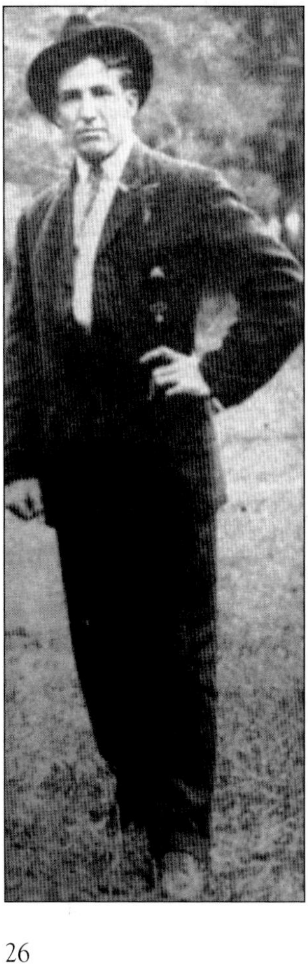

The photograph above is from 1913, shortly after the construction of the Crosby jail and courthouse on Reidland (Sixth) Street, west of Main Street. It was affectionately known as the "Blue Goose" due to its blue exterior paint. It served as a temporary jail for prisoners who would later be transferred to Houston. The county approved its construction in 1910, and an April 21, 1912, newspaper article chronicled the transfer of land, which was gifted by the Dr. Hollingsworth family. On October 21, 1919, the jail was destroyed in a fire during an attempted escape, according to the *Post*, and it was not rebuilt. Constable Bill Smith (left) was the first man hired to operate the jail, in 1913–1914. The first judge was Charles A. Tomlinson. (Both, courtesy of the Leatherwood family.)

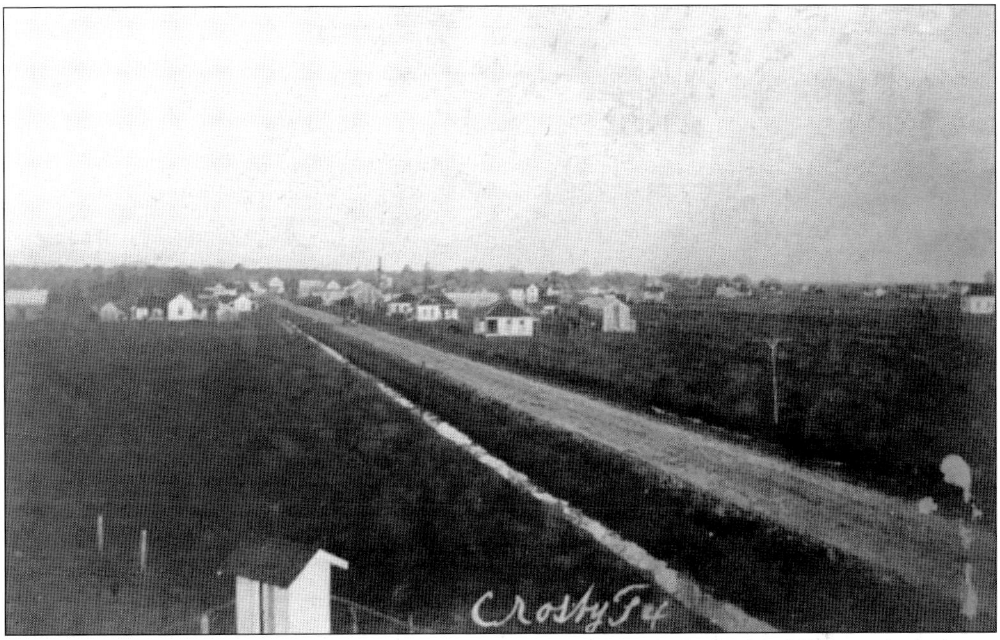

This photograph was taken around 1915 of Main Street (present-day FM 2100) from the balcony of the Crosby jail and courthouse, looking north toward the downtown area. The small white building in the foreground was the outhouse for the jail. (Courtesy of the Ewell family.)

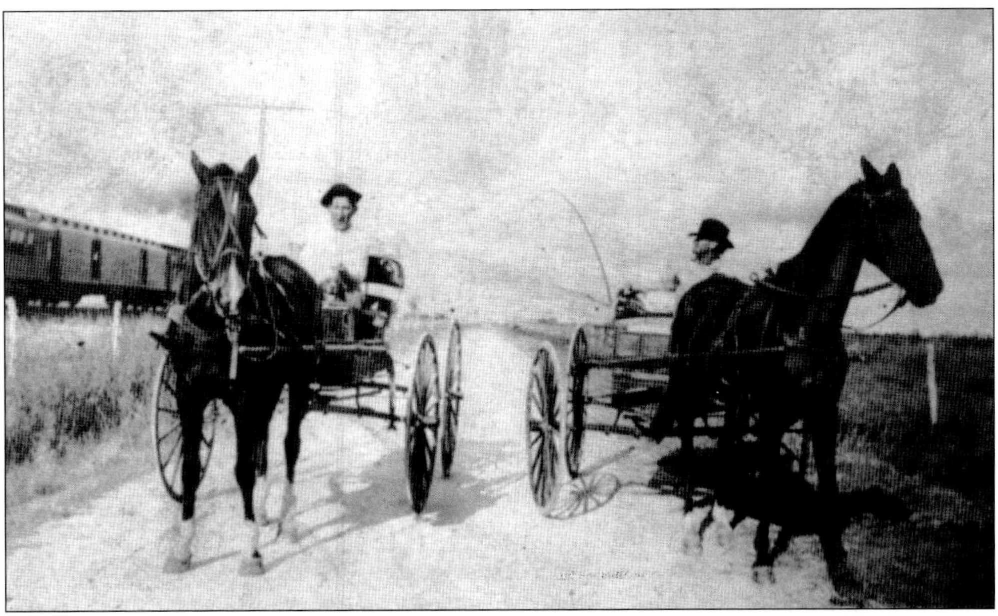

Clyde and Homer Johnson are pictured in this c. 1915 image. They are parked on Crosby Dayton Road, next to the railroad tracks. The brothers had moved to Crosby from Missouri. Clyde worked as a bartender at the Sirocka Saloon, and Homer was a carpenter. He lived just around the corner from where this photograph was taken. (Courtesy of the Johnson family.)

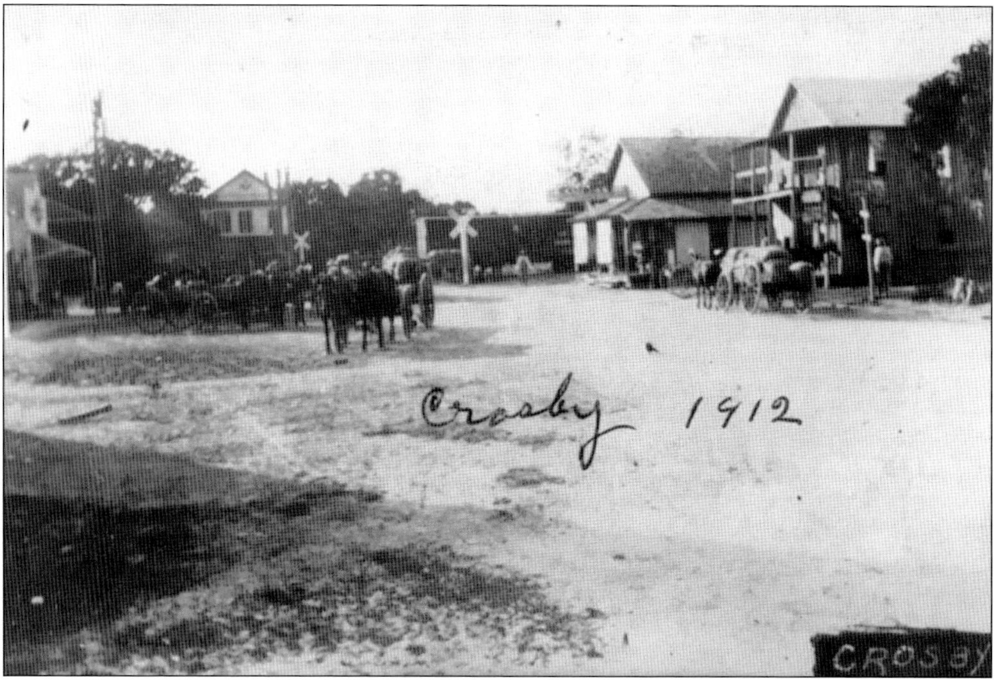

Pictured here is Main Street looking north in 1912. A number of wagons are gathered in front of the businesses near the railroad depot. These include the R.E. Dunks general store and Masonic lodge, Ramsey's confectionery, and Dr. Cutler's home and office. (Courtesy of the Hicks family.)

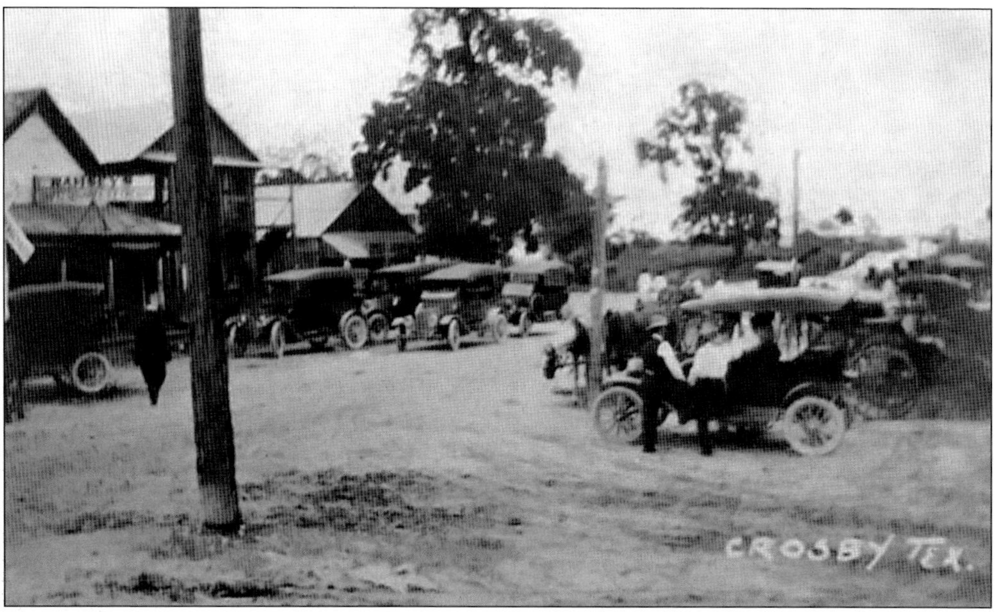

This image looks south down Main Street from the railroad depot, with a number of cars parked in front of the Sirocka Saloon. The roads in Crosby were more dirt trails than actual roads at the time of these photographs. The hanging tree at center was cut down a few years later. (Courtesy of the Hicks family.)

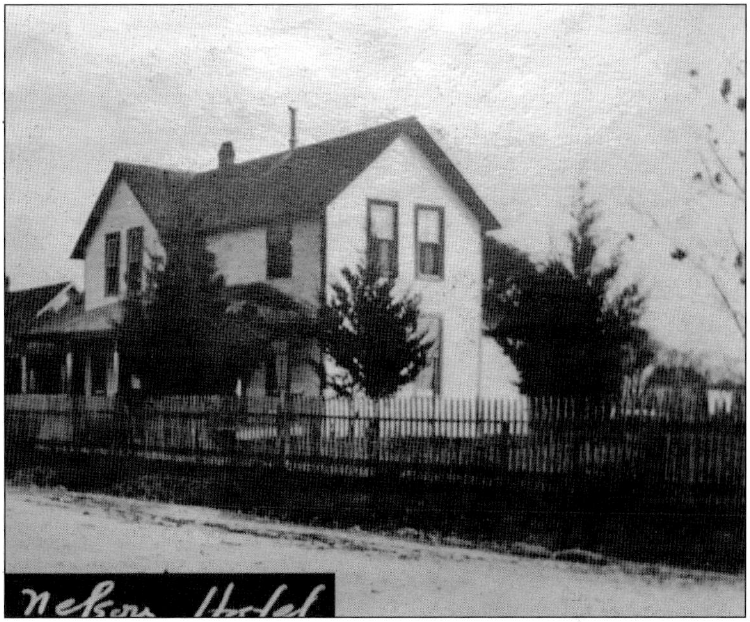

Lars Nelson and his wife, Mattie, moved to Crosby in 1896. They built a boardinghouse and ran a real estate agency. Over the years, he convinced several other Swedish families to relocate to Crosby for the land and mild winters. Pictured here is the Nelson boardinghouse at 506 Kernohan Street. (Courtesy of the Newton family.)

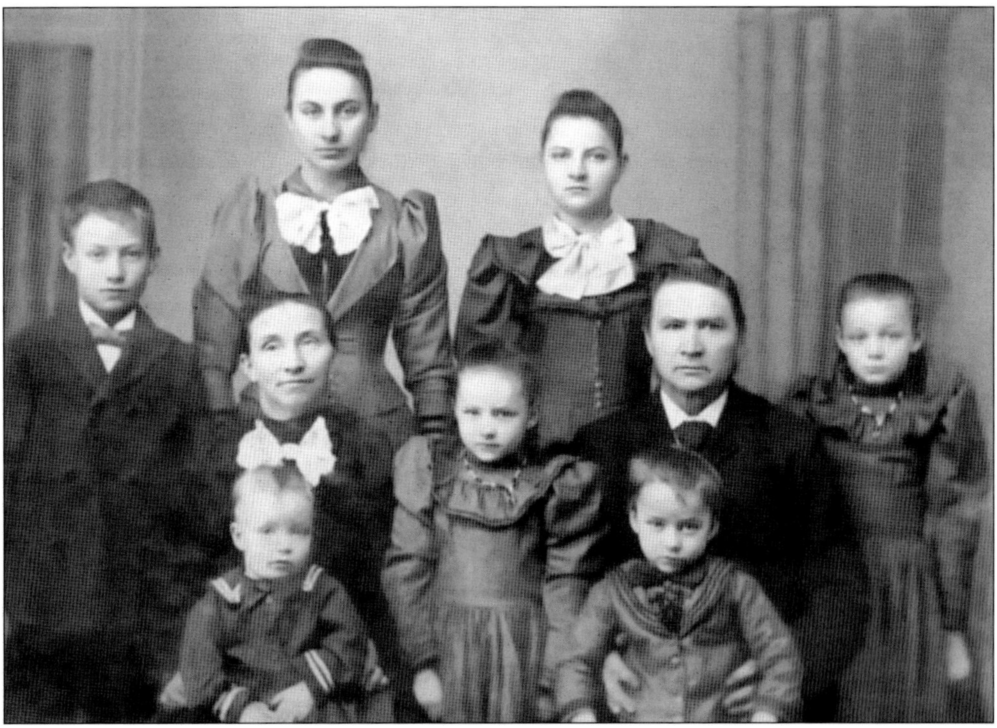

In 1907, the Nelson family's first home was destroyed by a fire. Afterward, they moved to Houston. In 1910, they returned and rebuilt their boardinghouse. At that time, Lars Nelson also opened a livery stable behind their house. Lars and Mattie Nelson, along with their seven children (Tillie, Annie, John, Ida, Mary, Oscar, and Emil), are pictured here. (Courtesy of the Nelson family.)

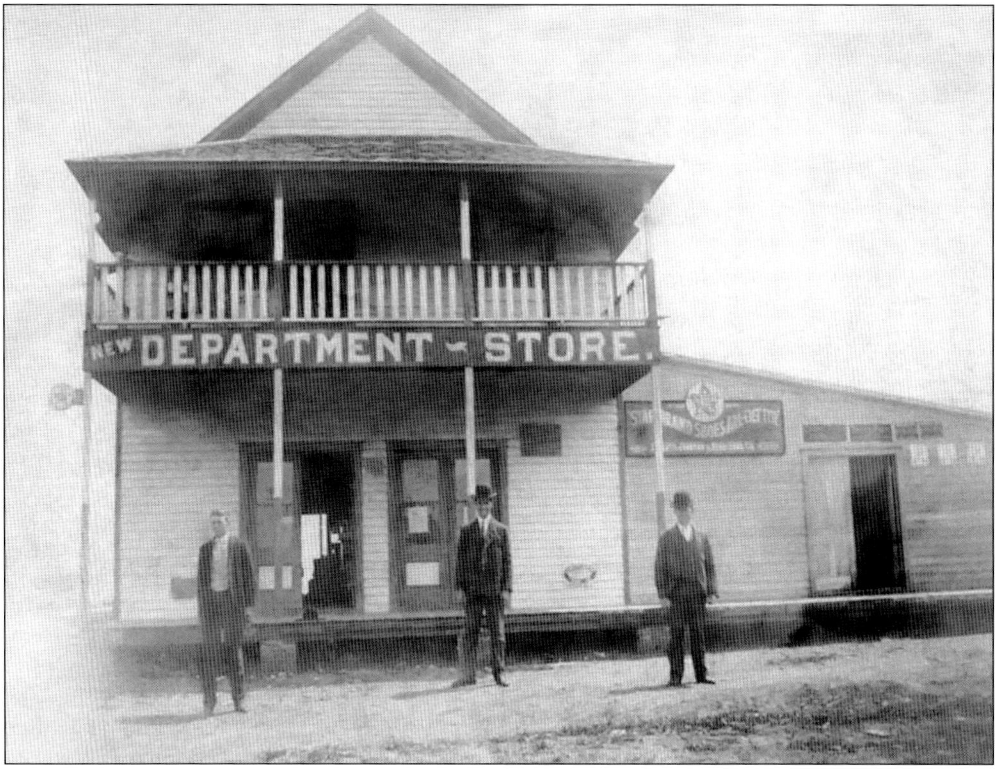

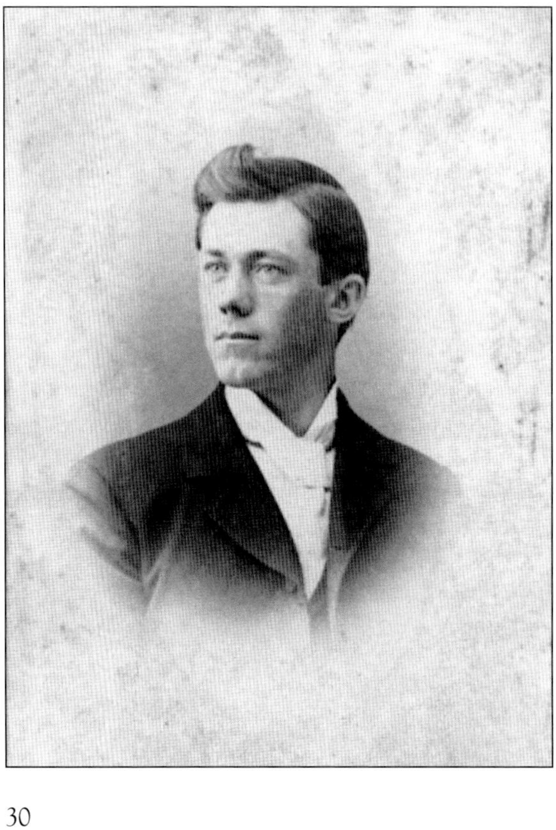

This is the Crosby Cash Store, built around 1900 in the 500 block of Runneburg Road on the southwest corner of the intersection with Crosby Dayton Road. R.C.J. Kenning (left) arrived in Crosby in 1894. He soon married the daughter of Lars Nelson. In 1900, the young couple built the store pictured above and originally lived upstairs. This was the third general store built in Crosby. The first was the Warehouse, built in 1865 by Charles Karcher. In 1897, Joe Anderson built the Anderson Store at 5815 Crosby Dayton Road. In 1904, Kennings and one of the Anderson sons (along with two other brothers-in-law) formed a partnership and built the Crosby Mercantile Company across the street from this building. (Both, courtesy of the Barrett family.)

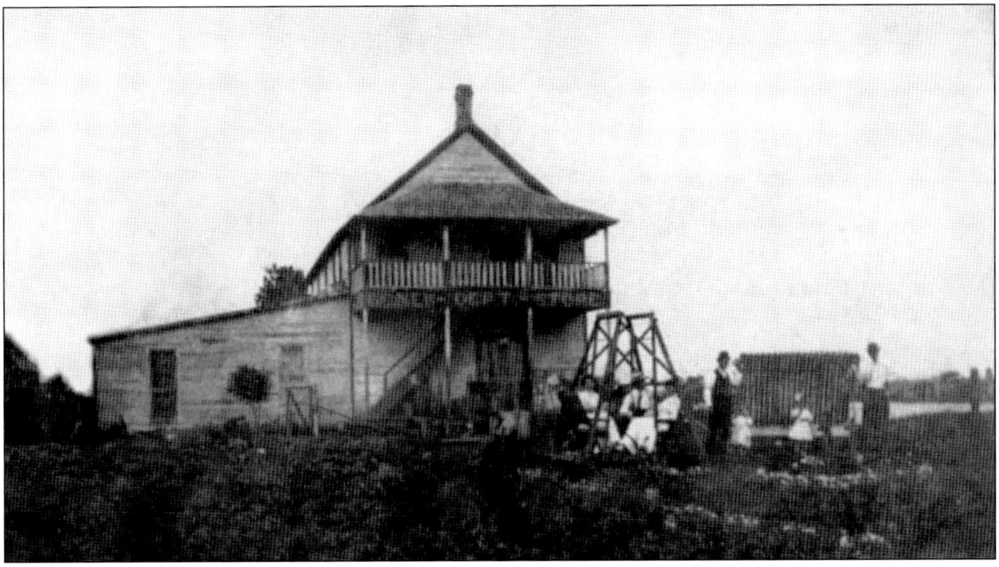

A rear view of the Crosby Cash Store is seen above. The upstairs was the Kenning home, and behind the store was their private space, which featured a couple's swing and their cotton field. Eventually, the couple purchased the Dave Reidland home across the street on the corner of Crosby Dayton Road and Kernohan Street and moved there. Below is a side view of the building. A water barrel with an angled board sits beside the structure. It was below the drip line of the roof to capture drinking water. Later, a water well was drilled across the street at the Crosby Mercantile Company, and this building became a warehouse and feed store. (Both, courtesy of the Barrett family.)

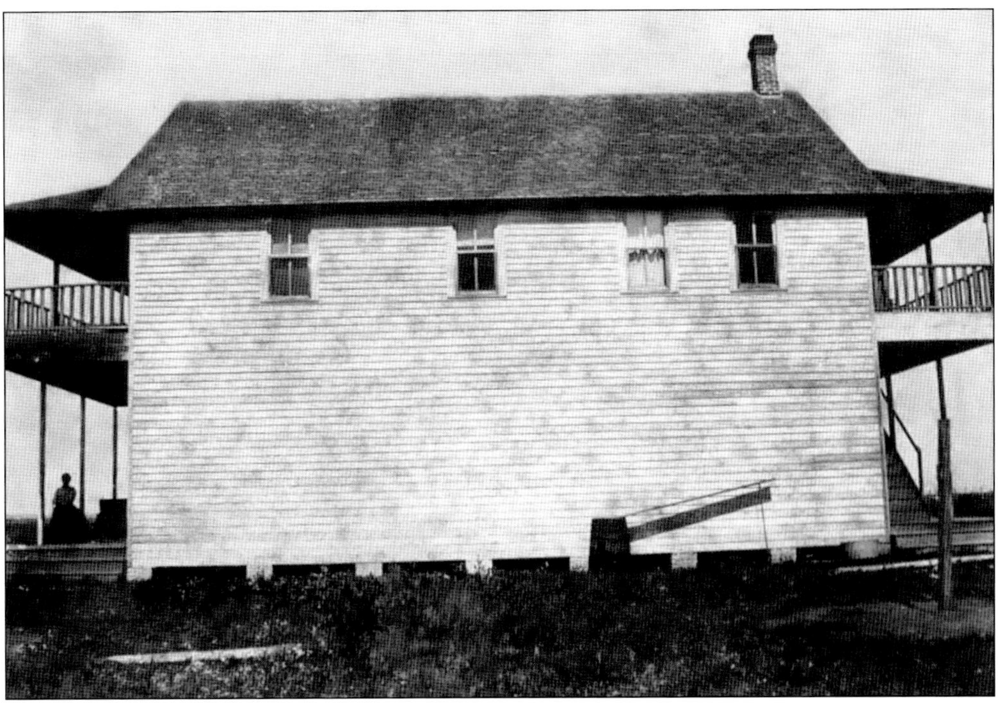

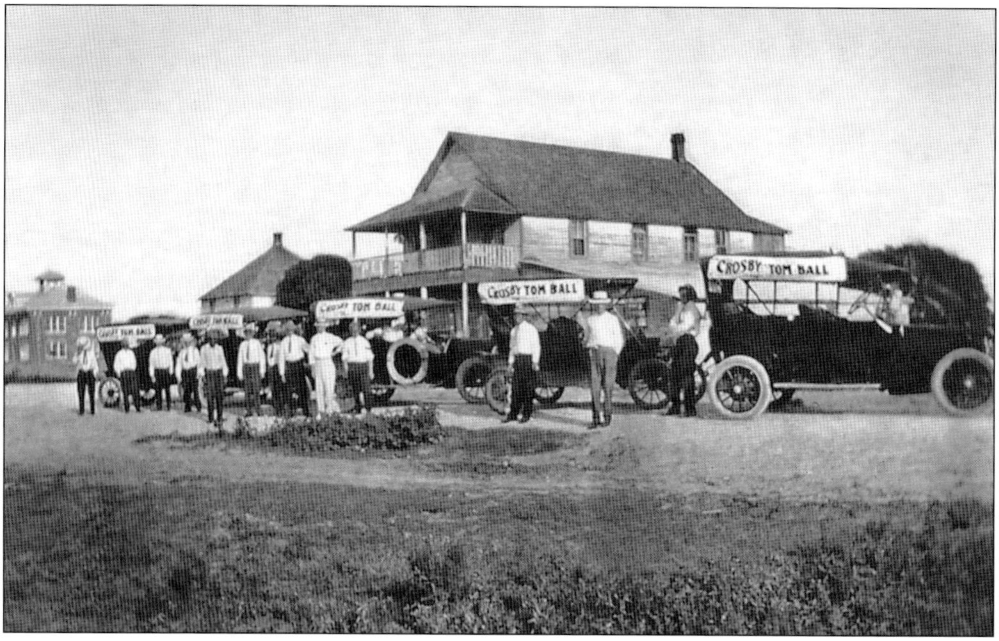

Above is another view of the original Crosby Cash Store, on Runneburg Road near Crosby Dayton Road. Behind it is the Pira Home, and farther back is the 1910 Crosby School. In this c. 1920 photograph, a group of cars are parked in front of the store before embarking to Tomball for a chamber of commerce community promotion. Driving to Tomball would have been an overnight trip in this era, because of the poor roads and slow cars. Starting around 1935, this building was used as the home for the Dawson Mattress Factory. Below is the Crosby Mercantile Company in 1906, which replaced the Cash Store. In the background is the Anderson general store.

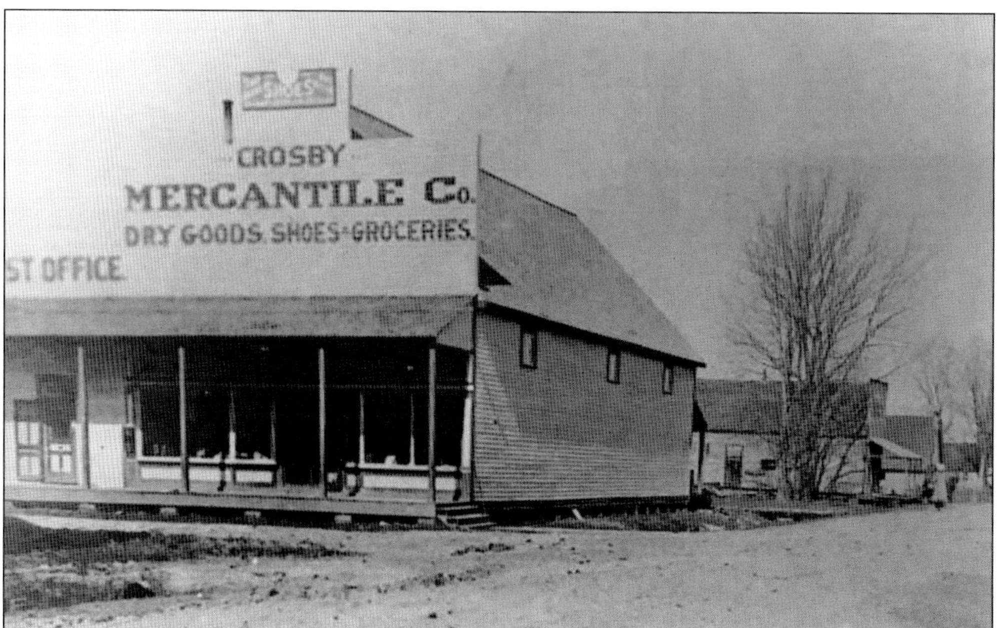

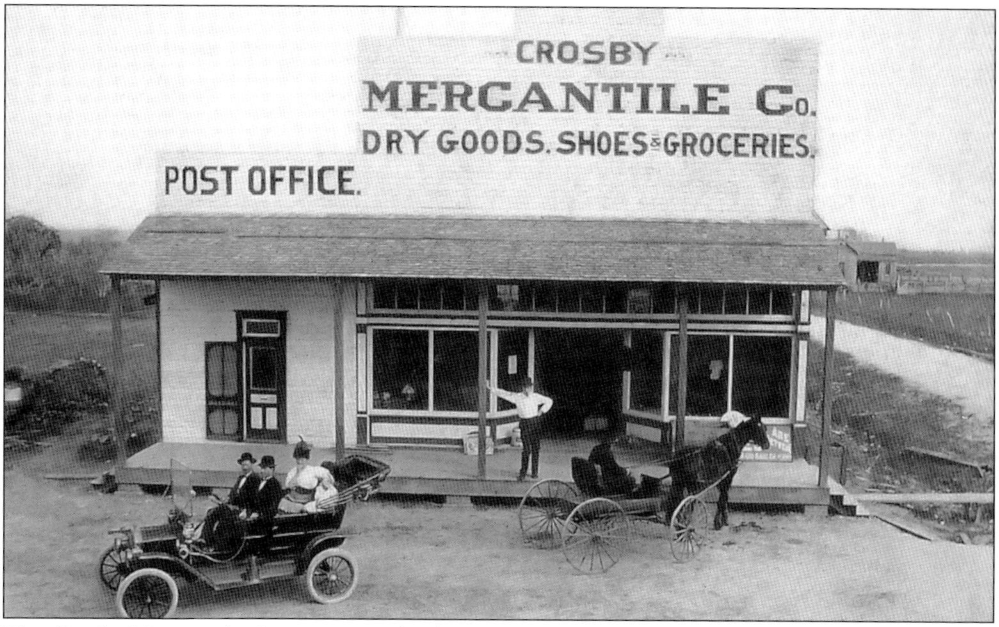

The Crosby Mercantile Company was built in 1904 at the intersection of Runneburg and Crosby Dayton Roads on the northwest corner and facing Runneburg. The post office was relocated to this building on April 4, 1905. In 1909, R.C.J. Kenning established the first car dealership in Crosby in this building, which sold Buicks. These two photographs are from around 1911–1912. They were taken from the balcony of the Crosby Cash Store. Crosby's first firefighting equipment was stored beside this building. The equipment consisted of some water barrels stored on a wagon with a hand pump. (Both, courtesy of the Barrett family.)

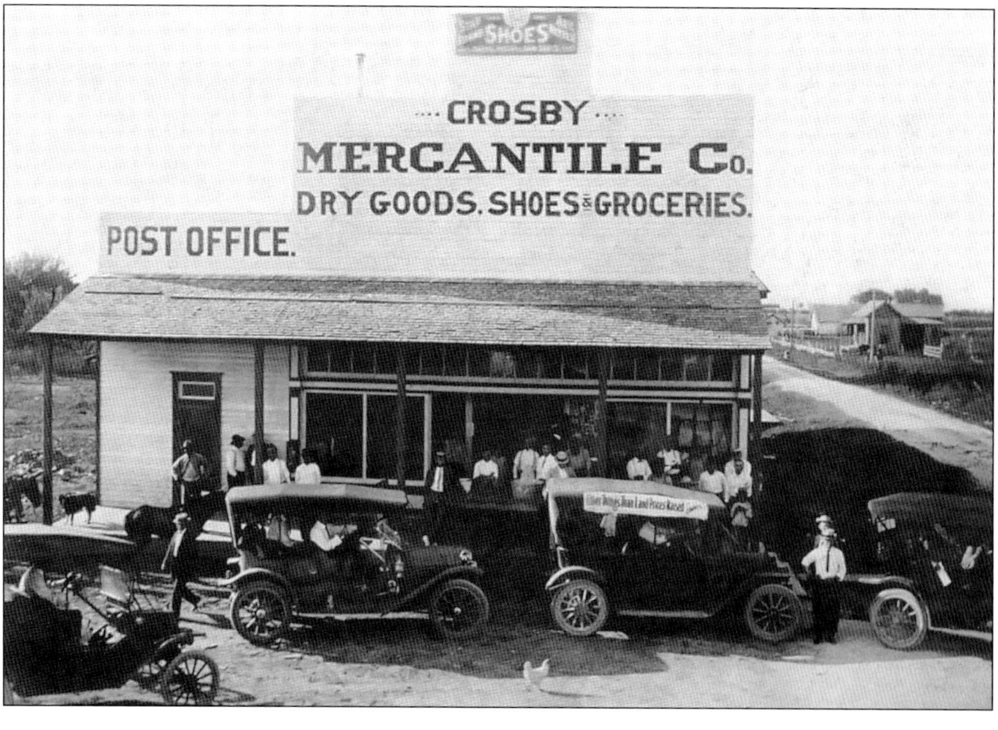

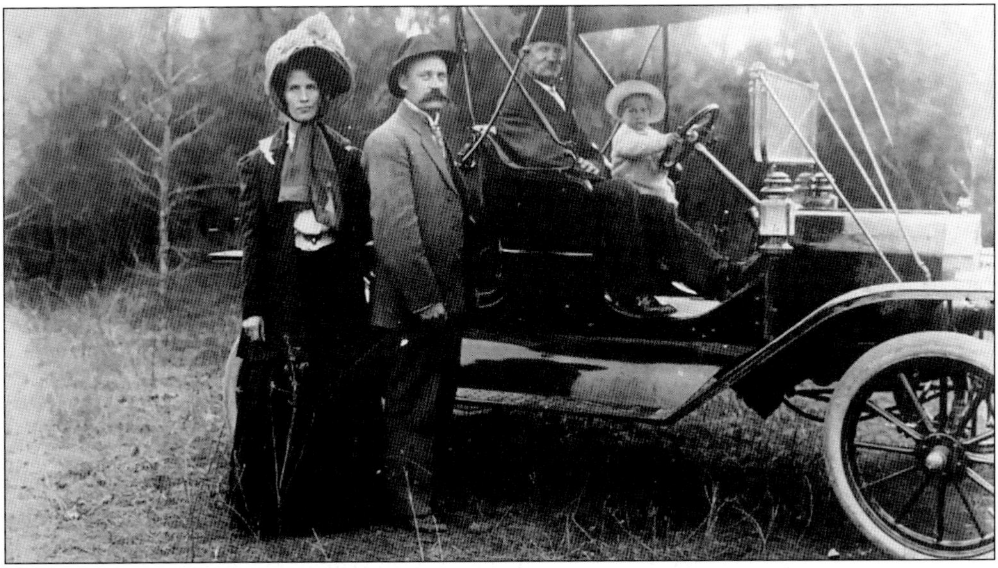

Pictured below is the interior of the Adolph Ehrlund blacksmith shop, built around 1912. Adolph Ehrlund and his wife, Tillie Wahl Ehrlund, are pictured above. Her father, Henry, and Adolph Jr. are in the car. The shop was at 5909 Main Street, next to Jackson Bayou. Adolph sold the business to John Sirocka, and it became the Sirocka blacksmith shop. Eventually, Sirocka became partners with a couple of other blacksmiths: a Mr. Naiver and Lewis Edward "Lige" Dillard. In the late 1920s or early 1930s, Joseph Shipula from Czechoslovakia purchased the business, and it became the Shipula blacksmith shop. Joseph Shipula Sr. is pictured below with his son Joe Jr. around 1939. (Above, courtesy of the Swanson family; below, courtesy of the Baumbach family.)

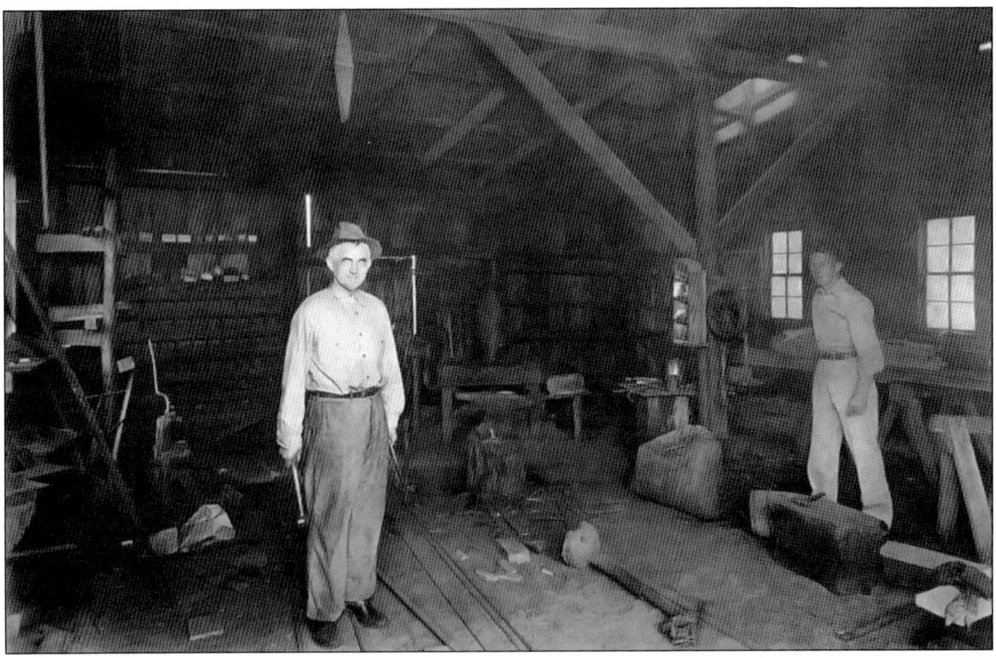

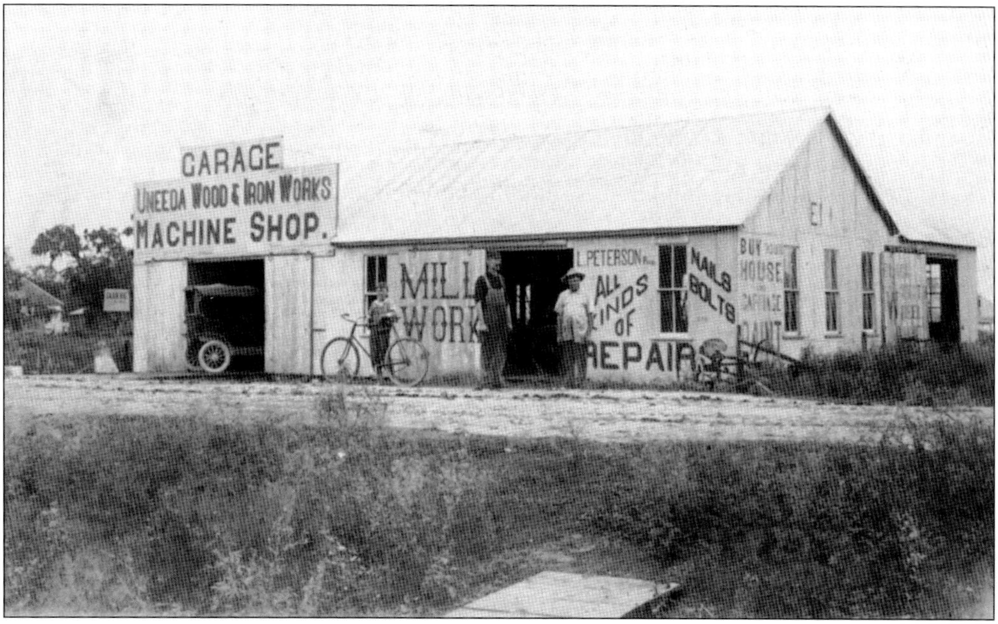

Uneeda Wood & Iron Works was at 5506 Main Street, on the northeast corner of the intersection with Wahl Street. It was a blacksmith and machine shop. The c. 1915 photograph above is a very early view of the business. The owner, Ludwig Peterson, is standing at center wearing overalls. The same building is pictured below a few years later with a number of the town's automobiles parked out front. The dirt trail is present-day FM 2100. Peterson was constantly expanding his building and adding new signs. (Both, courtesy of the Peterson family.)

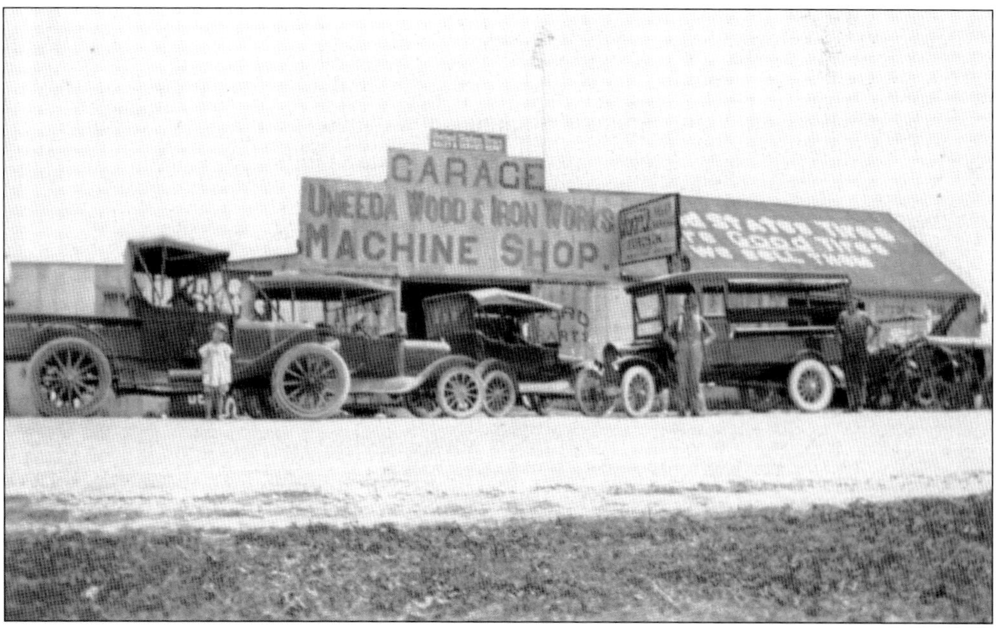

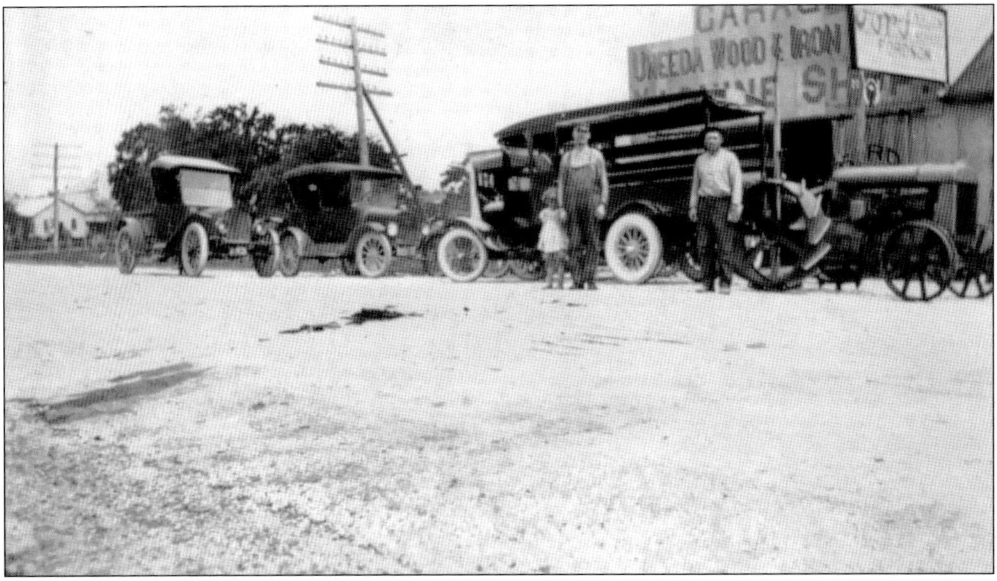

In the c. 1920 image above, Ludwig Peterson, the owner of Uneeda Wood & Iron Works, holds a small girl's hand. Pictured below are an older Ludwig Peterson and his car in front of his business after he added a gas pump and portico out front. The sign above the gas pump points south to Houston and north to Beaumont. In this era before Highway 90, all traffic between the two cities came right down Main Street and turned onto Kernohan Street. Ludwig Peterson and his wife, Anna, lived around the corner from the shop on Wahl Street. They helped start the First Baptist Church in Crosby and had built a church in Genoa (southeast Houston), before moving to Crosby. (Both, courtesy of the Peterson family.)

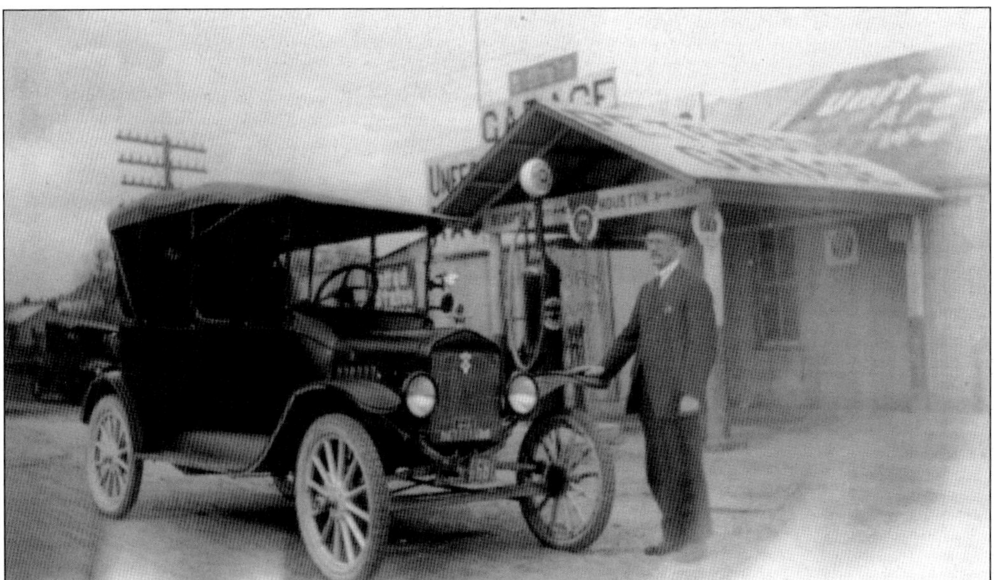

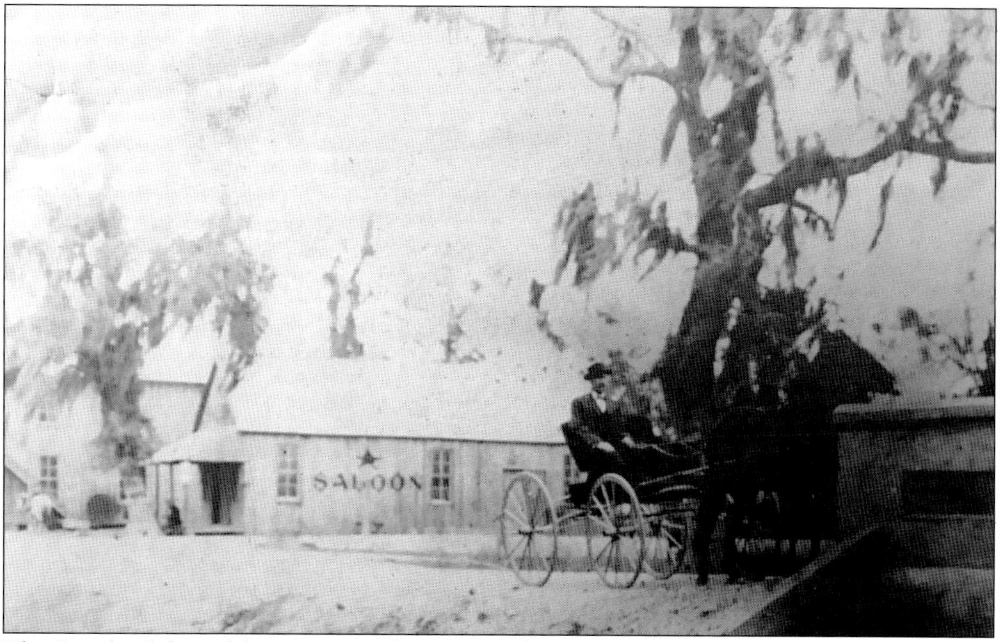

The Sirocka Saloon (above) was at the corner of Kernohan and Main Streets. Below, several patrons stand next to the bar in the Sirocka Saloon in 1916. Signs on the back wall read, "Lunch in Rear," and "No Minors Allowed." From left to right are Clyde Johnson (bartender), Peter Celestine Ulrich (one of the largest ranchers on the Texas coast), Sheriff Dave McKinney, Joe Sirocka Sr. (dark coat and light pants), four unidentified, George Maxey (sitting on barrel), unidentified, Earl Hilliard (in overalls, with drink raised), unidentified, and Joe Franta Sr. (Above, courtesy of the Swanson family; below, courtesy of the Prochazka family.)

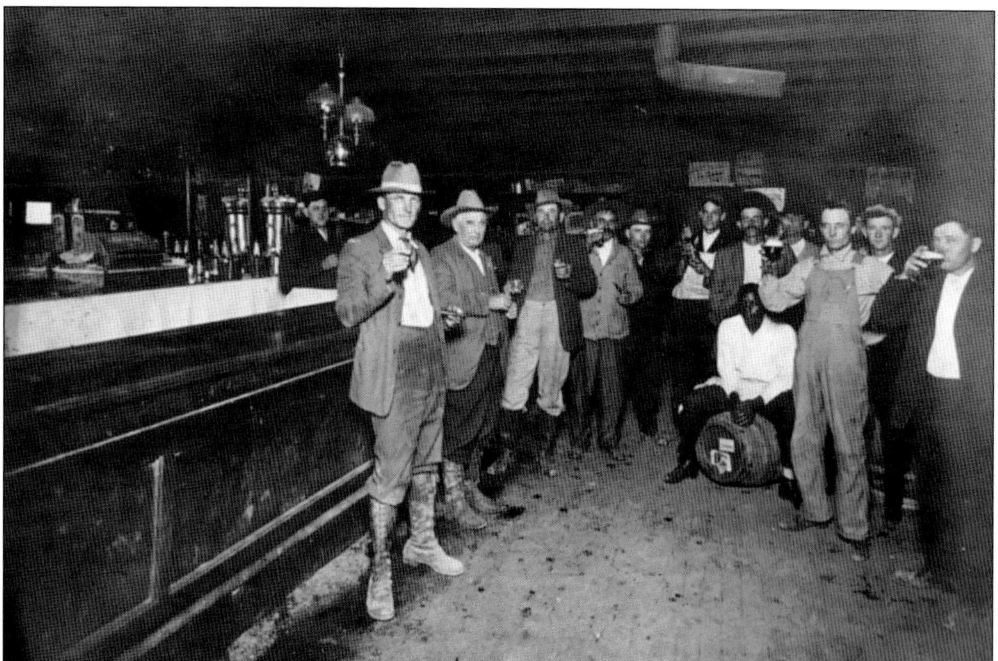

LIQUOR LICENSE OF CROSBY SALOON KEEPER WAS REVOKED

County Judge Ward Ruled That H. H. Moore Was Interested in the Business.

The liquor license of Joe Sirocka, who conducted a place on the Crosby road, near the San Jacinto river, was revoked by County Judge W. H. Ward, Thursday The matter has been under consideration since last week, when the case was tried.

Judge Ward decided that H. H. Moore was an interested party in the business and shared in the profits as a partner. In the affidavit upon which the license was granted Sirocka had stated that no one else was interested with him.

The license would have expired Friday, and the decision of Judge Ward will make it impossible for Sirocka to secure a renewal or a new license.

In 1910, women were given the right to vote and slowly began to exercise that right. Most women of the era preferred Prohibition. Public sentiment on alcohol had always been pretty evenly divided in Crosby. The Czech and pioneer citizens mostly favored a wet community, while the Swedes more often favored Prohibition. In a September 3, 1904, election, Crosby voted against Prohibition by one vote, 40 to 39. Elections in 1916 were strongly against Prohibition by 42 votes. In May 1917, Prohibition was defeated yet again, 153 to 77. However, in 1919, Crosby voted to go dry by two votes, 87 to 85. In 1920, the entire country decided to enact Prohibition. During this period, a number of stills were raided in and around the Crosby farming community.

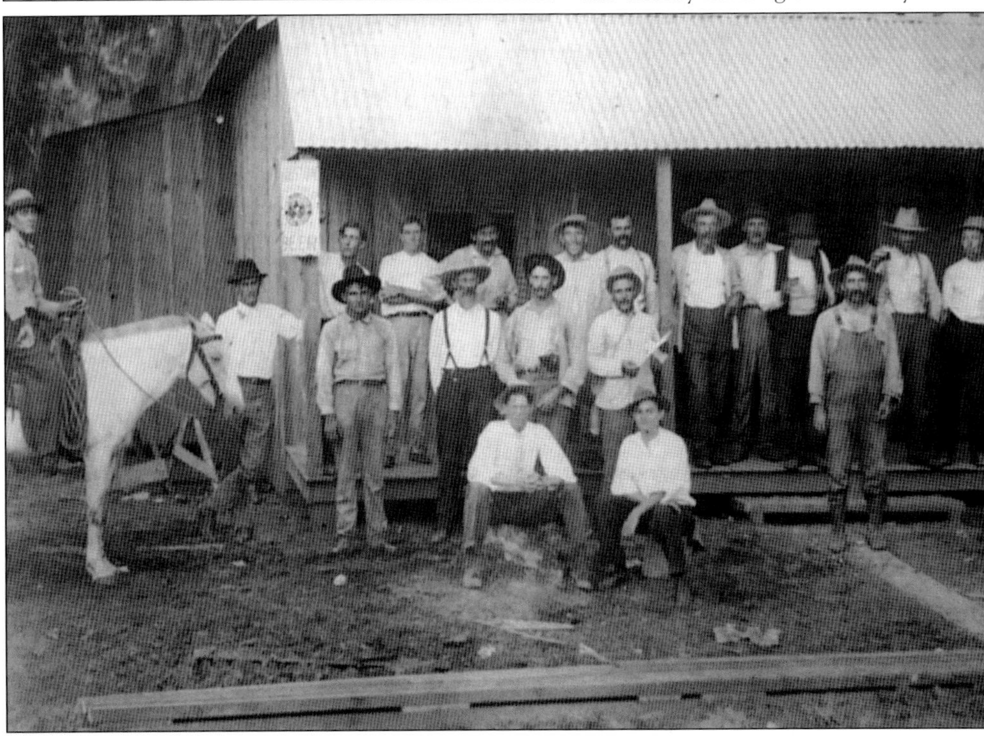

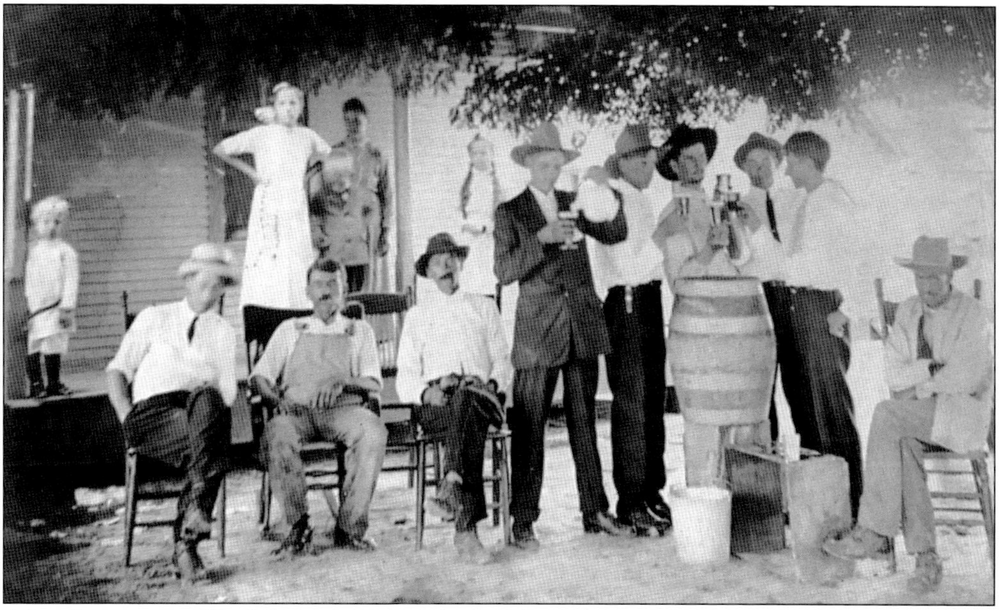

After the passing of Prohibition, many of the Czechs and Germans in the community continued to make their own alcohol at home. These families had already been brewing their own beer, wine, and whiskey before Prohibition, but now it became a riskier proposition. In the above photograph, members of the Otto Adlong (German) family drink from their private beer keg during Prohibition with friends. Prohibition ran from 1920 until December 1933, when the federal law was repealed. Pictured below is a 1933 Prohibition bust by East Harris County police. This stockpile was confiscated in Old Pelly (Baytown). After Prohibition ended, many counties and towns in Texas voted to remain dry—but not Crosby.

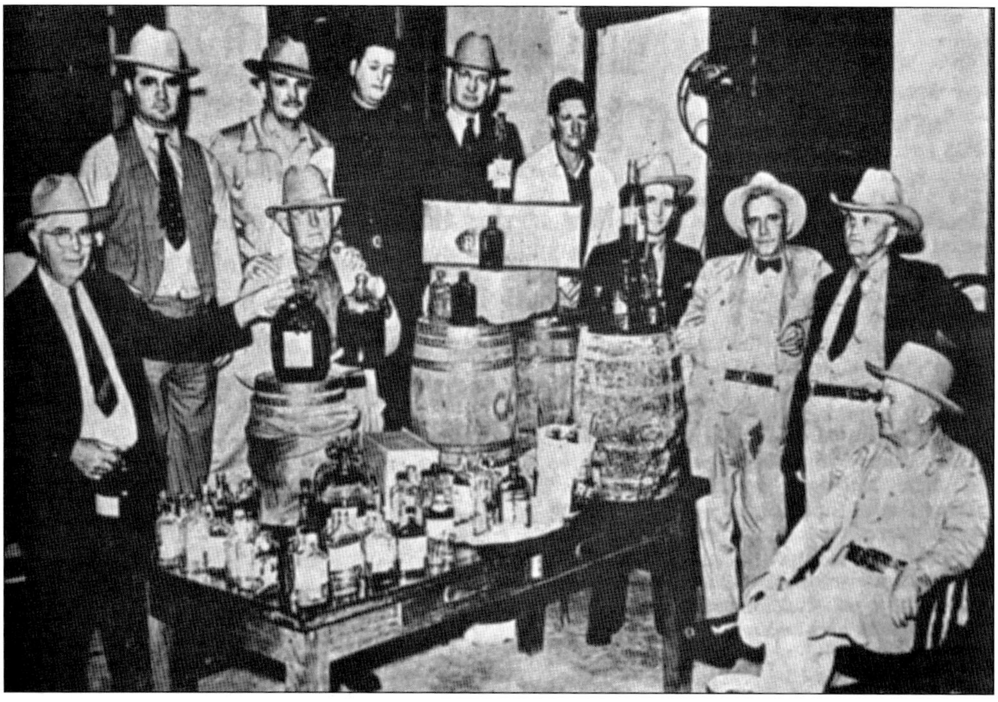

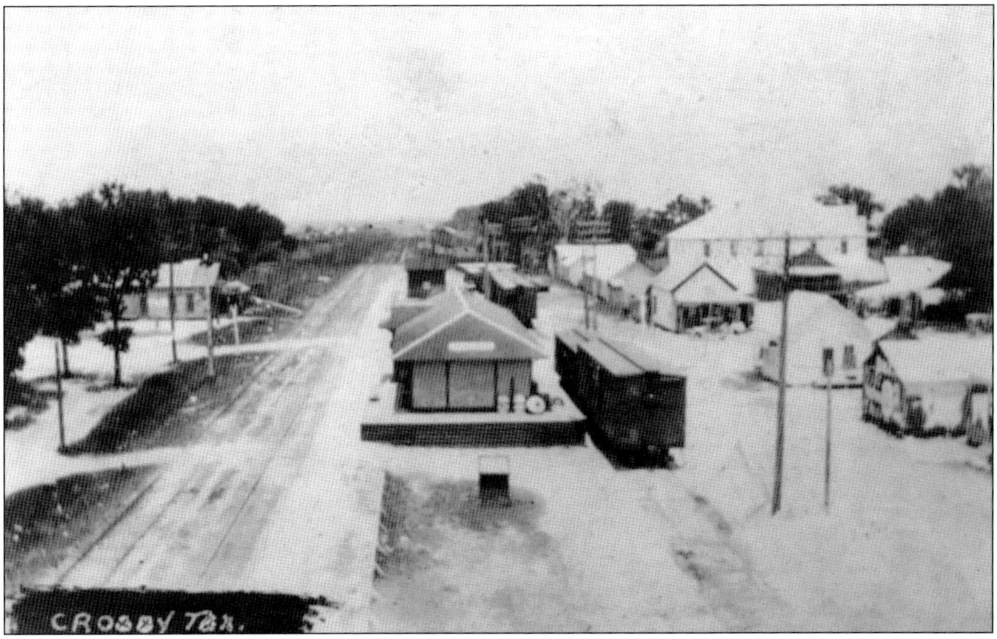

These photographs were taken sometime between 1913 and 1914, from atop the railroad water tower looking east toward Main Street. The train depot is in the foreground. On the north side of the railroad tracks is Ira Matthews' meat market and saloon. In 1909, he added an icehouse for the meat and for selling ice to the public. The Crosby State Bank building was erected in 1913, and is visible at right below. On the west side of Main Street is a structure in the future location of the Ramsey drugstore building (the small white building near the depot). It could be a railroad survey office. (Both, courtesy of the Newton family.)

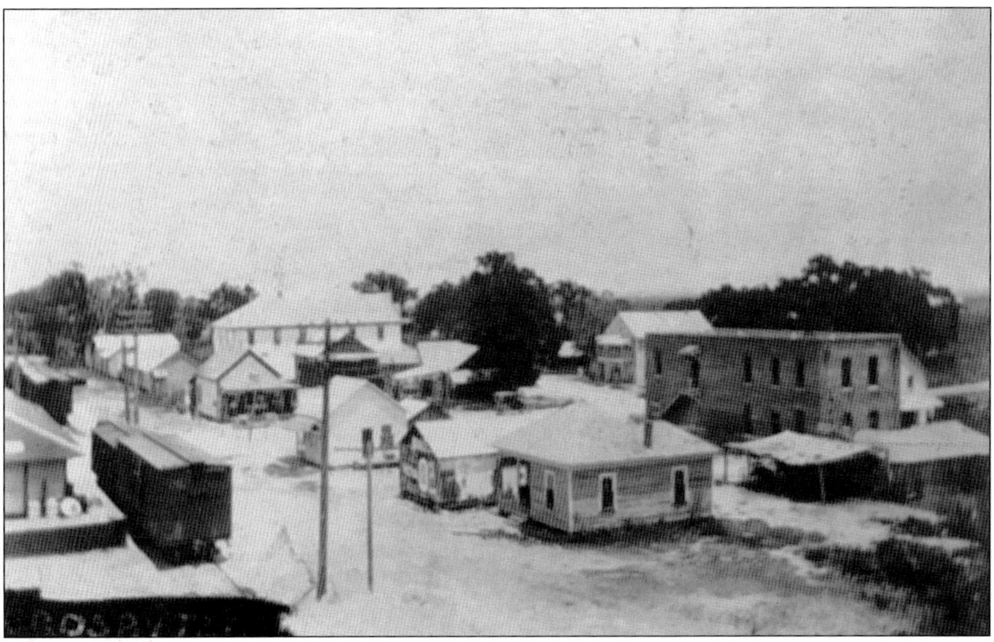

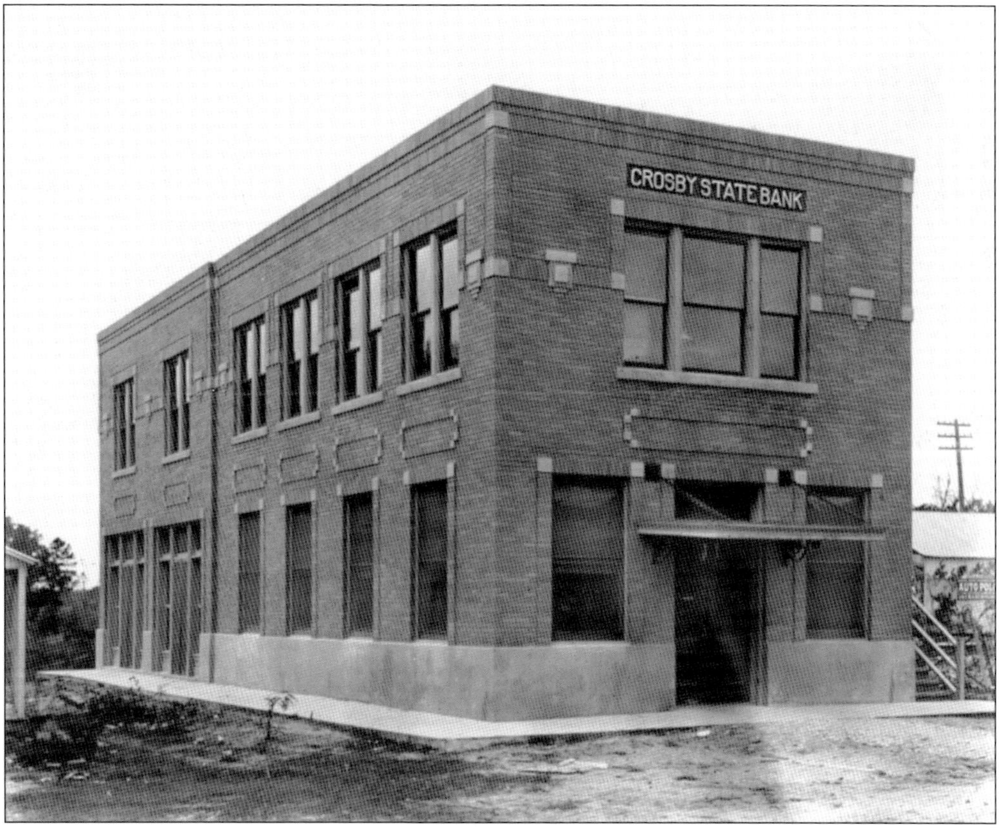

The photograph above was taken in 1913 shortly after completion of the Crosby State Bank. The building is still located at 5613 Main Street, south of the railroad. At the rear of the bank was the post office, with access on the side of the building. Office space was available on the second floor. A stairwell to access the upstairs was on the north side of the building. The bottom three feet of the bank's exterior walls were solid poured-in-place concrete. It is rumored that John T. Hare threw some $20 gold pieces into the concrete as it was being poured, which are still there today. At right is the bank's high-security safe, which was inside a walk-in safe on the first floor. (Both, courtesy of the Hare family.)

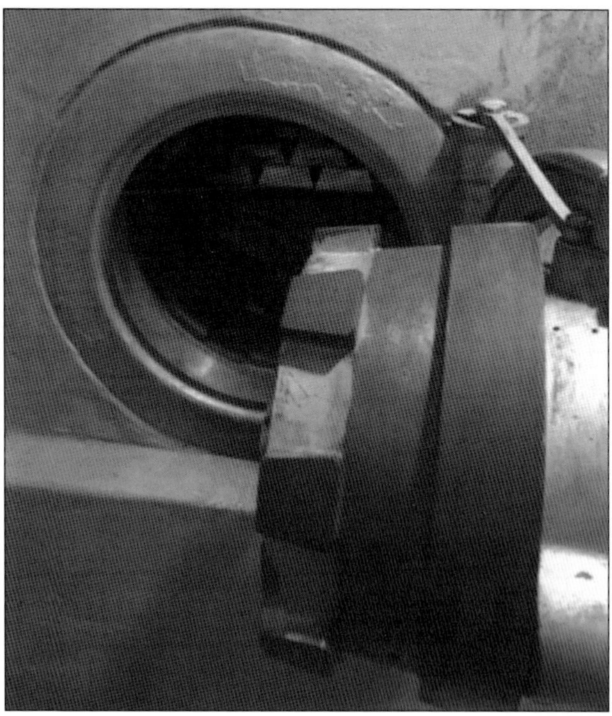

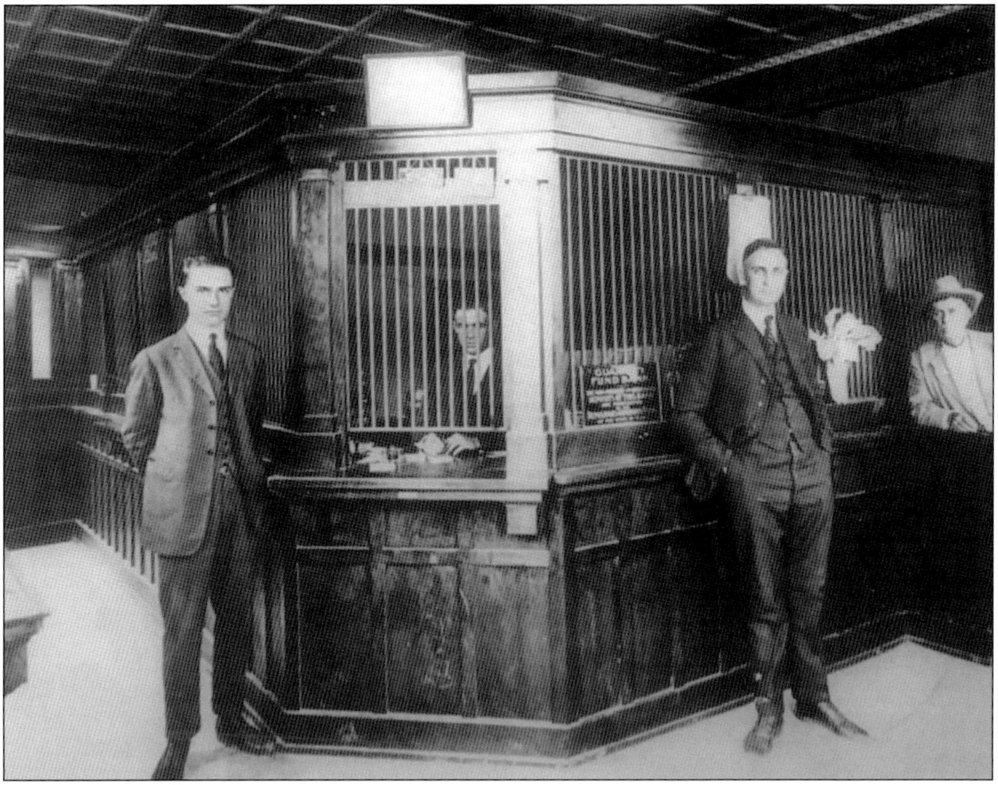

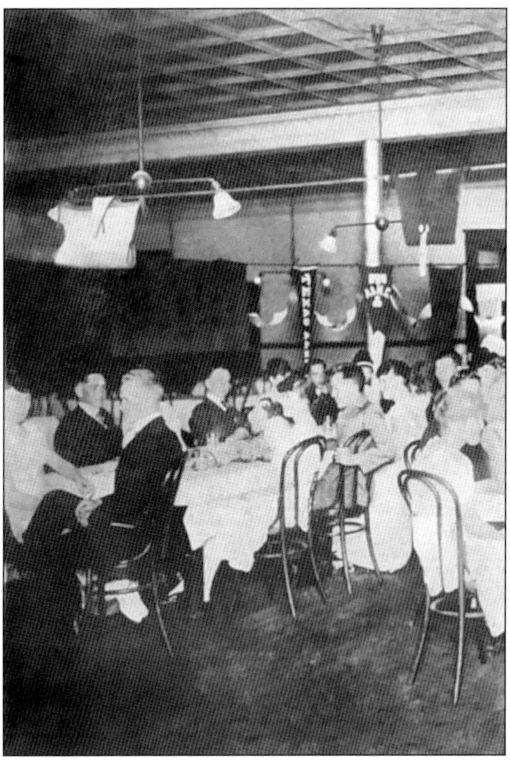

Pictured above is the interior of the Crosby State Bank. The Crosby Post Office, which occupied the back half of the bank, was established in 1877 at the home of Capt. John Simms. The bank was its fifth location. At left is the banquet room located upstairs. The space was rented out for birthday parties, beauty pageants, dances, and dinners, like the one being held here. The man seated closest on the left is Othello Hare. The Texas A&M banners may have been for his college graduation party. (Both, courtesy of the Hare family.)

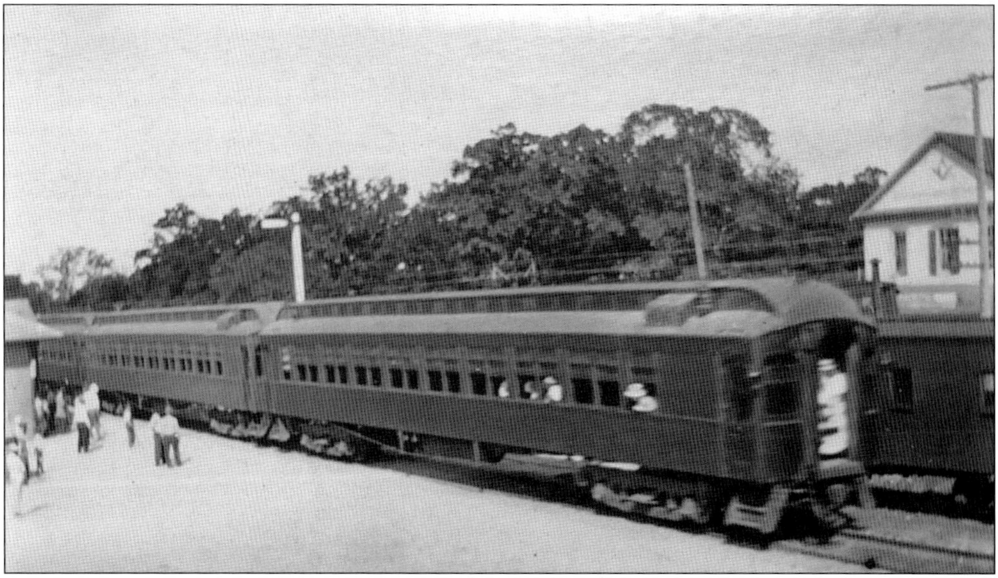

Crosby had four passenger trains that stopped daily, with two headed west and two headed east. The downtown area was a hub of activity, with people arriving and freight being delivered. In this image, a passenger train is pulling away from the Crosby depot on its way to Houston. The Dunks general store, with the Sampson Masonic Lodge upstairs, is at right in this c. 1910 photograph. (Courtesy of the Newton family.)

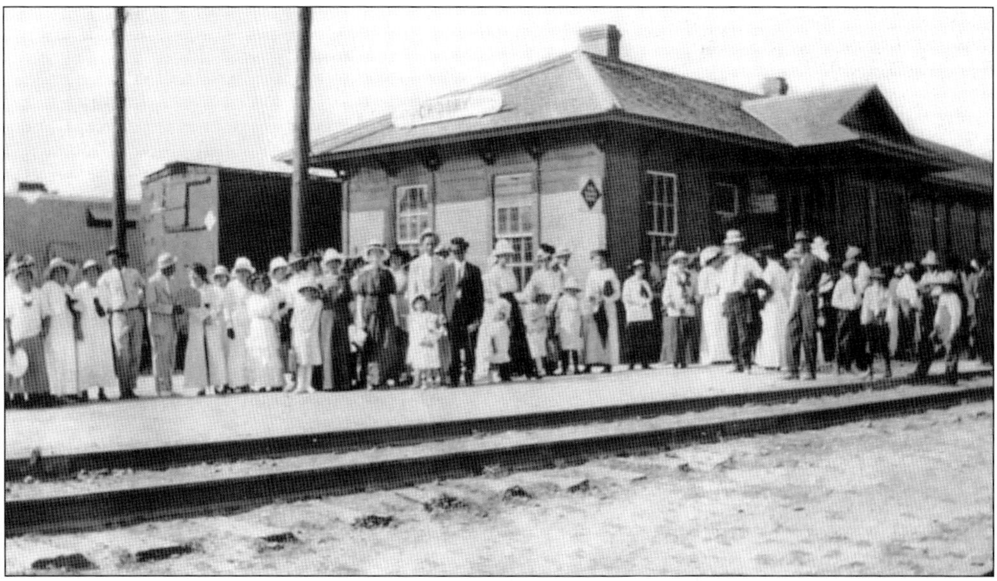

This is a photograph of the train depot in 1914. On many Sundays, residents would gather on the depot platform to visit with the passengers when the train stopped for water and supplies. News of what was going on outside the community was exchanged during the brief visits. Travelers would shop at the nearby stores and mingle with the townsfolk. (Courtesy of the Barrett family.)

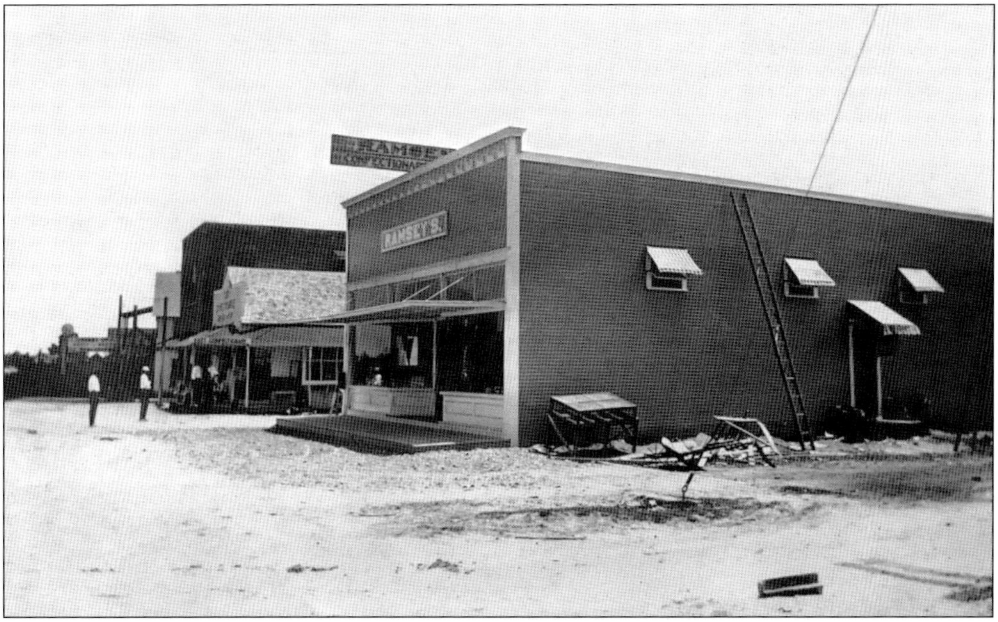

Above is the newly opened Ramsey's Drugs at 5623 Main Street in 1914. It was next to the railroad depot. A competitor, the Cozy Confectionery, was next door. It was owned by Sol Aron. His brother Abe owned a dry goods store across the street. When oil was found in Goose Creek, the two brothers quickly moved there to profit from the growth. They opened a theater and a dry goods store in what became Baytown. Pictured below is the interior of the Ramsey drugstore. Jesse Newton was the manager of the popular establishment. It served train travelers and locals as well. (Both, courtesy of the Newton family.)

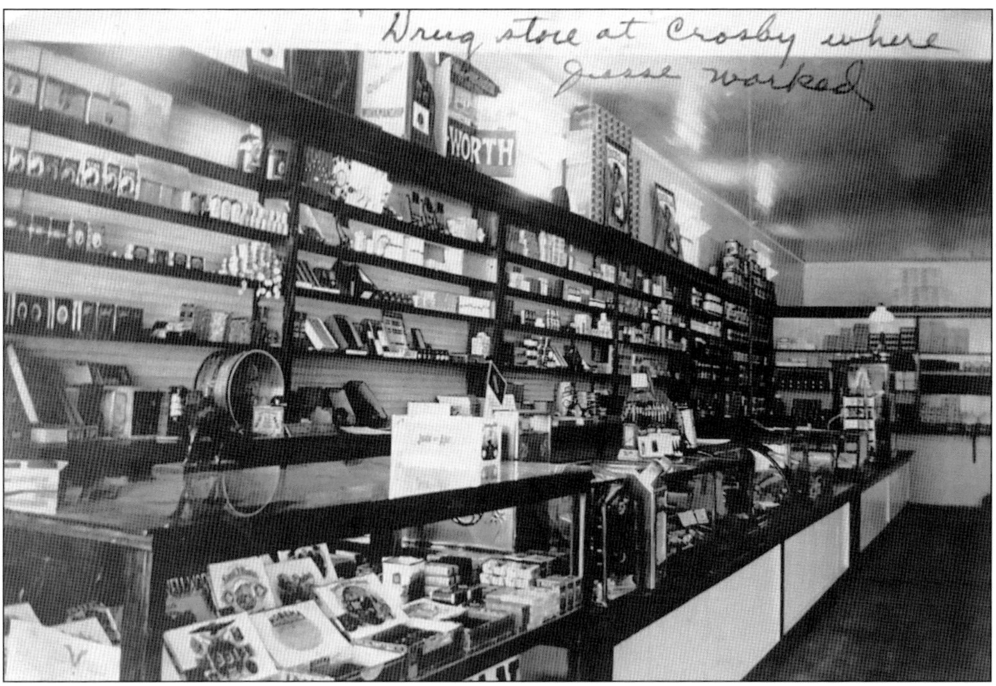

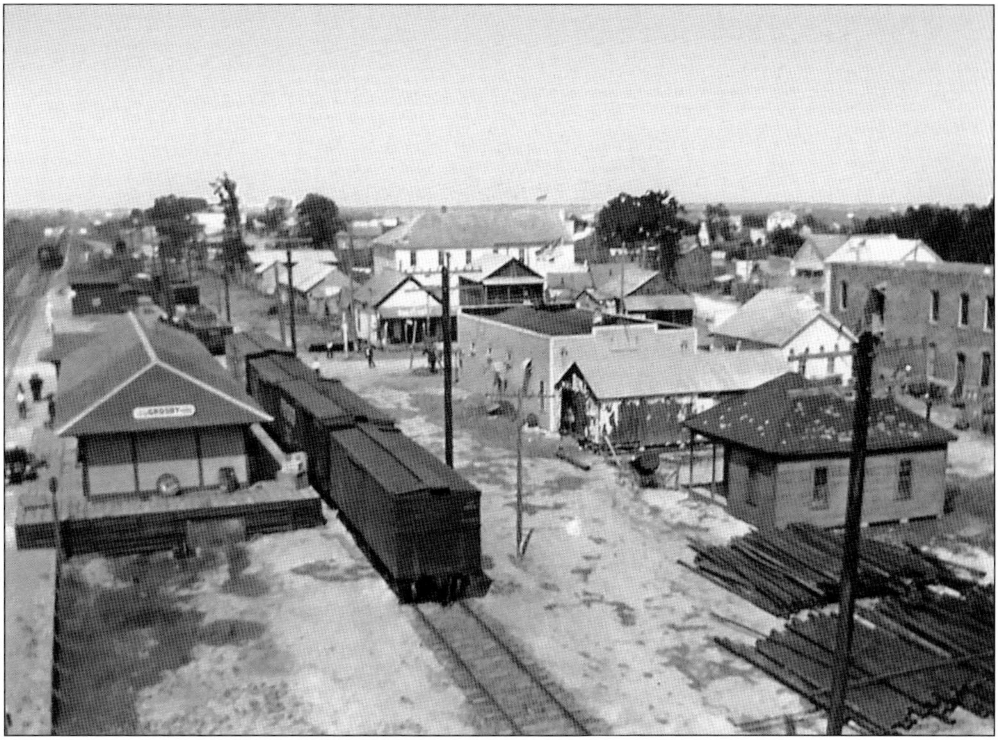

In 1915, the Gulf Pipeline was being installed, and loads of pipe have been offloaded in the foreground. Several other pipelines would also be built in the area. Crosby had a number of out-of-town workmen who lived in the various boardinghouses. The photograph above was taken from the top of the railroad water tower, looking east at Main Street. Ramsey's drugstore is on the west side of Main Street, and the Crosby Auto Supply Co. has moved into the old Ramsey Confectionery building, on the east side of Main Street. The photograph below offers one of the clearest views of the rail yards. (Both, courtesy of the Swanson family.)

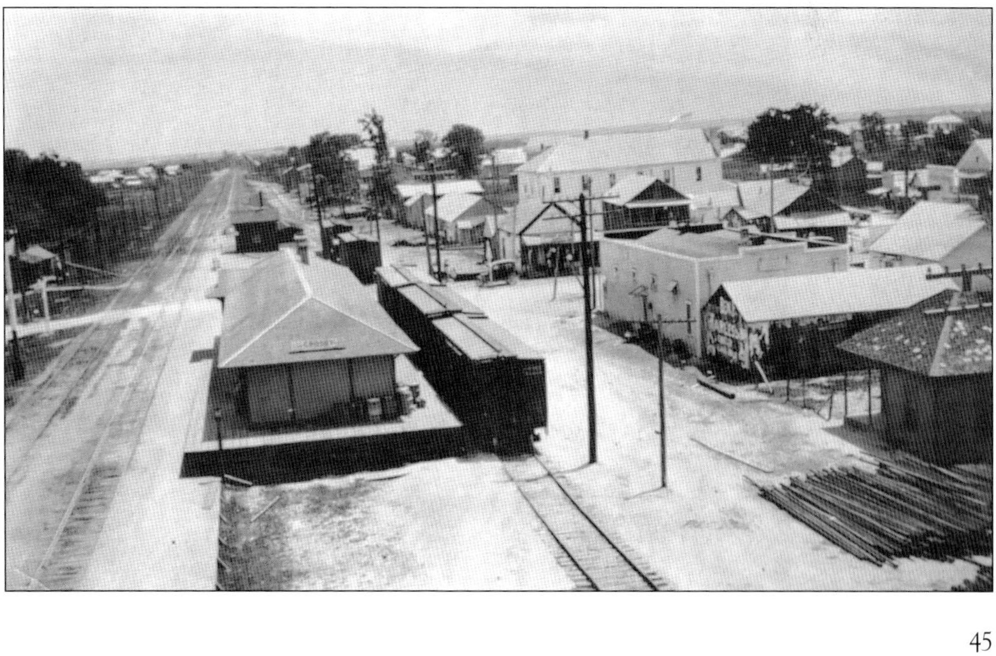

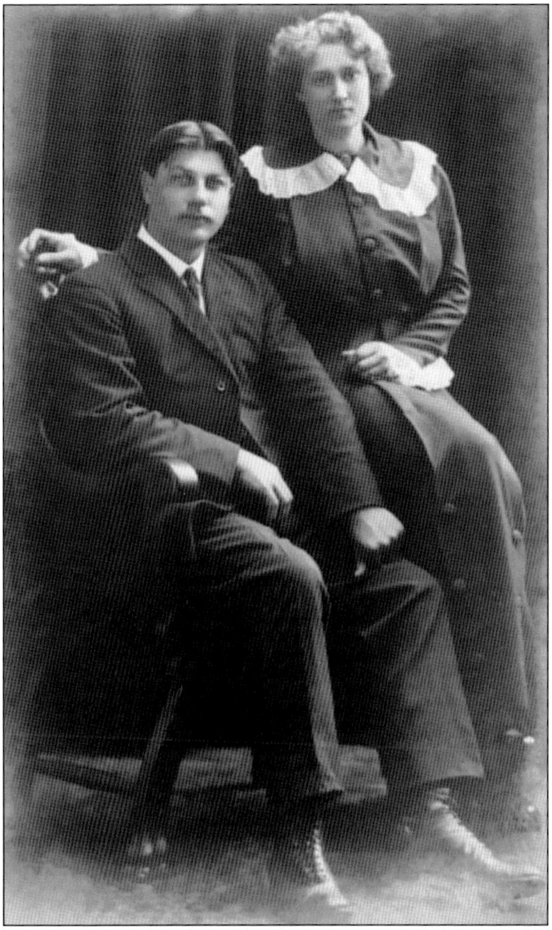

William M. Truxaw owned the Texas Mercantile store. He and his wife, Amanda Hare Truxaw, are pictured at left. William and his father established the Crosby Telephone Company in 1914. It was originally housed in the lean-to addition on the east side of the Texas Mercantile Co. building at 125 Kernohan Street. The store also housed the post office at the time. In 1920, the telephone exchange was moved to the second floor of the Crosby State Bank building. The Crosby Telephone Company served Crosby, Huffman, Mt. Belvieu, Cedar Bayou, Elena (Highlands), Lynchburg, and Goose Creek. William eventually moved the company headquarters to Goose Creek (Baytown) and renamed the business the Goose Creek Phone Company. It later became General Telephone Company of the Southwest. (Both, courtesy of Klaus Duda.)

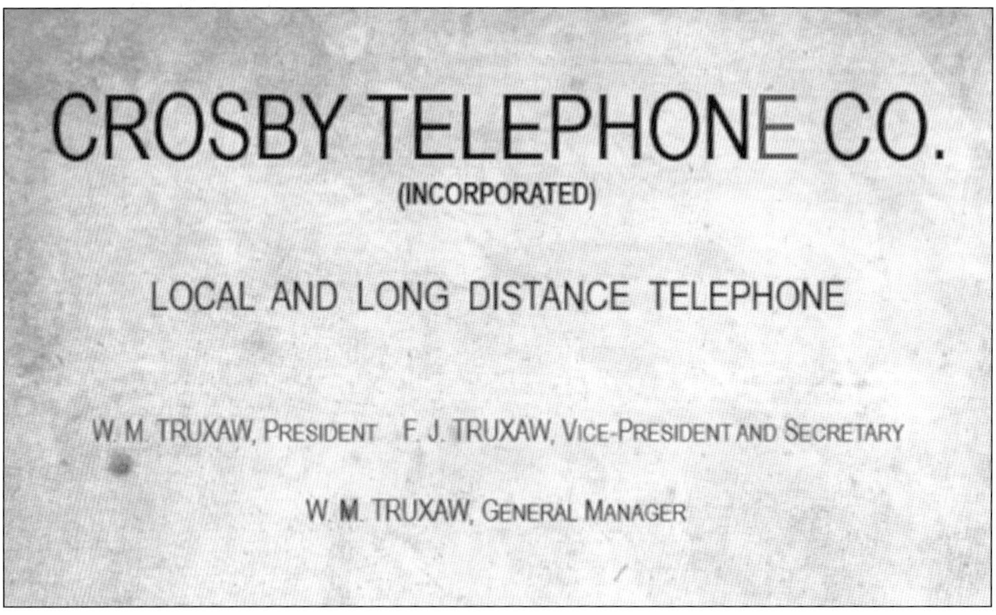

CROSBY TELEPHONE CO.

(INCORPORATED)

LOCAL AND LONG DISTANCE TELEPHONE

W. M. TRUXAW, PRESIDENT F. J. TRUXAW, VICE-PRESIDENT AND SECRETARY

W. M. TRUXAW, GENERAL MANAGER

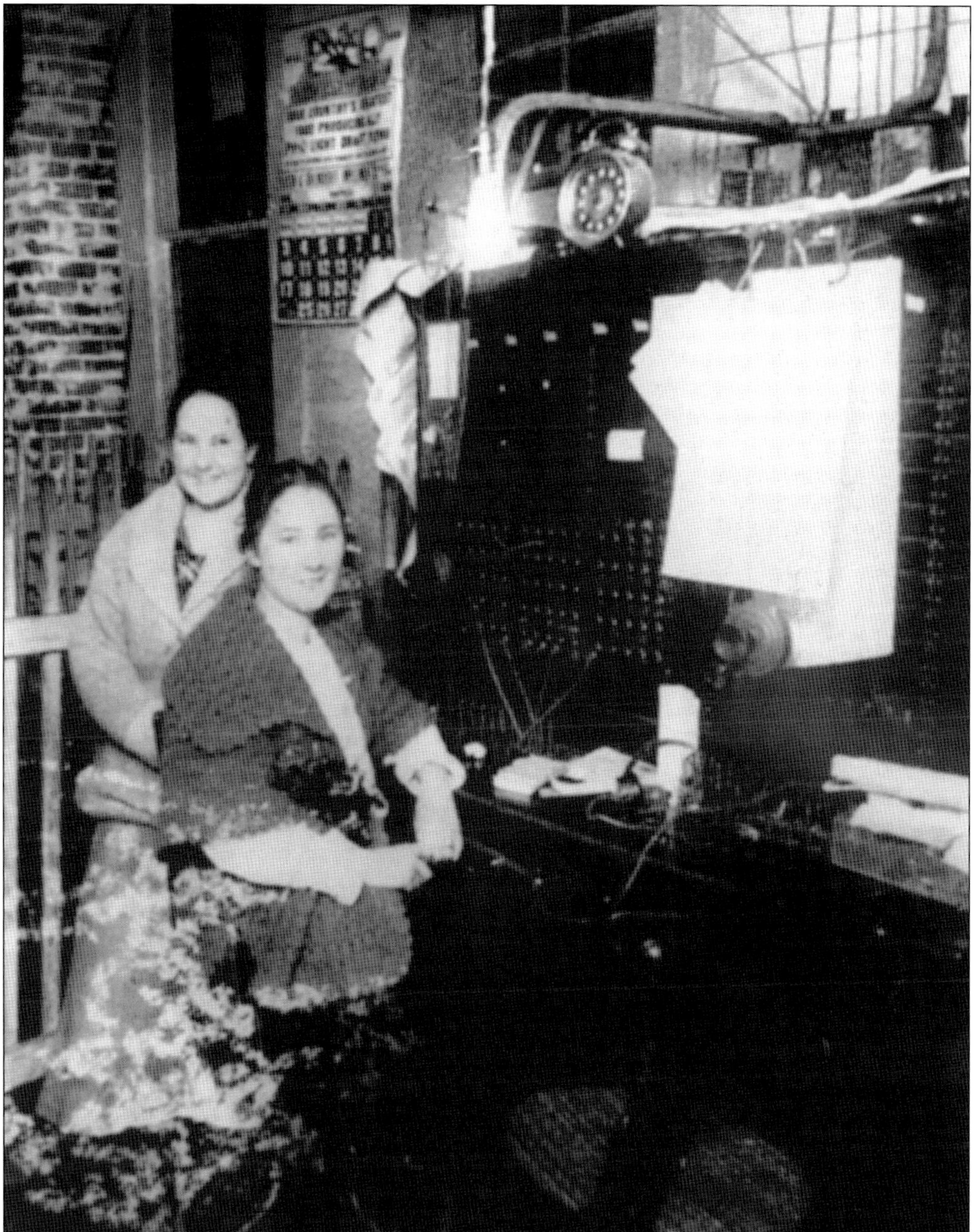

This photograph of Crosby Telephone Company switchboard operators Ora Harvey (standing) and Mable Lynch was taken in January 1916. This image was captured at the second-floor bank building location. Mable's parents owned the Lynch boardinghouse. Ora's father was a local blacksmith. She met her future husband, Othello Hare, at the phone company. He originally worked for the company stringing wires, but later worked for the Crosby State Bank on the first floor. By 1924, the two were married and had opened Crosby's first movie theater that played talking movies. (Courtesy of the Hare family.)

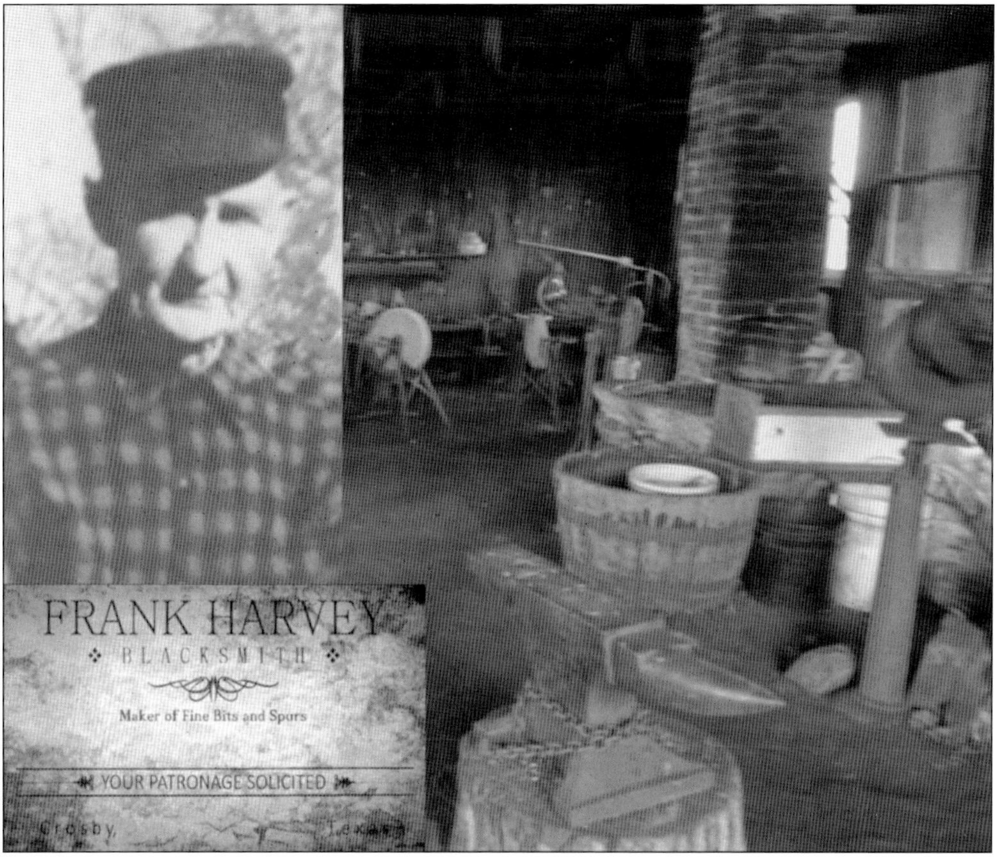

Frank M. Harvey's father, Joel Harvey, was a wheelwright who began making spurs and bits to supplement his income. The spurs and bits were more profitable, and so Frank decided to concentrate on only making them. He built a home at 218 Kernohan Street with a blacksmith shop next door. Across the road from his home were the railroad stock pens, where all the cattle were corralled for inspection and shipping. Harvey not only sold his spurs to the local cowboys there, but the Houston landmark store Stelzig's Saddlery also sold them as its top spur. They were lightweight and had a proper shank and rowel. Frank Harvey spurs have been passed down from one generation to the next and are highly sought after by collectors today. (Both, courtesy of Klaus Duda.)

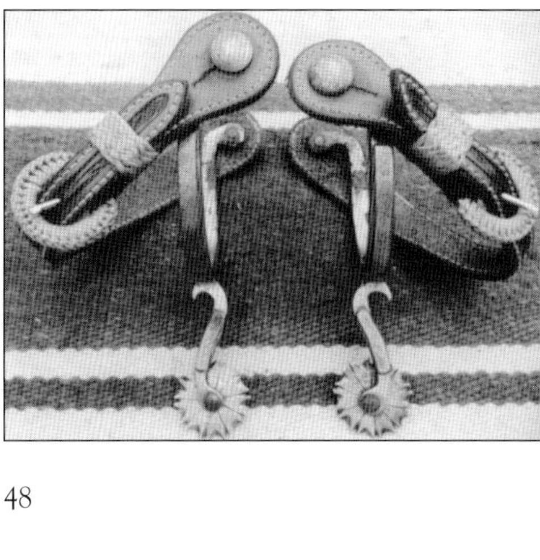

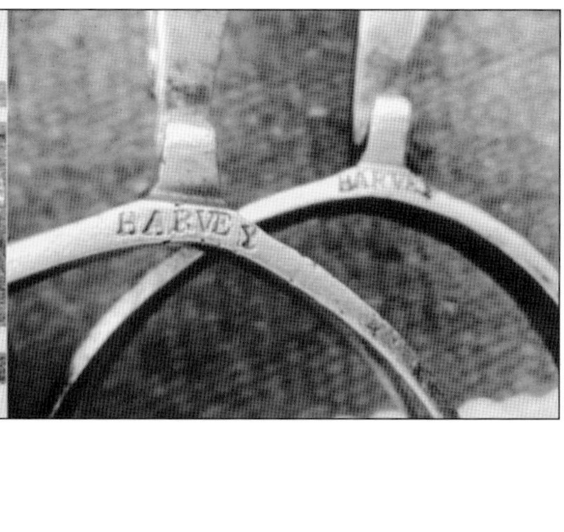

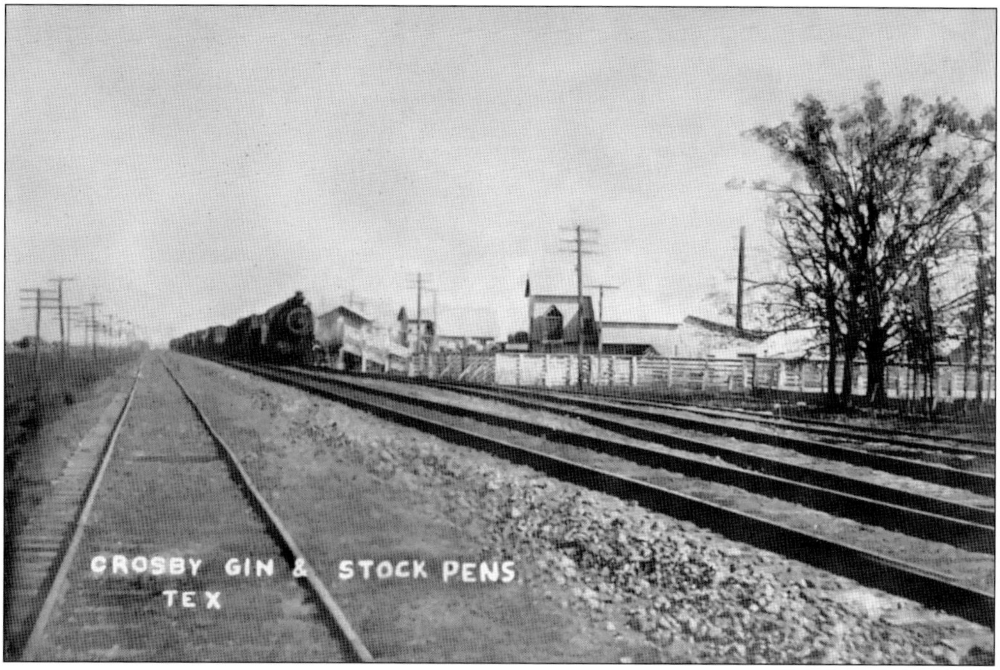

Pictured above and below are the railroad stock pens around 1911. The stockyards were in the 300 block of Kernohan Street. The photograph above looks east toward the stockyards with two of Crosby's cotton gins in the background. The railroad had a siding adjacent to a loading ramp connected to the pens. Wild horses and cattle were held in the pens until specialized stock cars could be sent to pick them up. The photograph below shows two workers feeding wild horses hay. The Gregory Gin is at center, across the tracks. (Both, courtesy of Klaus Duda.)

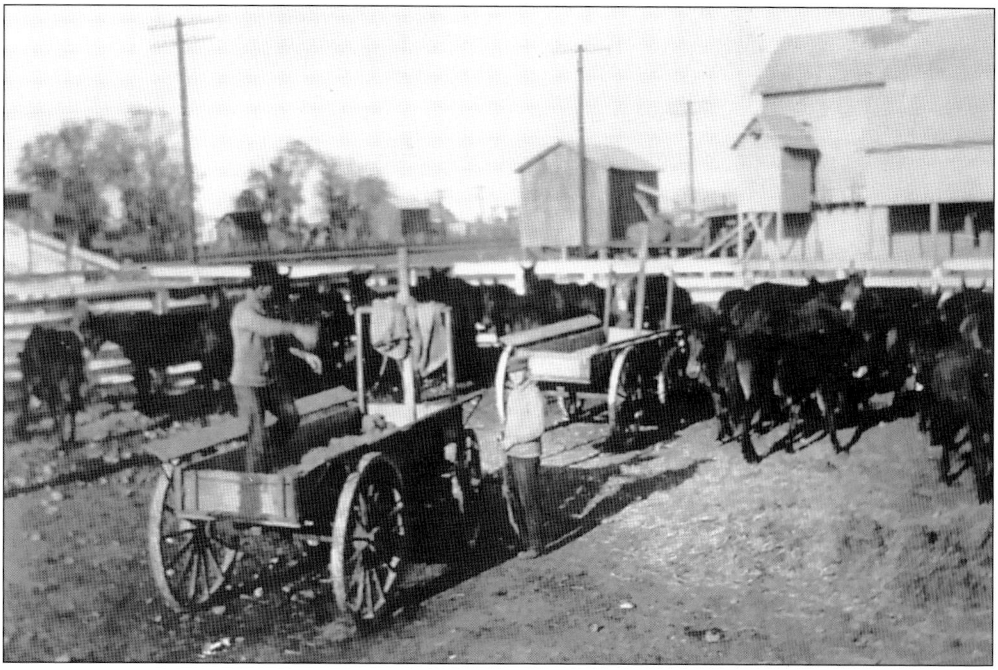

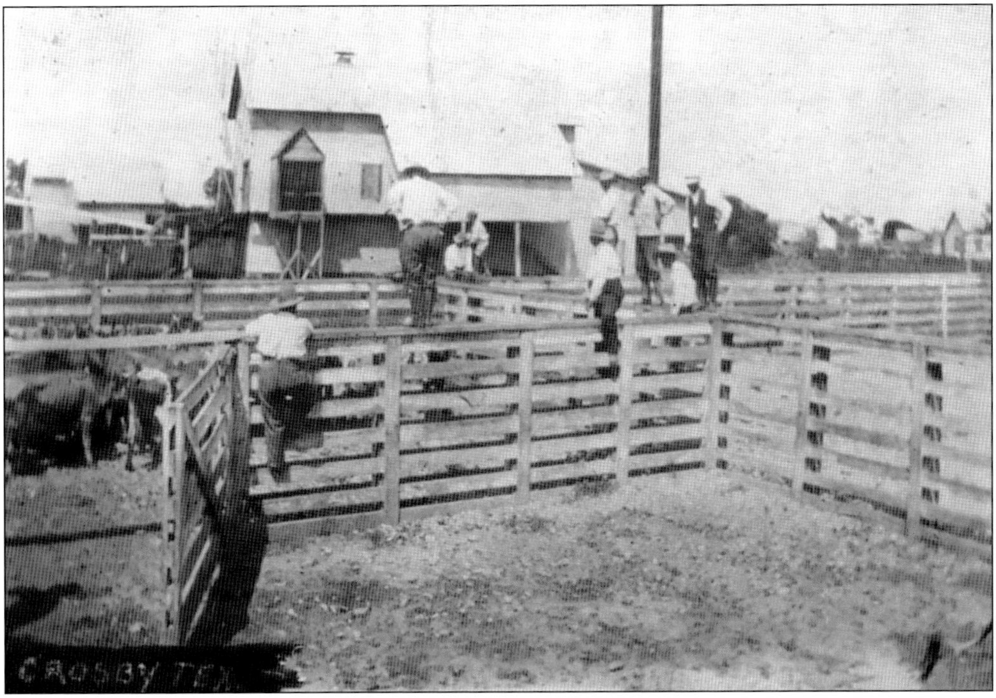

In 1898, the grasslands around Crosby held an estimated 8,000 free-roaming cattle. Rounding them up and herding them to the stockyards was one of the first big sources of income for early residents. Choice beeves brought $3.50 per head, and common heifers brought $2 per head. The cattle were so plentiful that fences were placed around farms to keep them and the hogs out, rather than to fence them in. The railroad cattle holding pens pictured above around 1913 were built in 1897. These pens had space for 500 head of cattle and were used until the 1920s. (Above, courtesy of Cecil Newton; below, author drawing.)

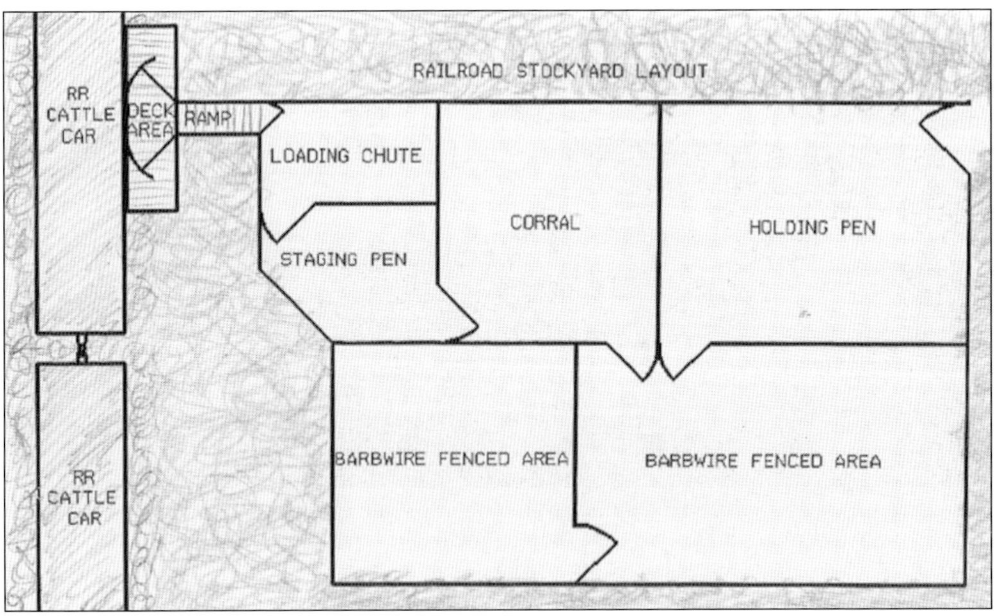

Three

King Cotton, White Gold

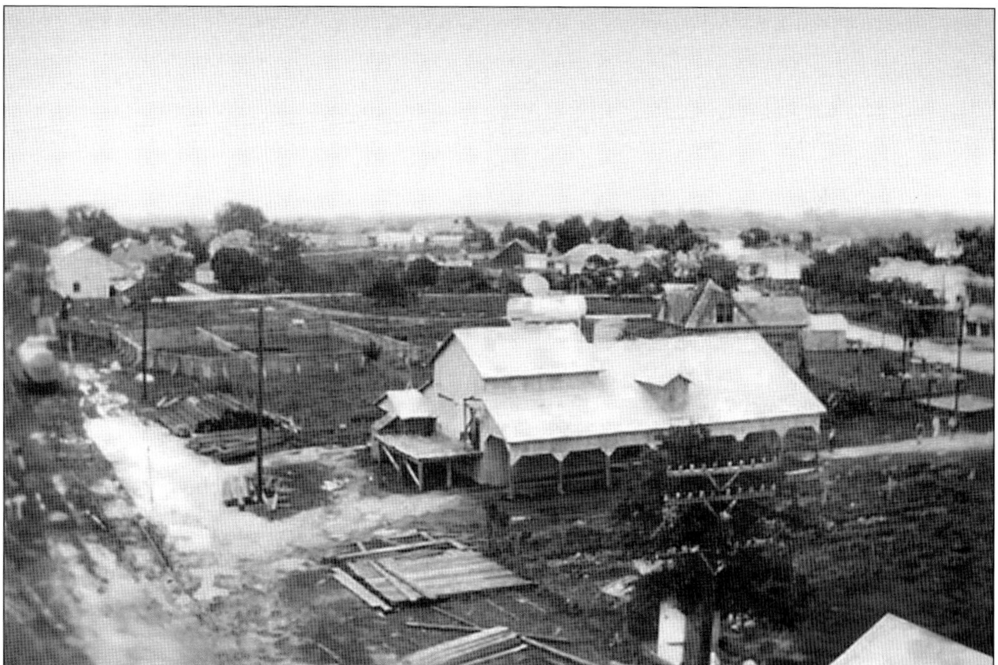

Cotton was the most valuable commodity grown during the early days of Crosby, with a value very similar to oil today. It became the driving force in the growth of Crosby. The land here was regionally famous for its fertile soil, which yielded nearly a bale of cotton per acre. The first gin in Crosby was built in 1897 by Albert McKinney.

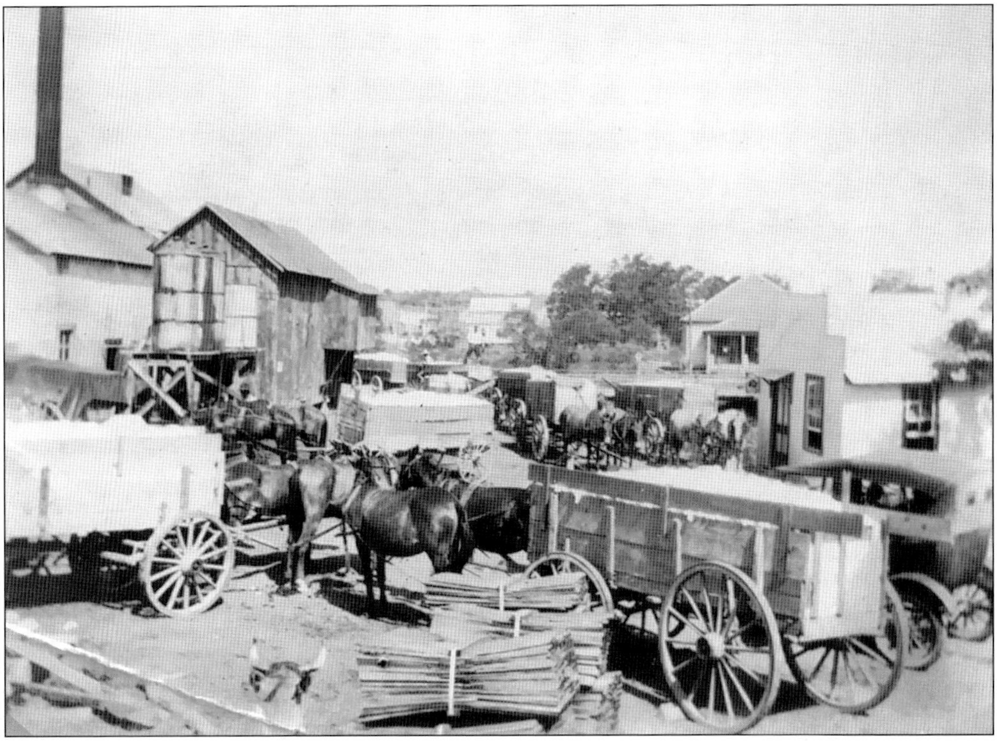

In 1909, C.A. Gustafson built a second gin in Crosby, pictured above in 1917. It was on Main Street near the southeast corner of the intersection with Wahl Street, and included a sawmill at the southern end of the property (pictured below). It was the first steam-powered gin in the area. Gustafson was probably the wealthiest Swede in Crosby and purchased much of the land along the waterways. He had a number of workers who would clear the land to supply his sawmill. Afterward, he would sell the land to ranchers or farmers. (Both, courtesy of the Anderson family.)

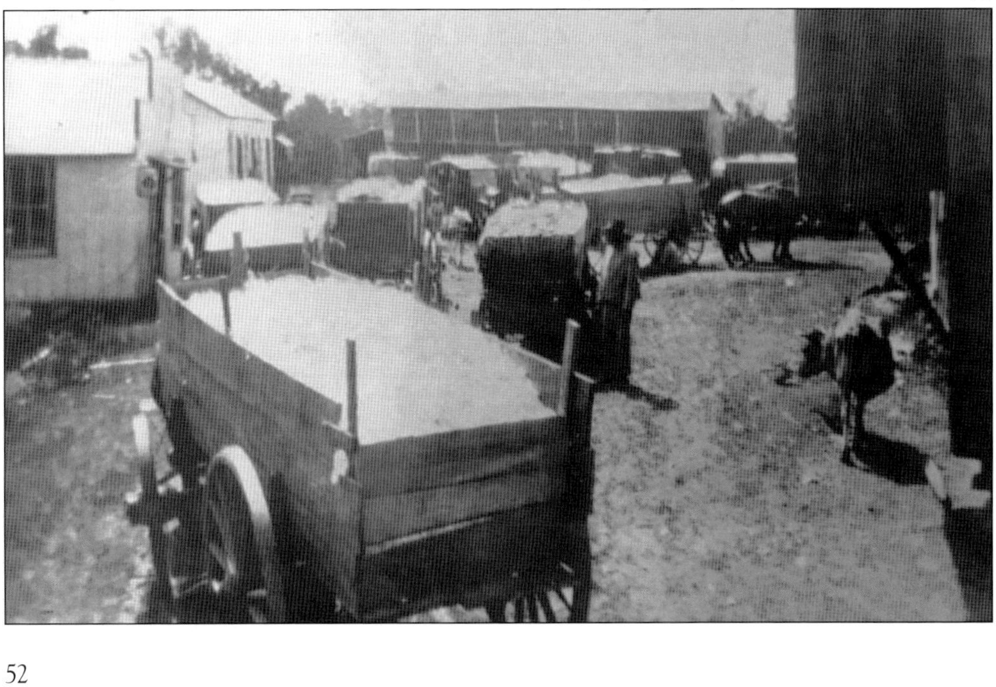

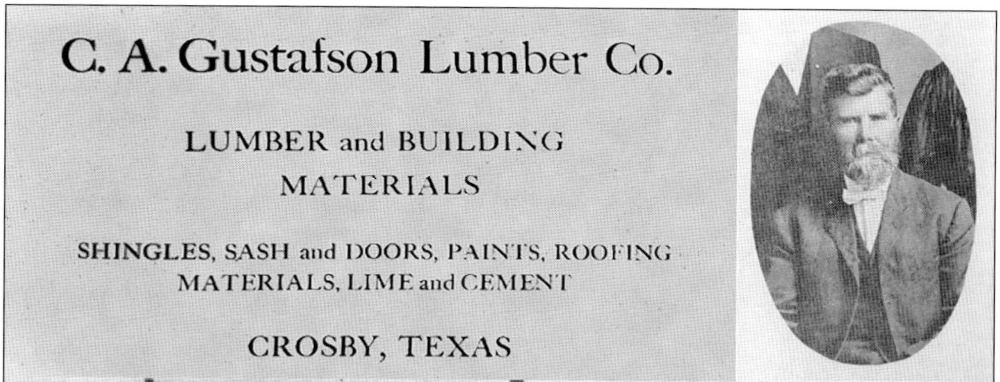

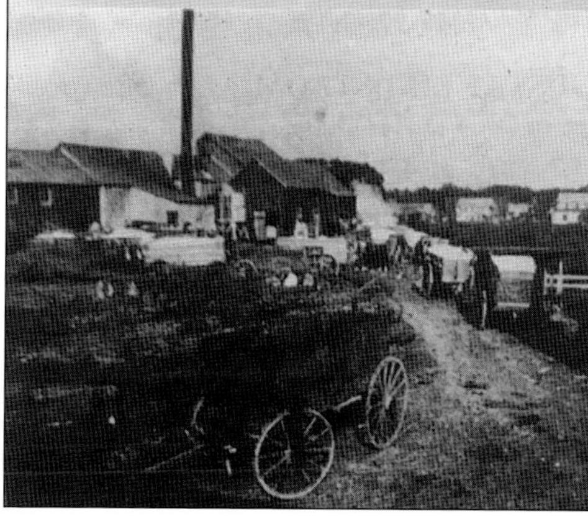

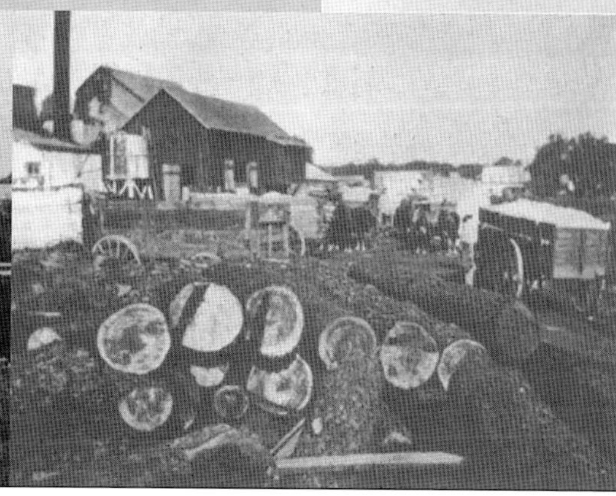

The C.A. Gustafson gin and lumber company was on Main Street, with the lumber company on the corner of West Reidland Avenue. Record cotton crops brought prosperity to Crosby in 1917. An infestation of boll weevils the following year caused the town to be quarantined. The year 1918 was very difficult for Crosby cotton farmers, so many cut down trees for the sawmill instead.

NEW GIN AT CROSBY

Will Be a Convenience to the Farmers.

(Houston Post Special.)

CROSBY, Texas, August 1.—Improvements for the week ended yesterday show a number of new buildings and improvements.

The big modern gin plant of the Crosby Gin and Lumber company has just been completed. It will be a great convenience to the farmers of this section as one gin is not able to handle all the cotton that is raised in this section.

R. E. Dunks has begun to remodel his house.

C. M. Matthews has just completed his ice house and has sold two cars of ice this week and he expects to handle more this coming week.

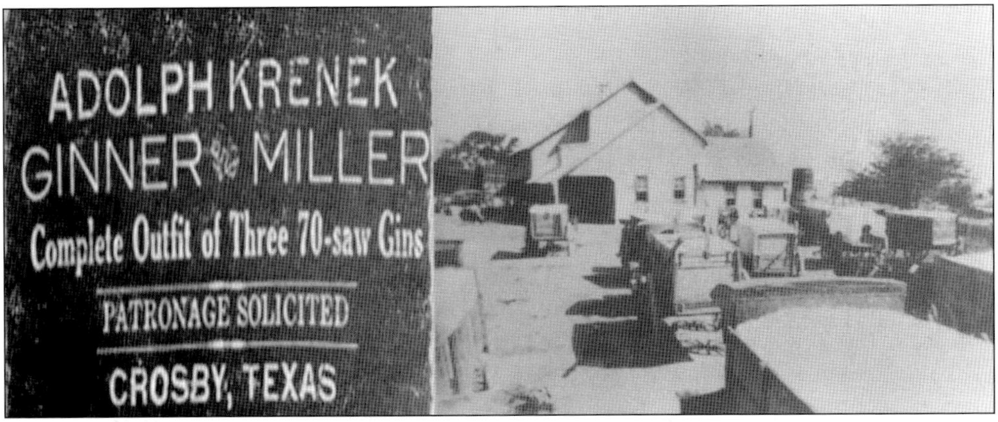

In 1910, local farmers sold shares of stocks and built a cooperative gin, because the other two gins in town at the time (McKinney and Gustafson), couldn't keep up with the amount of cotton local farmers were producing. In 1915, Ike and Helen Krenek (pictured below), along with Ike's brother Adolph, built the Krenek Brothers Gin (above). It was adjacent to the Farmers Gin on Kernohan Street. This gin also had a grist mill on the property, which ground corn during the corn harvest. The grist mill was powered by an old tractor. It was at the western end of Runneburg Road and later was used as a Woodmen of the World dance hall and event space. (Both, courtesy of the Krenek family.)

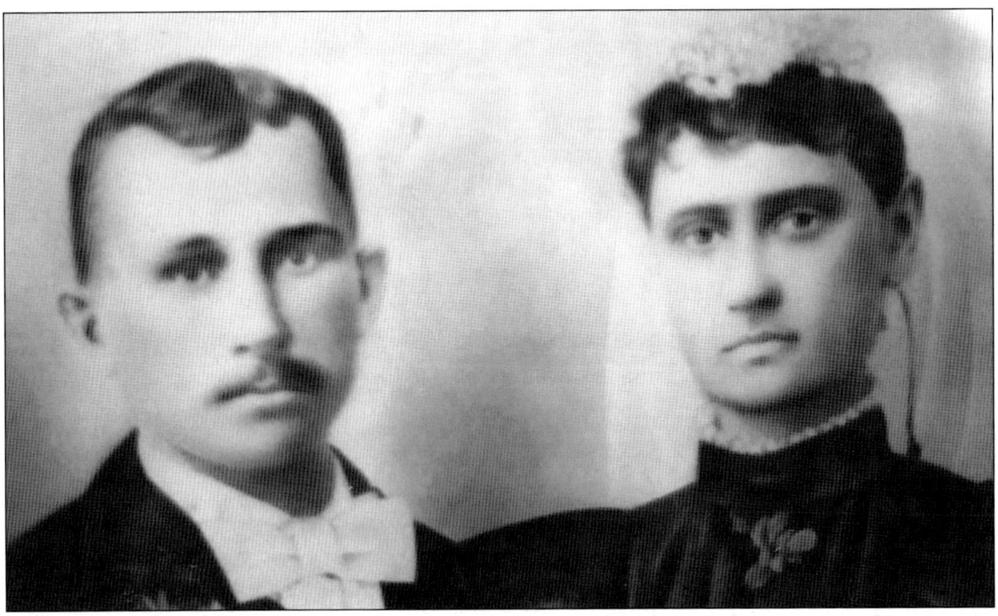

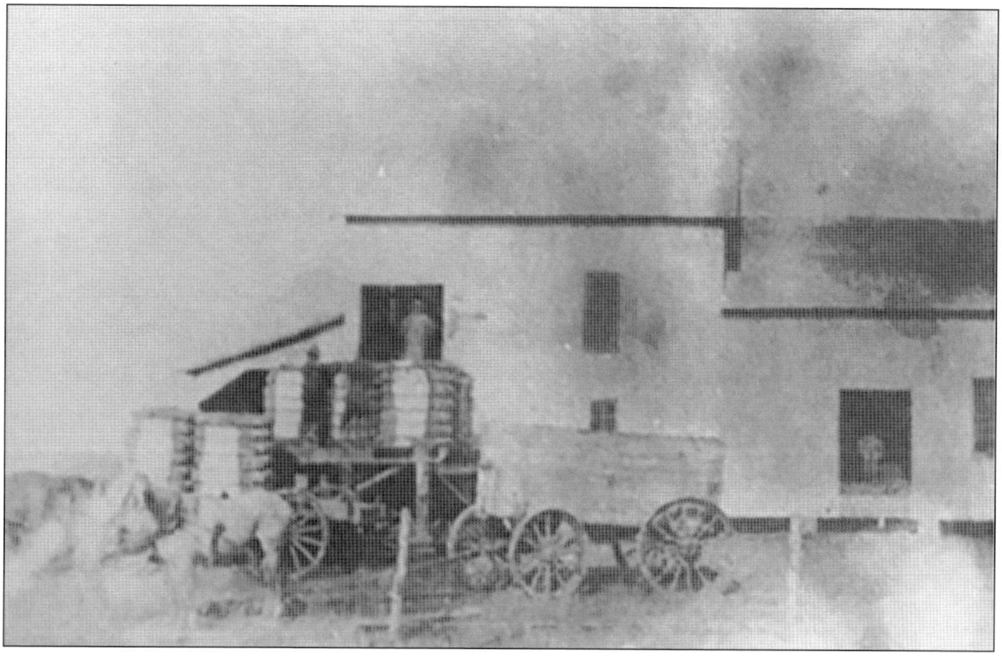

Pictured above is the Gregory Gin, located in the 300 block of Live Oak Street, at the east end next to the railroad tracks. It was built by Albert McKinney in 1897, but it was acquired by Joseph Gregory in 1915. During the peak of the cotton harvest, the numerous Crosby cotton gins operated 24 hours per day to keep up with the local farmers. It was reported that over 17,000 bales of cotton were ginned in Crosby in 1915. Pictured below is Gus Stasney in 1927, with a group of cotton pickers that he hired from Port Arthur to help with his harvest. (Both, courtesy of Karen Randall.)

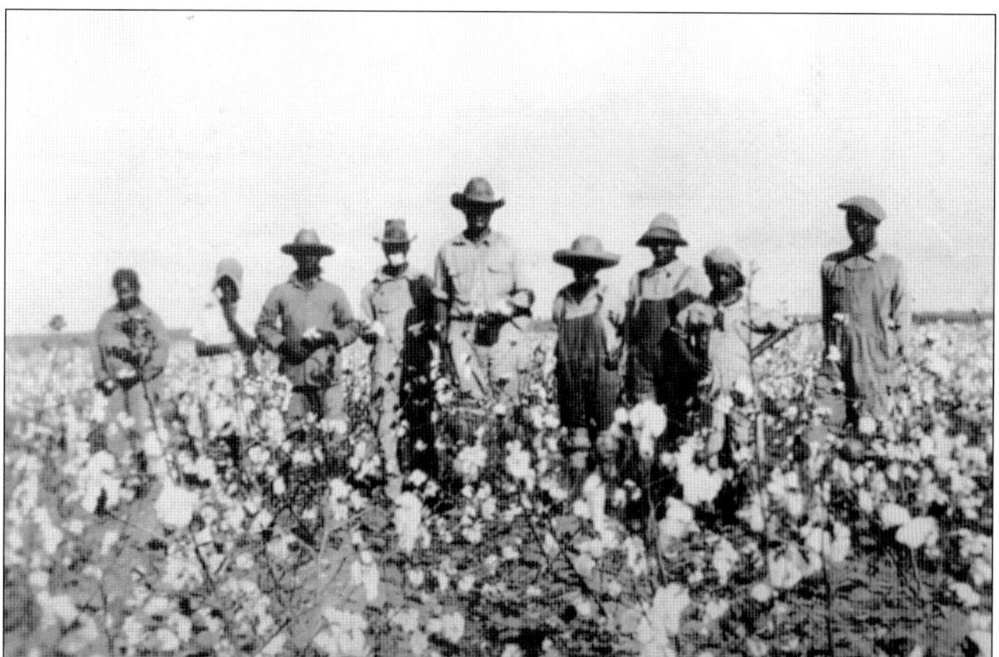

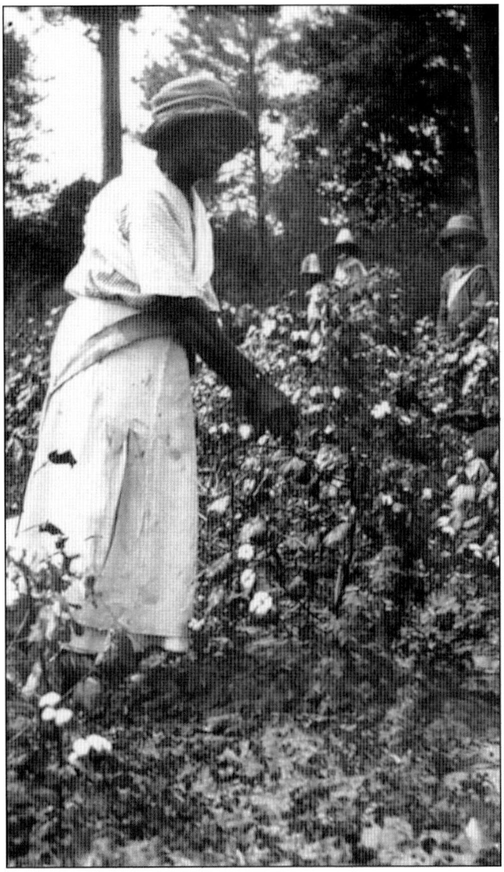

In 1926, the Crosby Chamber of Commerce passed a motion by Oscar Reidland that a standing offer of $50 would be given to the farmer who brought in the first bale of cotton each year that met standard grades. This set off a rush among farmers trying to be the first to deliver, and races to the gins soon ensued. Below, Joe Franta Sr. is pictured with a wagon load of cotton in the Krenek brothers' cotton field near Bohemian Hall Road. At left is Betty Thomas and her family picking cotton on the McKinney farm. (Left, courtesy of the McKinney family; below, courtesy of the Lostak family.)

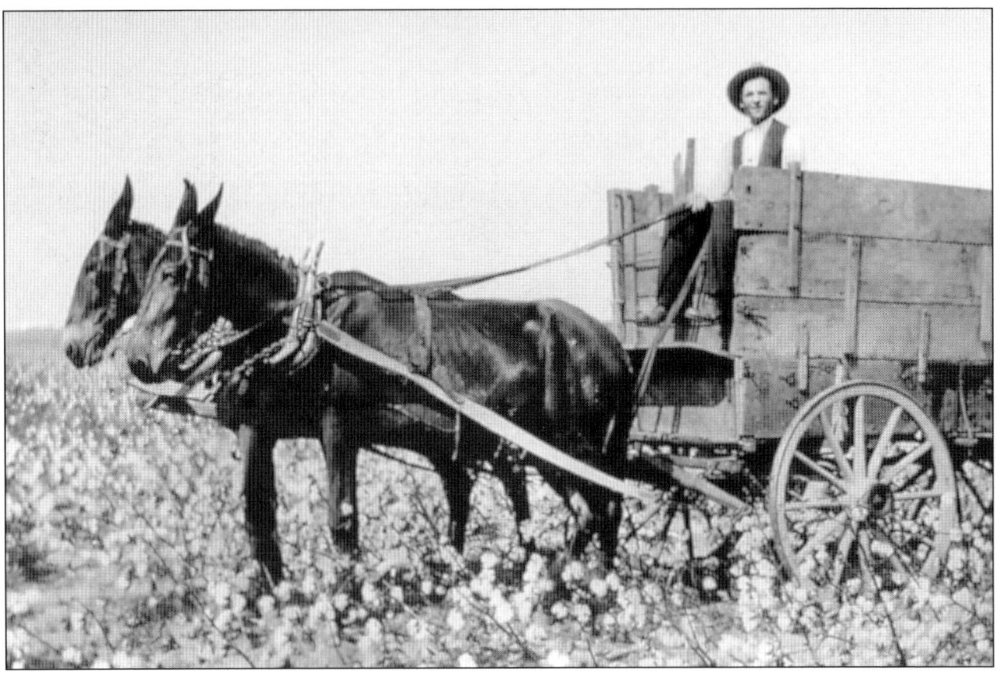

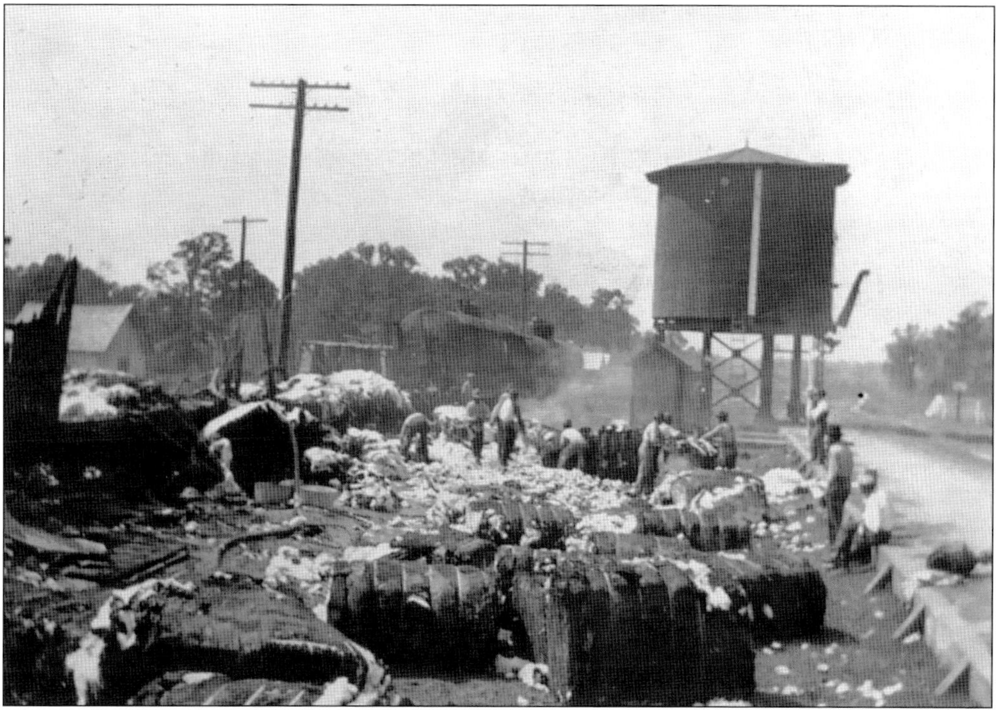

Workmen clean up after a load of cotton caught fire in 1915 at the Crosby railroad terminal. Remnants of burnt cotton bales and pieces of a boxcar litter the area. The photograph above is one of the best images of the railroad water tower, where so many early photographs of the town were taken. The tank was moved to Dayton in 1925. Photographers would climb to the top of the tower to get a good vantage point. The men below are Reynold Johnson (1), Charlie Swanson (2), William Lynch (3), Fred Burkland (4), and Elmer Jackson (5). (Both, courtesy of the Swanson family.)

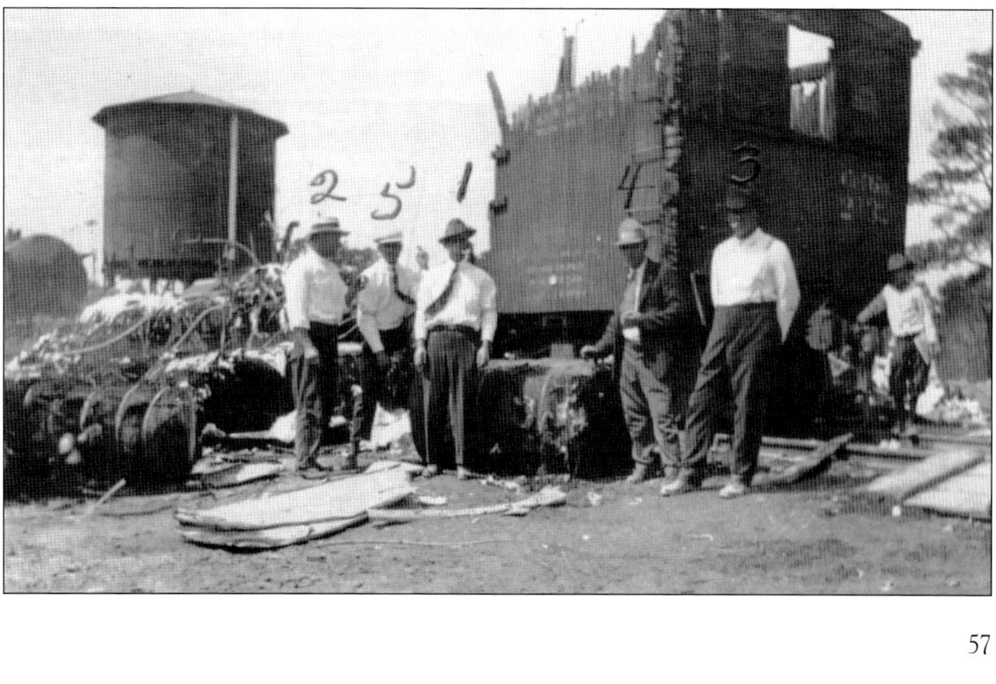

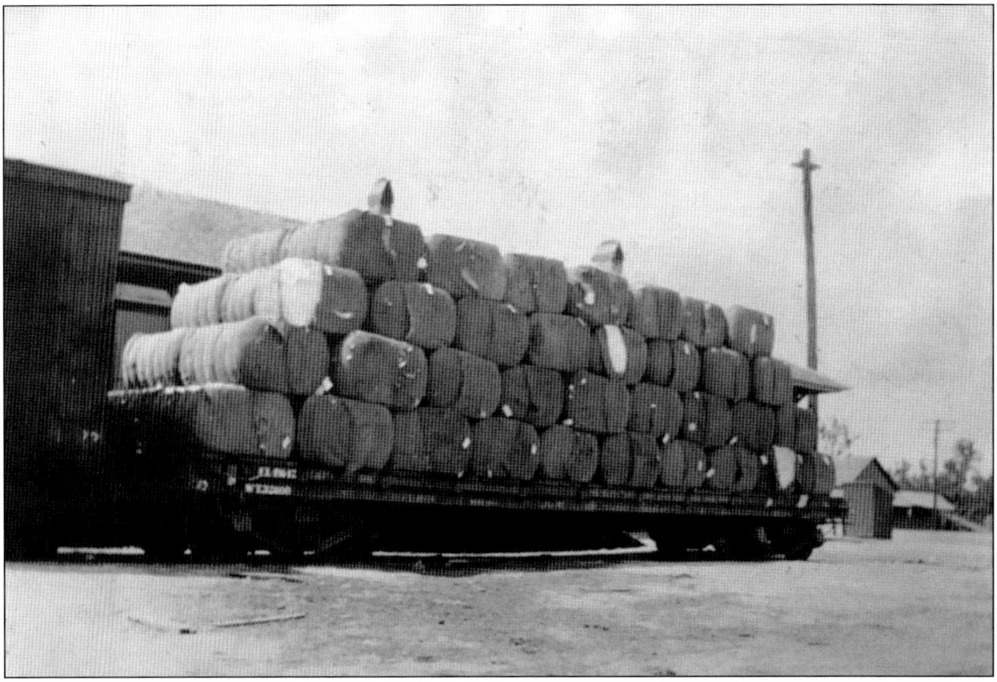

The Crosby Mercantile Company bought raw cotton from local farmers and had it ginned and compressed into bales. It was then loaded on train cars and shipped out. The photograph below shows just how good the 1917 harvest was. The four owners of the Crosby Mercantile Company (Oscar Reidland, R.C.J. Kenning, John Nelson, and Theodore Anderson) are standing on top of a load of cotton bales headed to Houston. From there, the bales were loaded onto barges and sent to Galveston, where they were loaded onto ocean freighters and sent to textile mills along the East Coast.

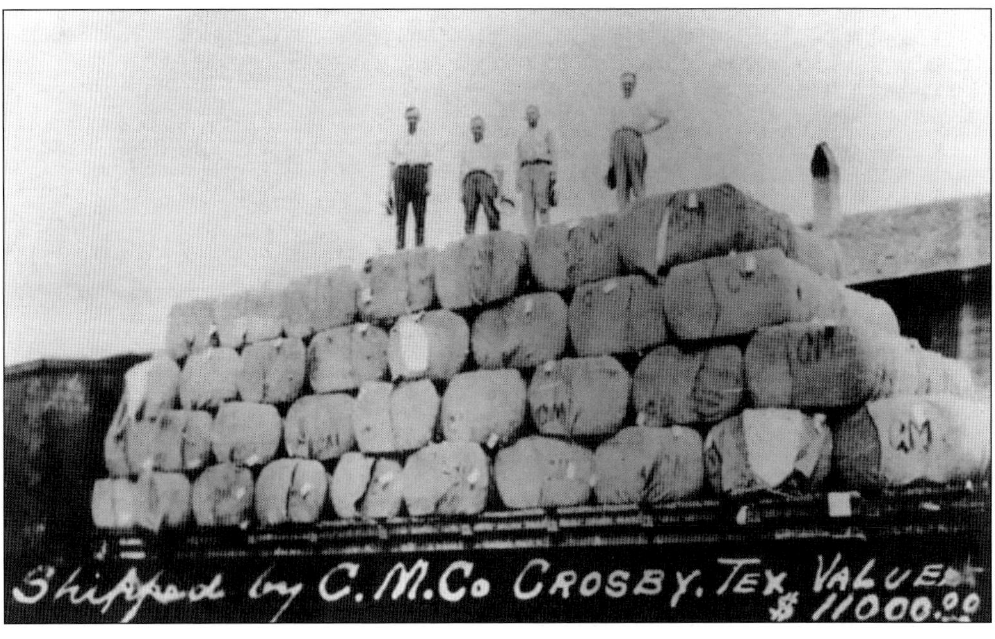

Four

Crosby, the Regional Center

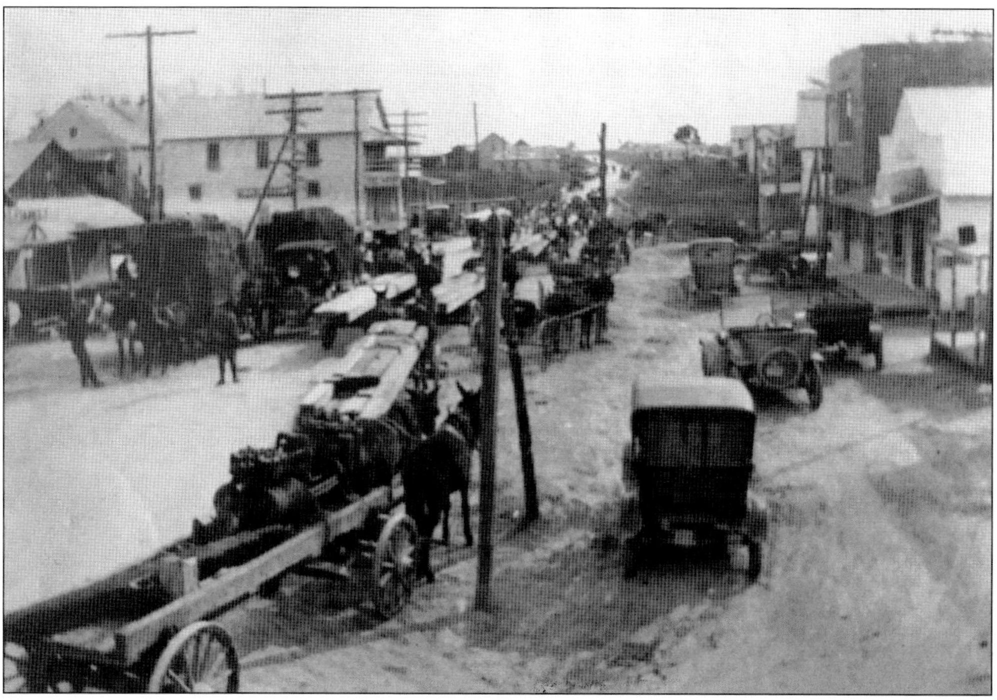

By 1915, Crosby had become the commercial center for East Harris County. However, the development of oilfields in Baytown changed that. Construction soon began on the Humble Refinery. With no direct rail lines into Baytown, everything was shipped by rail to Crosby and then loaded on the wagons of local farmers, who were paid to haul it. Pictured here is Crosby's Main Street. (Courtesy of the Evans family.)

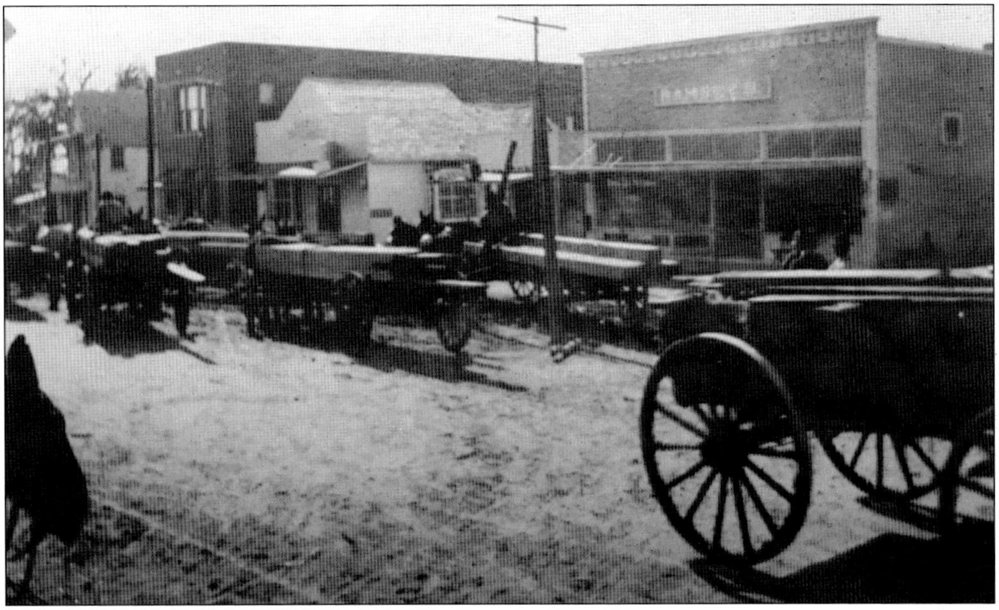

Above is another photograph of lumber and supplies headed from the Crosby depot to the Goose Creek oil fields in 1917. Oil had been discovered at Goose Creek in 1903. By 1917, hundreds of oil derricks were being built with lumber like that shown here. Below is Earl Hilliard's meat market and ice house, also in 1917. It was in the 100 block of Kernohan Street. The market closed in 1929, but Earl's son "Butch" would later run a locally famous seafood restaurant in Crosby for a number of years. From left to right are Joe Franta Sr., Joe Franta Jr., Earl Hilliard (owner), and two unidentified. Joe Sr. died the same year this photograph was taken. (Above, courtesy of the Evans family; below, courtesy of the Lostak family.)

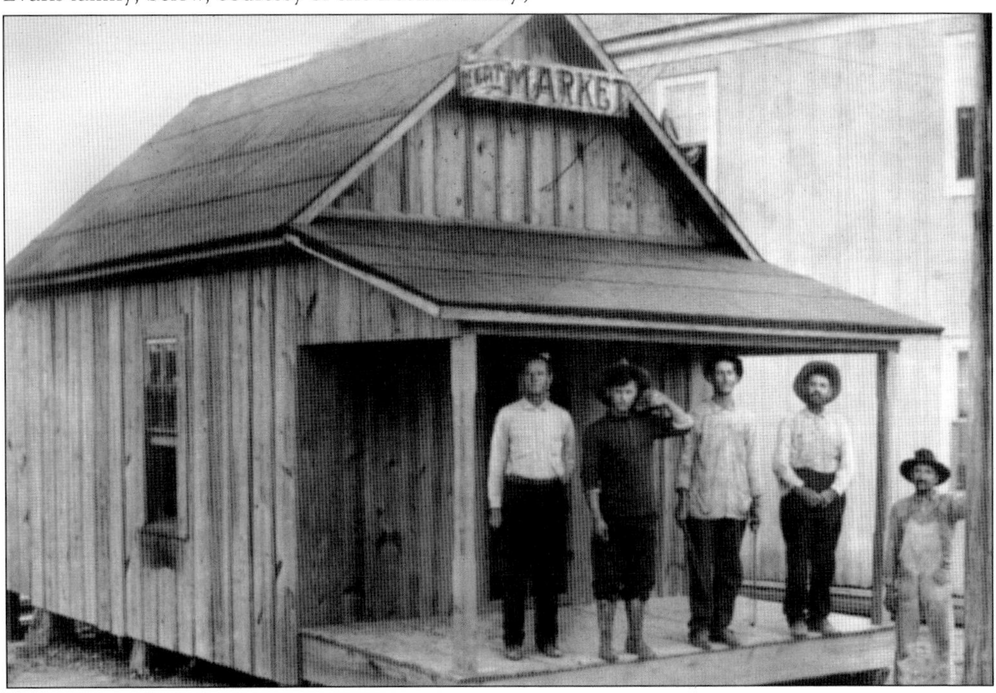

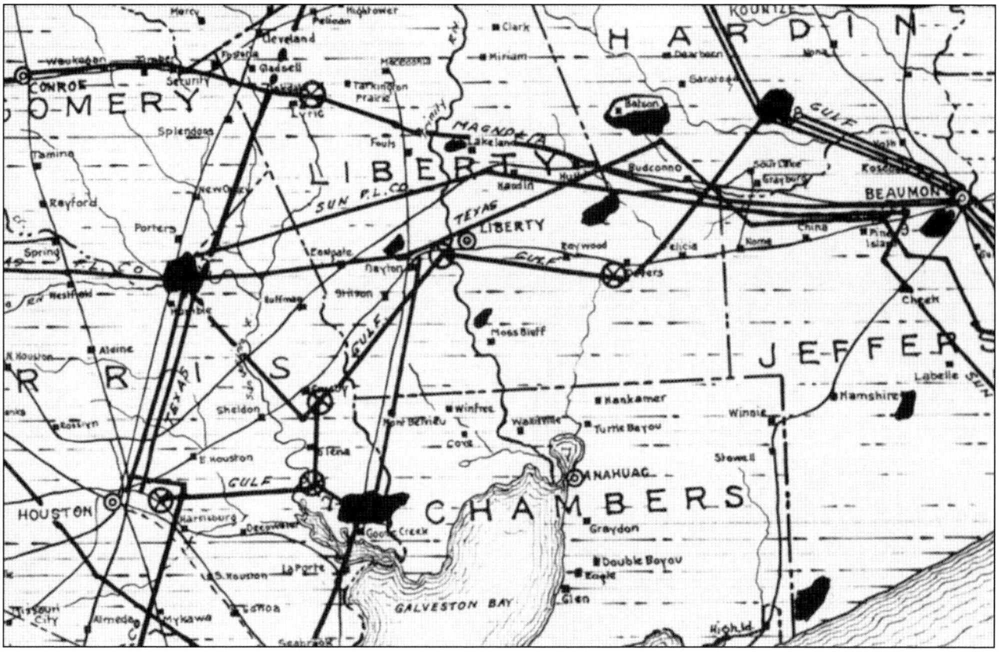

The oil discovered in the surrounding area led to the construction of a number of pipelines. The 1921 oil map above shows several pipelines that had already been constructed. The dark blots indicate known oil reserves. The circles with an "x" indicate pumping stations. The Gulf Pipeline pumping station seen below was in Crosby at Jaegers' Corner. It was built around 1920 and was one of a series of pumping stations built along the pipeline's path. Other pumping stations were in Lynchburg, Dayton, and Devers.

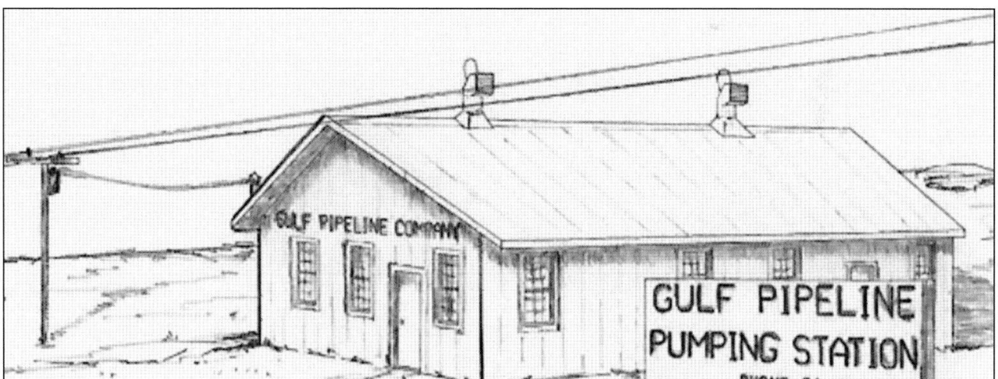

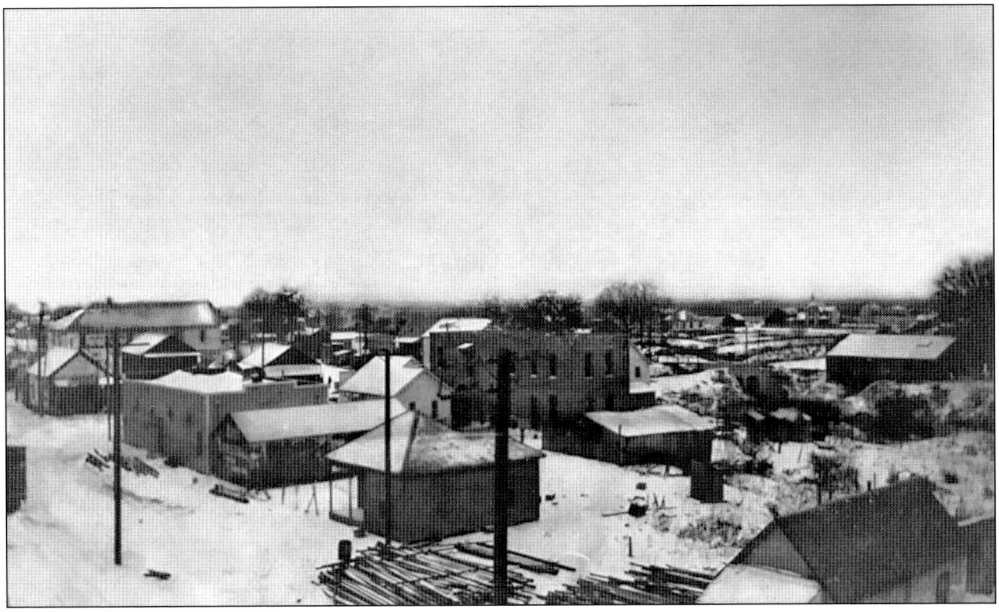

On January 11, 1918, it snowed enough in Crosby for a fairly decent snowball fight. Pictured below in a view looking north are the R.E. Dunks general store and the Matthews meat market and saloon on FM 2100. Snow in Crosby is rare, but on Valentine's Day 1895, the Houston area received 22 inches, with four-foot drifts. Single-digit temperatures are also quite rare; however, on February 13, 1899, the Houston area had a record low temperature of six degrees. It was so cold that all the area rivers froze over, and thousands of free-ranging cattle froze to death. The record-high temperature for Crosby is 109 degrees, set on September 4, 2000. (Above, courtesy of the Newton family; below, courtesy of the Swanson family.)

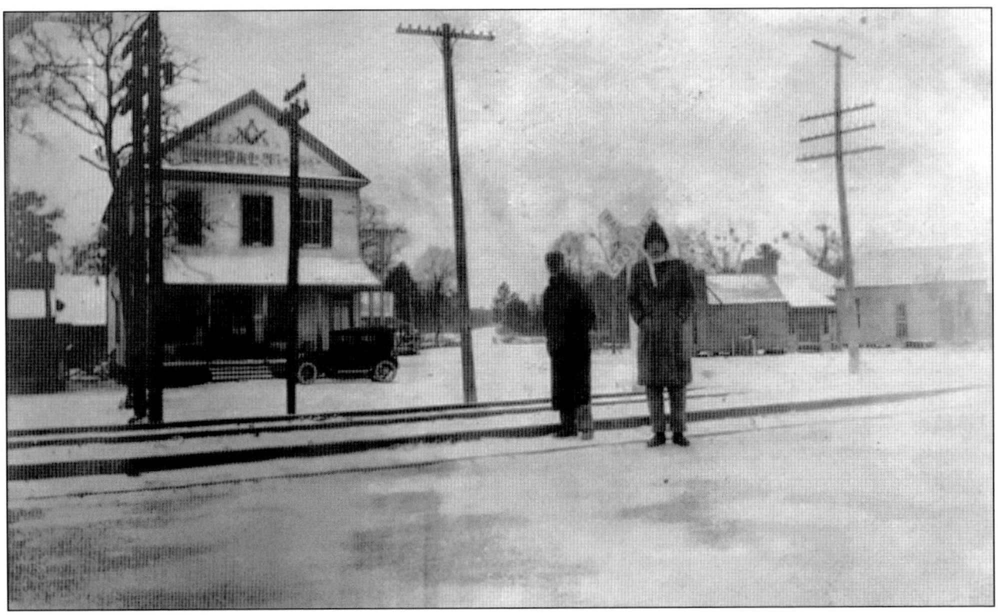

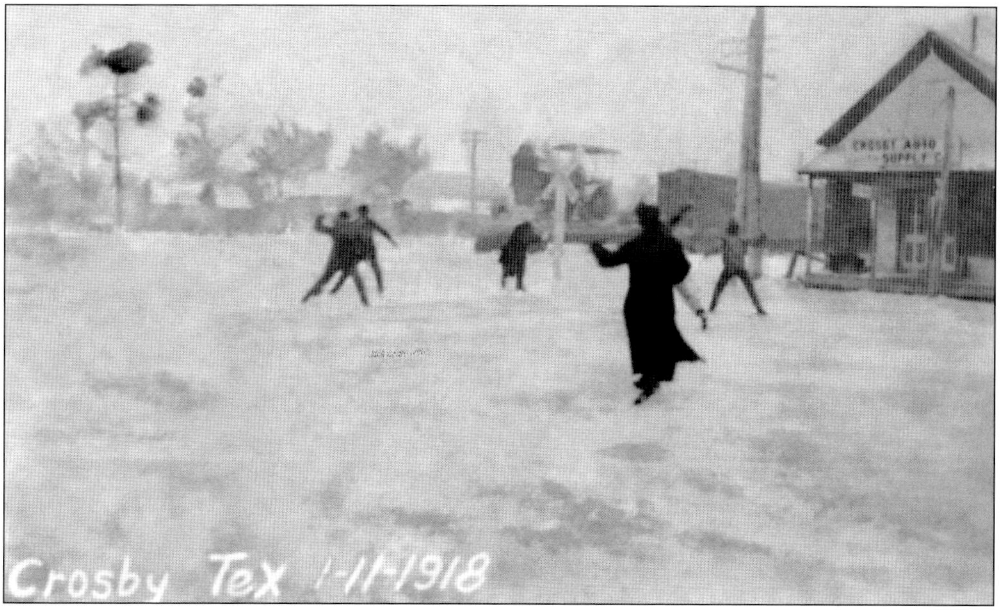

The snow led to an all-out snowball war on Main Street near the railroad tracks, captured in these photographs. The photograph above looks north with Crosby Auto Supply at right. A large steam-powered tractor waits to be unloaded off a flatcar. In the background is the Matthews meat market and saloon. The following year, Crosby went dry and ended all liquor sales in the area. The image below is on the railroad tracks just east of Main Street, looking east. The small building in the background may be a pump house. It is located where an artesian well was indicated on the 1903 plat of the town. (Both, courtesy of the Swanson family.)

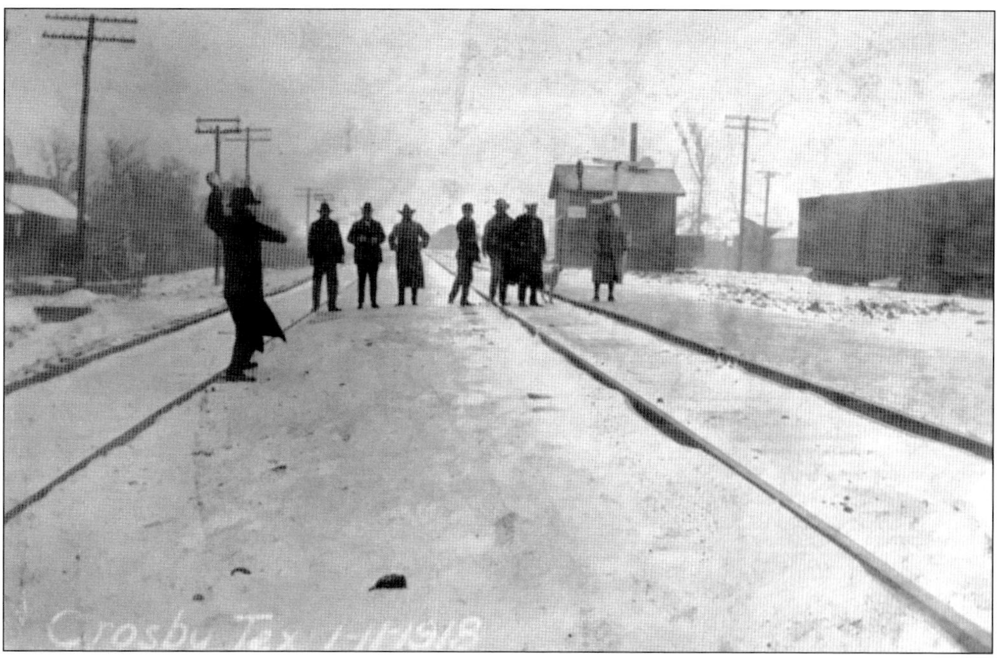

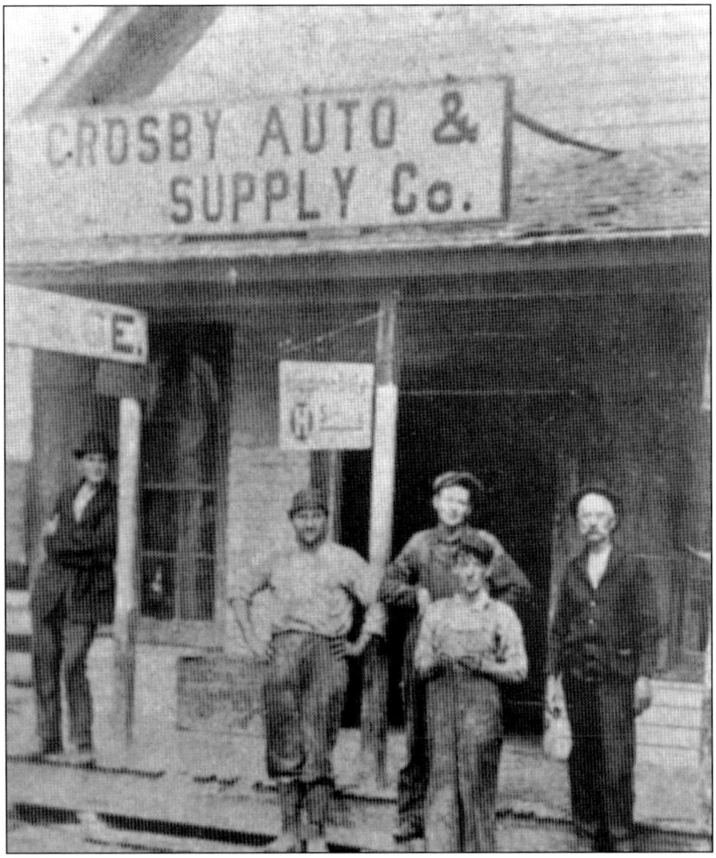

These photographs were taken in 1918 of Crosby Auto & Supply Co., which offered free compressed air to its customers. It was on Main Street next to the railroad tracks on the southeast corner, in the old Ramsey's Confectionery building. These are probably some of the same guys in the snowball fight on the previous page. The business was opened by J. Austin Smith in 1915. Smith went on to serve two terms as the Harris County road commissioner. The men below are local World War I recruits, headed off to basic training. (Both, courtesy of the Ramsey family.)

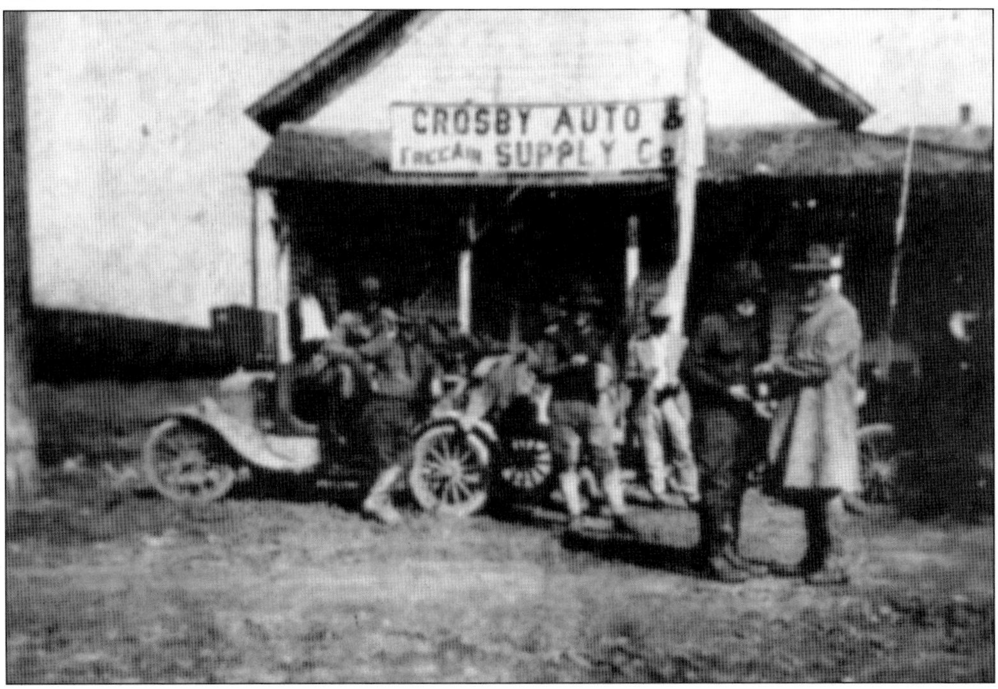

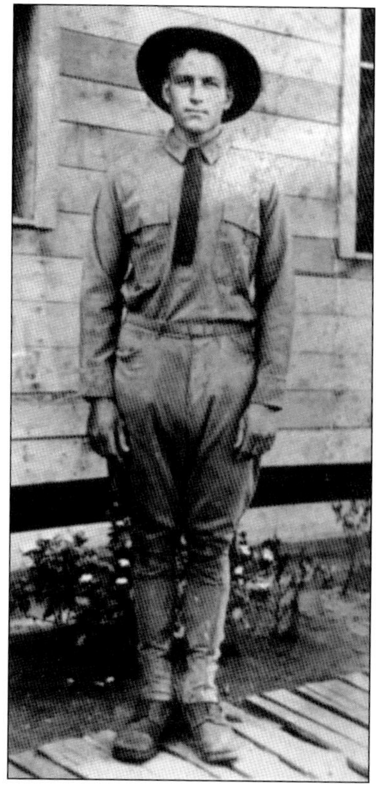

One of the many local young men who signed up for service in World War I was Louis Adlong (right). Another was Jesse Newton, who went to work at the newly built Ellington Air Base and the Park Place Air Base, which is today's William P. Hobby Airport. Newton worked in the mechanic's shop and acquired a number of great photographs, like the one below of airplanes flying in formation over the Crosby countryside. The planes often flew out to the Crosby area because a training field had been set up there. (Right, courtesy of the Adlong family; below, courtesy of the Newton family.)

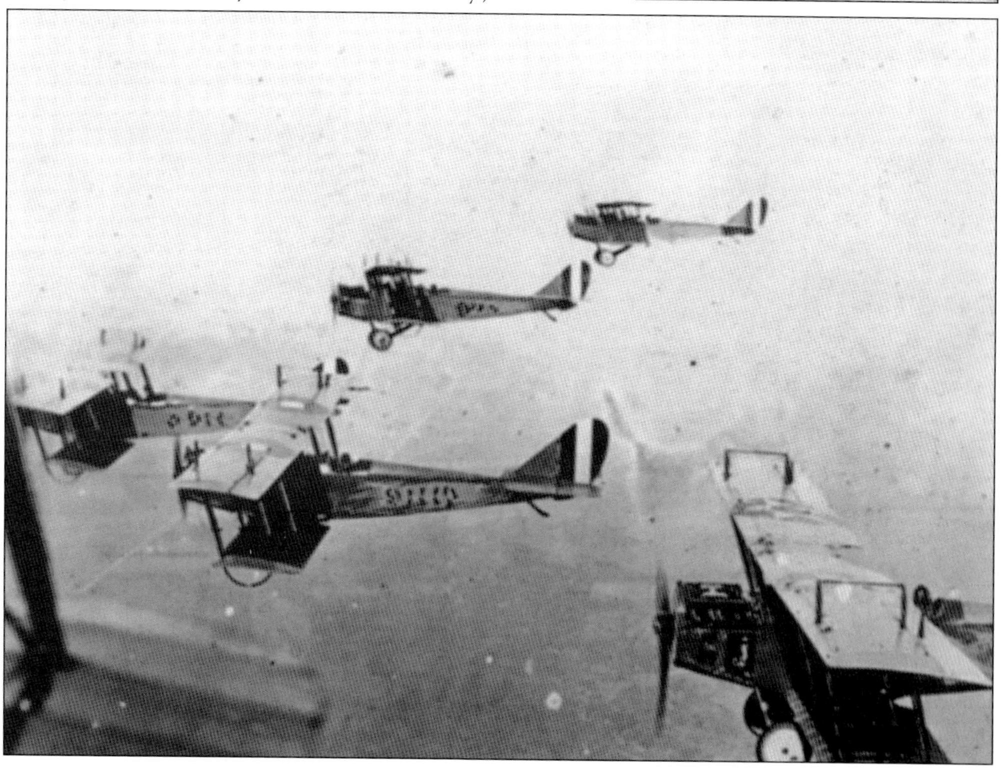

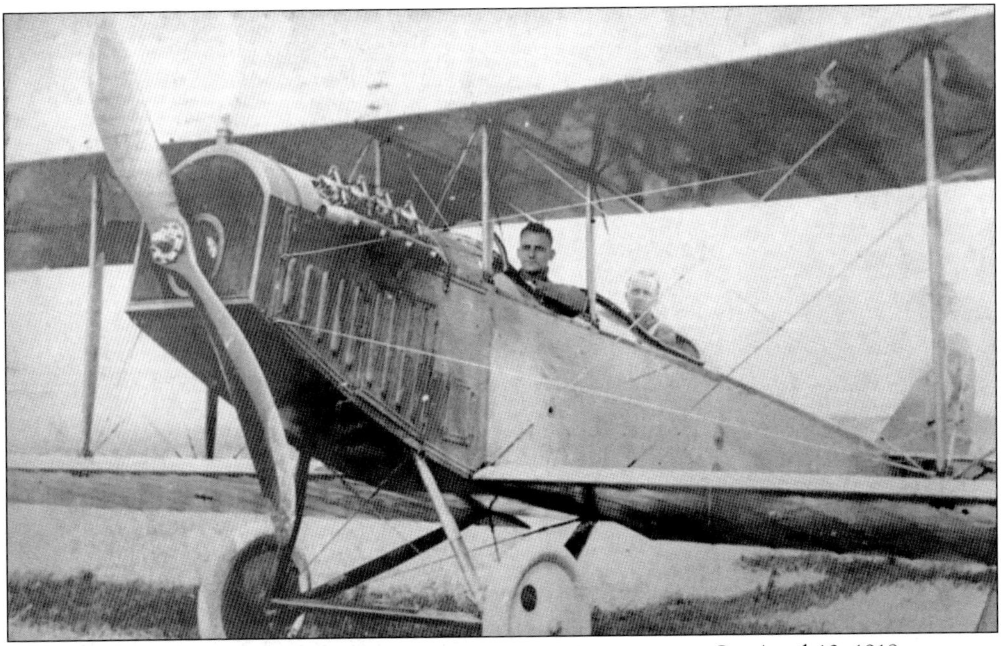

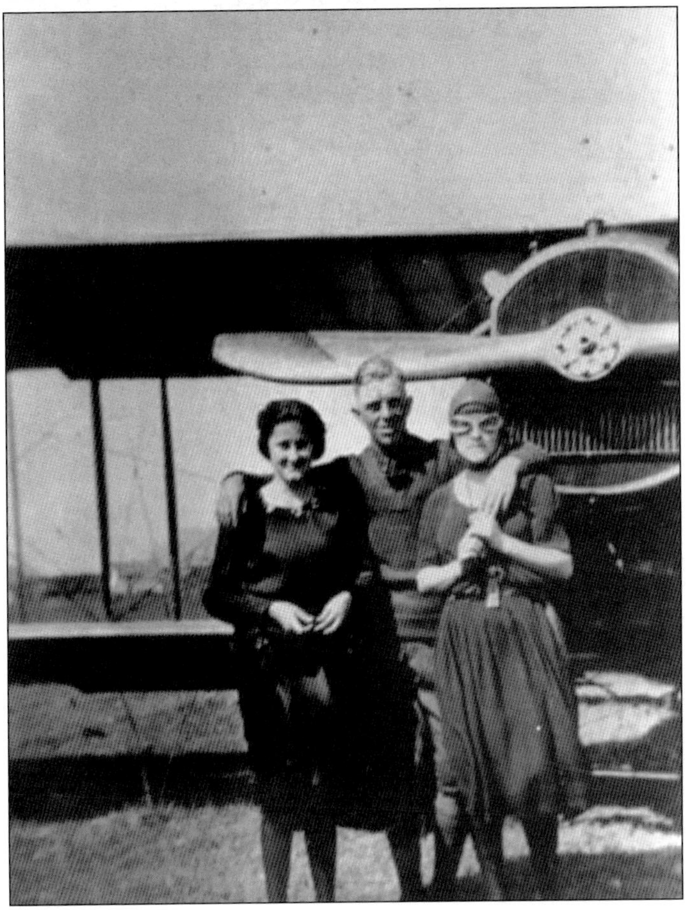

On April 13, 1918, an airplane landed in a makeshift airfield where the Nelson Addition is today. It was part of a fundraising effort for the Liberty Bond effort to raise money for World War I. It was one of the first airplanes to land in Crosby. Nearly every resident in Crosby went to see it. They also helped the pilot take off by holding the wings while he revved the motor. Pictured at left are Eleanor Henson and Gertrude Wilson with the pilot. By the end of the war, Crosby's airstrip had two to three planes landing per day for fuel and stopovers. (Above, courtesy of the Michalsky family; left, courtesy of the Blomstrom family.)

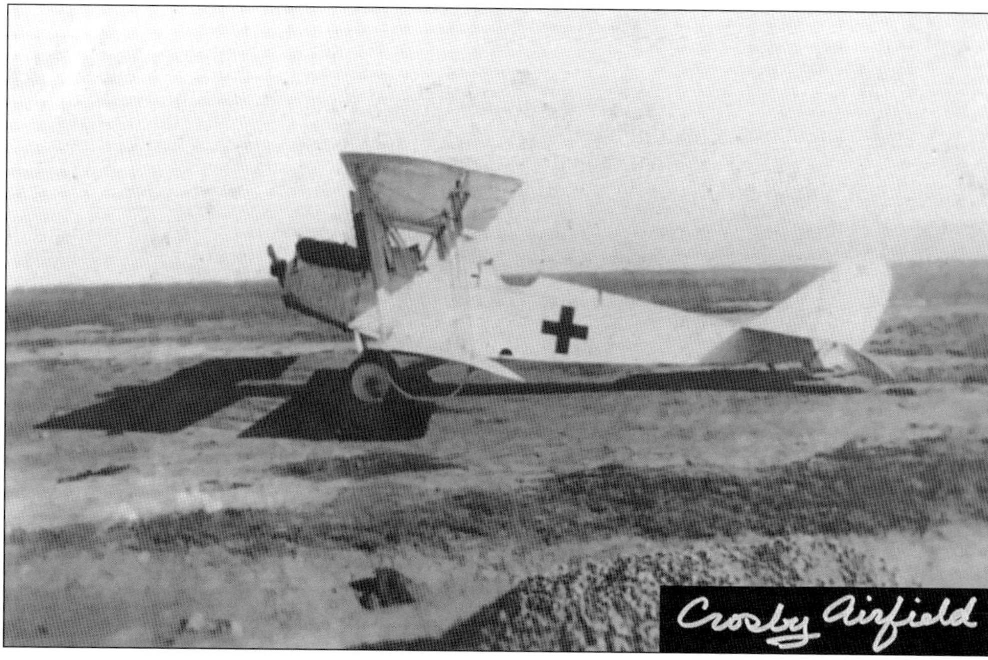

Above, a Red Cross plane from the Ellington Air Base is parked at the Crosby airfield around 1918. A newspaper clipping on June 26, 1917, documents the efforts of area officials to raise money for the Red Cross in Crosby. A number of Crosby women participated in the effort. The group portrait below was taken in front of the railroad terminal in 1918. Included are Mrs. Joe Burwick, Mrs. Ollie Dunks, and Mrs. C.A. Fortner, among others. Local businesses also played a huge role in helping to raise money for the group. Nearly 750 locals attended the event in June 1917, where Crosby's Bohemian Orchestra played patriotic selections at the barbecue dinner. (Both, courtesy of the Newton family.)

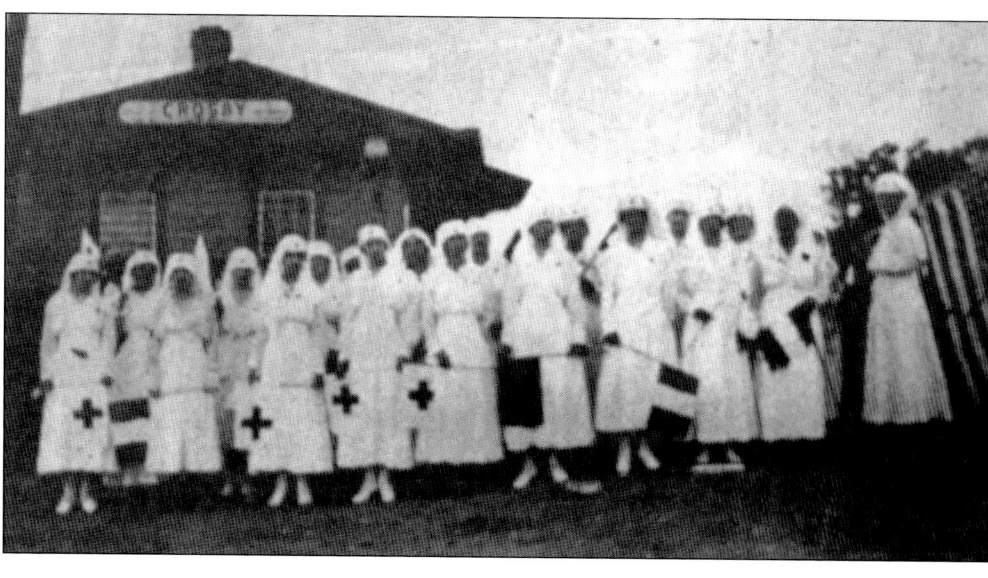

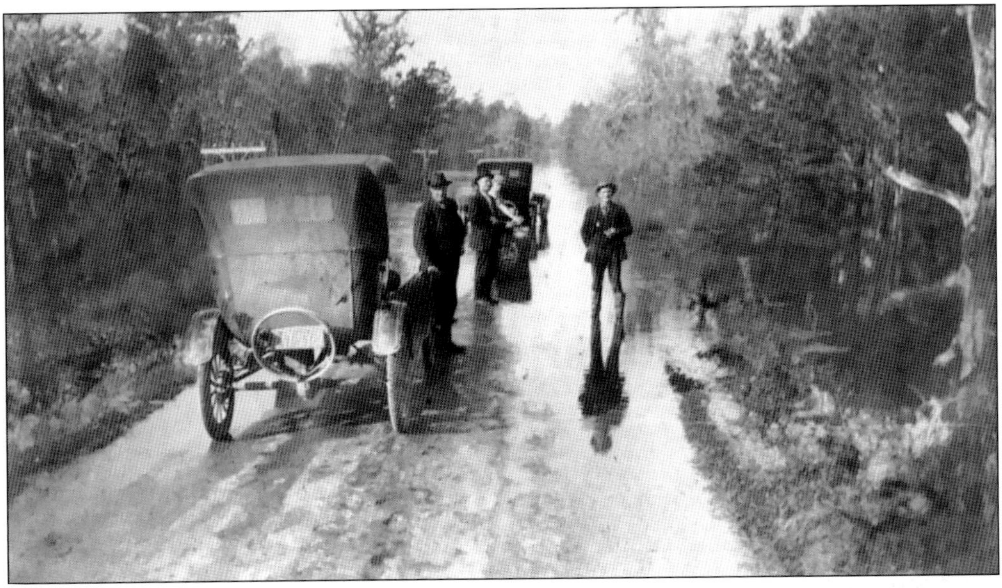

On August 16, 1915, a category four hurricane struck the Crosby area. It destroyed a number of structures in the community. The recently constructed Sacred Heart Missionary Catholic Church was destroyed, the railroad bridge was washed away, and the Crosby schoolhouse lost its cupula and ornamental dormer. The Union Church may have also lost its steeple. Flooding was widespread, as seen here. The photograph above was taken along the Crosby-Houston Road (Gulf Pump Road). The photograph below was taken on the railroad tracks near San Jacinto Road. (Above, courtesy of the Blomstrom family; below, courtesy of the Reidland family.)

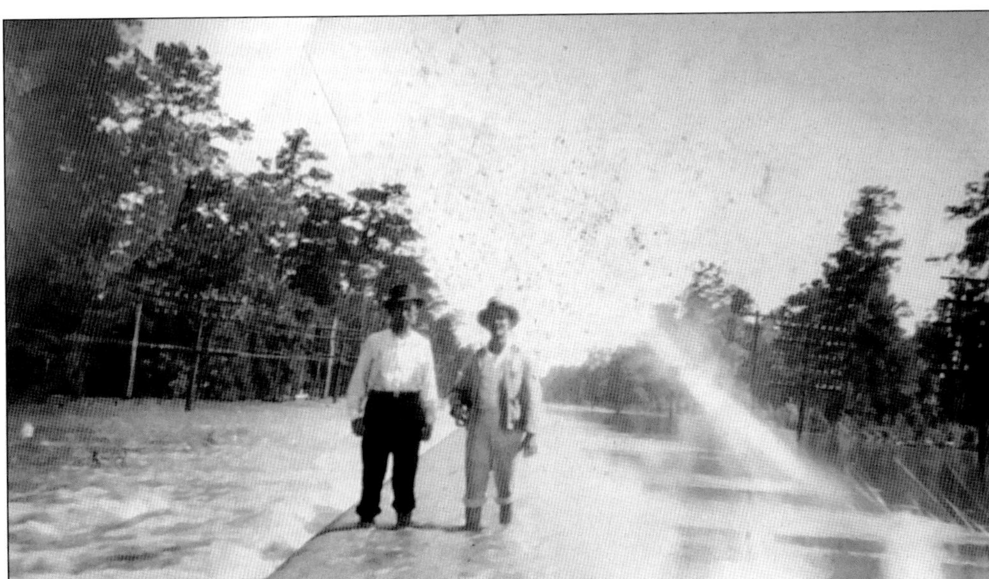

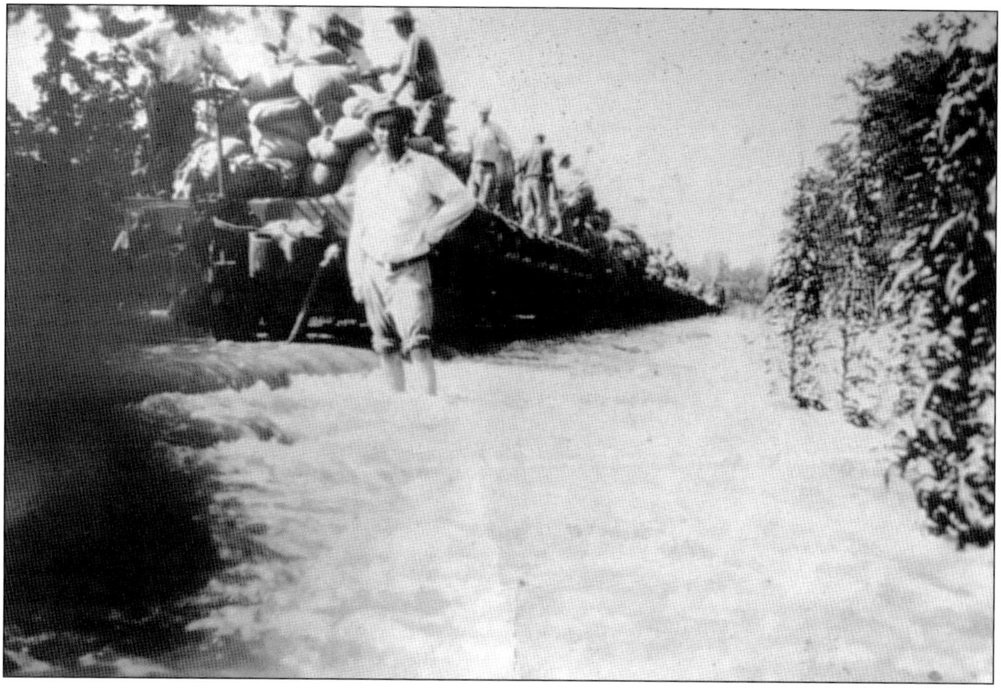

The flooding was widespread along the San Jacinto River, as these photographs document. The flood swamped the railroad tracks near the river. Above, a steam engine slowly backs down the tracks toward the river while the work crew tries placing sandbags along the tracks to limit the erosion. Unfortunately, the railroad bridge was washed out and had to be rebuilt. Most of the local crops were destroyed, and many of the farmers had to search for other jobs. Many ended up working at the nearby oilfields in Goose Creek. (Both, courtesy of the Reidland family.)

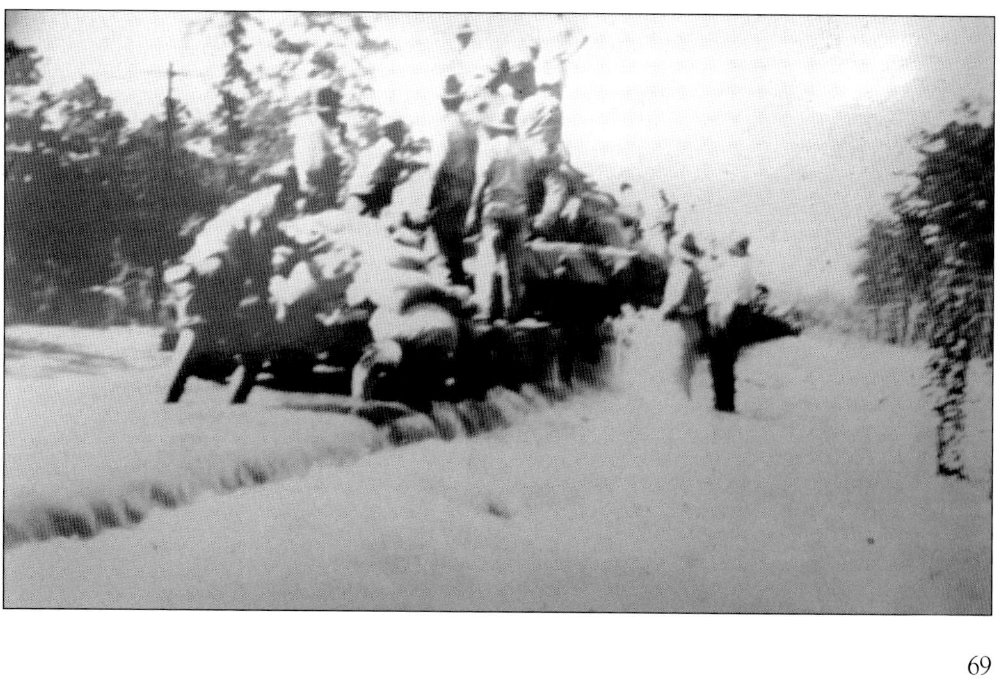

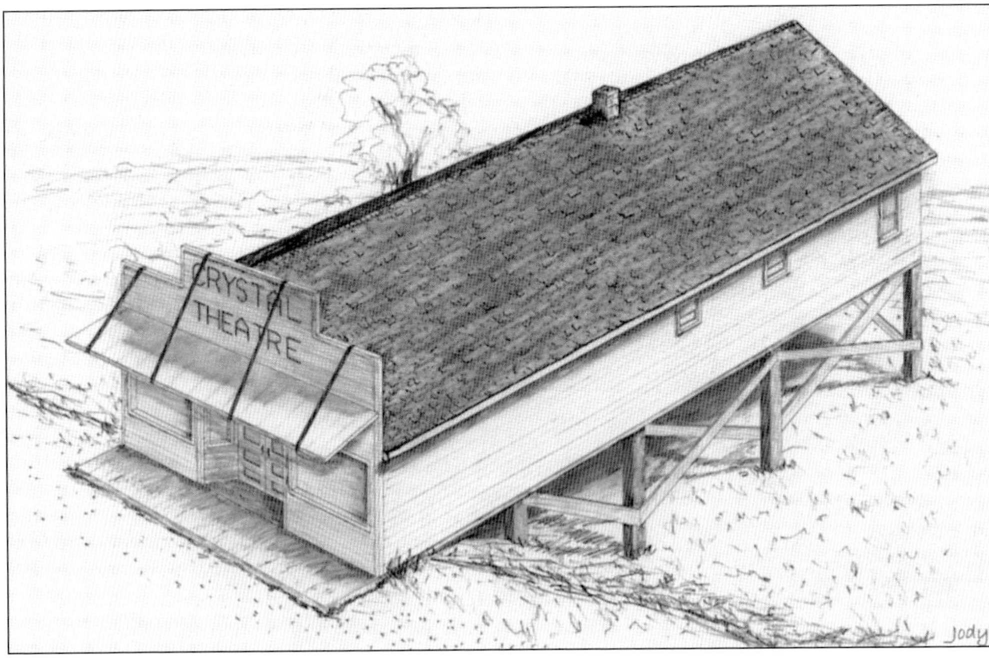

Pictured above is the Crystal Theatre at 124 Kernohan Street and owned by Anton Danek. Only silent movies were shown at the theater, with local musicians providing the accompanying score. Leroy Anderson played the violin, and Suella C.A. Fortner played the piano, based on what was going on in the movie. The rear of the building was raised on stilts near the edge of Jackson Bayou. Below is the first newspaper ad from August 16, 1918, for the new Crystal Theatre. The ad ran in the *Liberty Vindicator*. *Tarzan of the Apes* was the first movie played in a Crosby theater. (Above, author drawing.)

CRYSTAL THEATRE

Crosby, Texas

Friday and Saturday Nights, Aug. 30 and 31.

Tarzan OF THE Apes

From The Original Story by Edgar Rice Burrows.

See
Tarzan struggle with a Lion.
The elephant raid on a Cannibal Village
Battle between an Ape and Gorilla.
Abduction of a white girl by Apes.

The most Stupendous, Amazing Film Production in the World.

Elmo Lincoln, Enid Markey and 1000 others produced in the Wildest Jungles of Brazil.

Staged with Wild Lions, Elephants, Baboons, Apes and Cannibals.

Admission 25c and 50c.

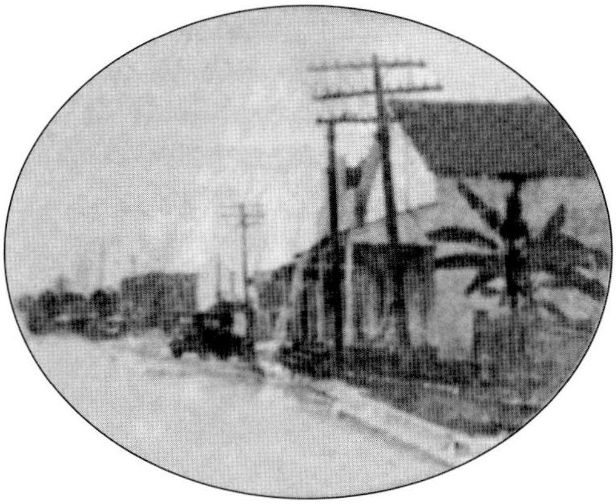
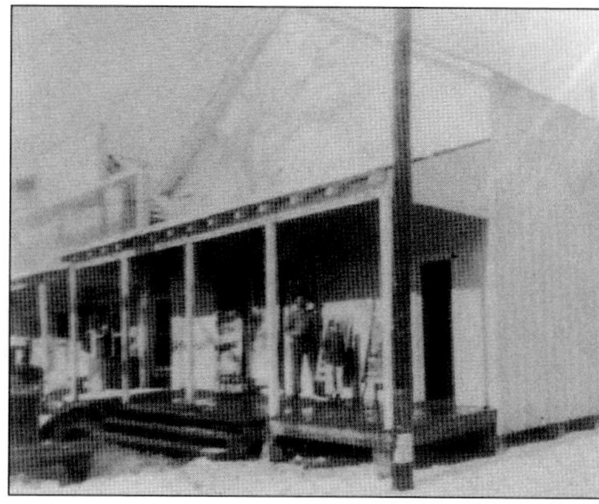

The Crystal Theatre was replaced by the Crosby Theatre in August 1924. Othello and Ora Hare (below) built a larger, more modern movie theater across the street. The building in the foreground of the photographs above is the theater the Hares built at 127 Kernohan Street. It featured movies with soundtracks. The Crosby Theatre ran movies four nights a week (Tuesday, Thursday, Friday, and Saturday). It charged 35¢ admission for adults and 9¢ for children. In 1940, the Hares replaced the Crosby Theatre with another larger, more modern theater on Main Street, which entertained the town until it closed in 1958. Ed Swanson purchased the building in the mid-1960s and reopened the theater for a few more years. The structure was torn down in the late 1960s. (All, courtesy of Klaus Duda.)

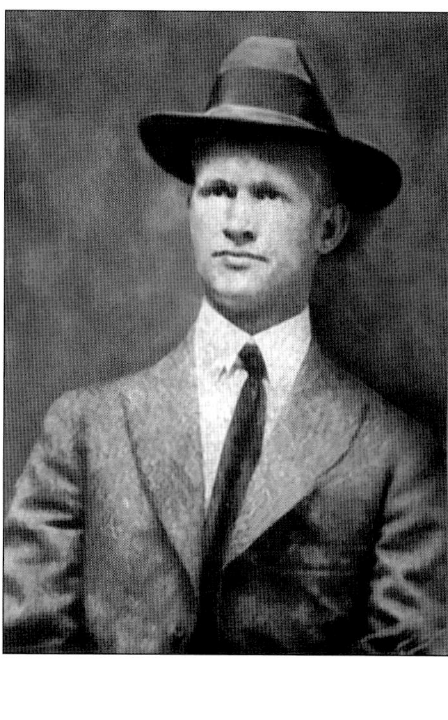
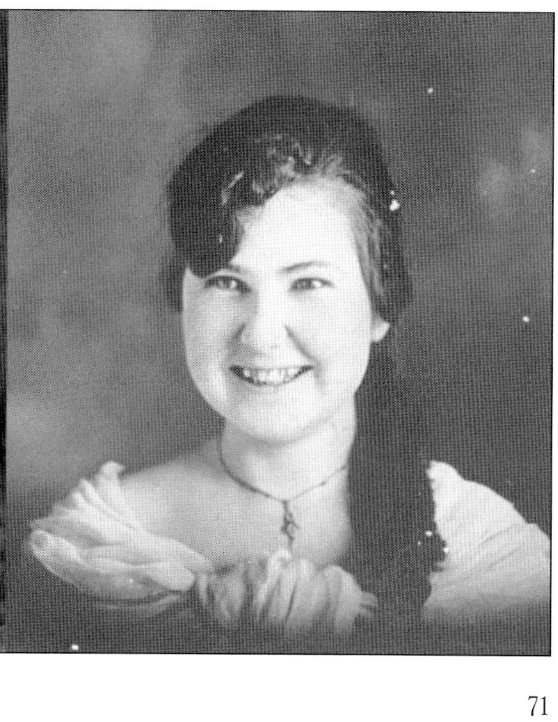

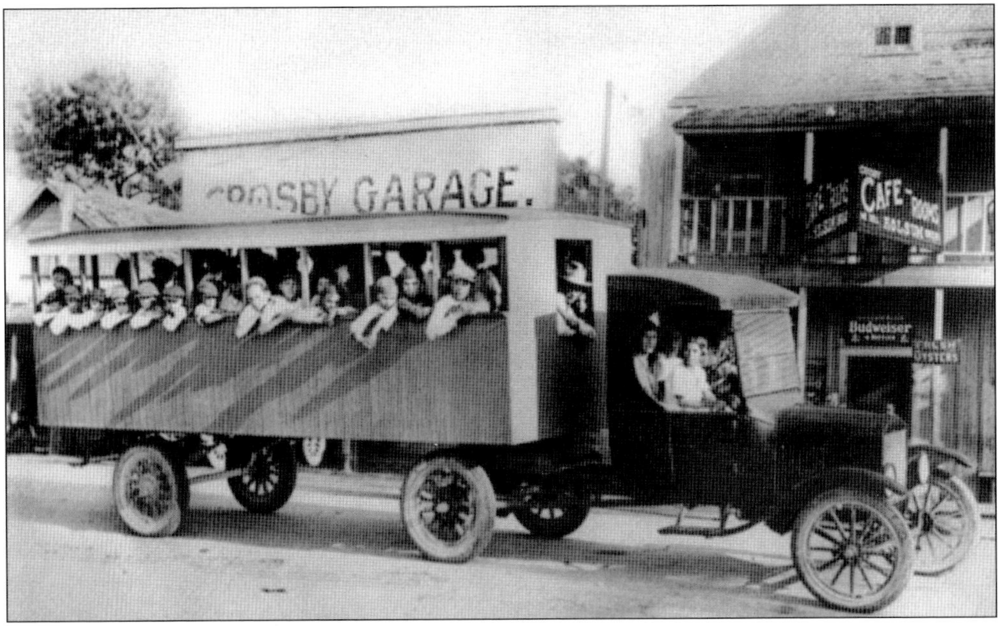

The photograph above was taken in 1923 on Kernohan Street in front of the Crosby Café & Hotel. This was Crosby's first school bus. It was made by local blacksmith "Lige" Dillard from a Model T chassis and featured canvas curtains. The bus was used to carry students from Elena (Highlands) to the Crosby School on Runneburg. It also picked up children from the Gum Gully School, Adlong School, Krenek School, and Clawson School every day. The Langdon sisters are riding in the cab with their mother, Anna, who was also the teacher. Their father, Clifford, is the driver. Below is the interior of the Crosby Café. (Both, courtesy of the Plocheck family.)

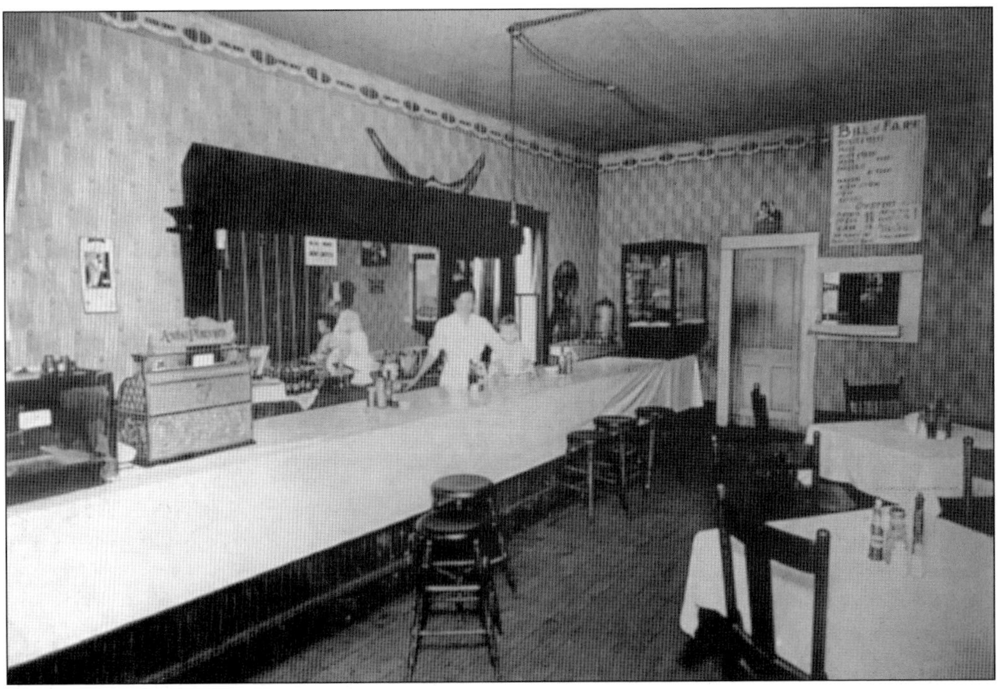

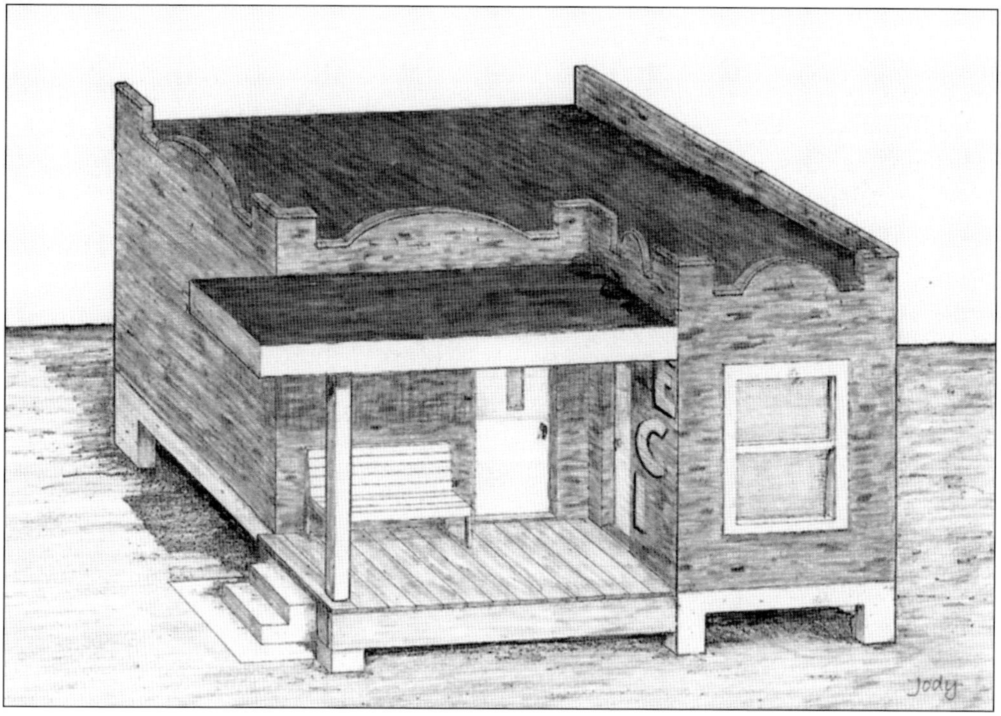

The first ice vendors hauled ice from Houston in the back of a Model T truck. Eventually, it was delivered in insulated boxcars. In the early 1920s, a brick building with a concrete floor was built at 123 Kernohan Street by I.C. Krenek (above). Fifty pounds of ice sold for 25¢. Having access to ice allowed early residents to refrigerate their food and enjoy an ice-cold watermelon picnic, like the Swanson family below. The icehouse was owned by Charles Prasek from 1936 to 1942. (Above, author drawing; below, courtesy of the Swanson family.)

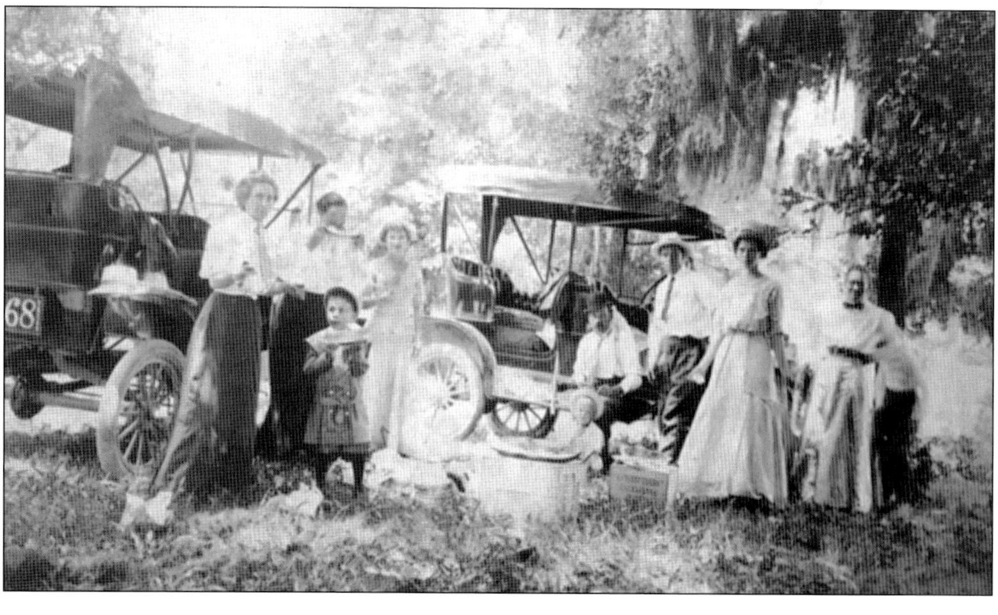

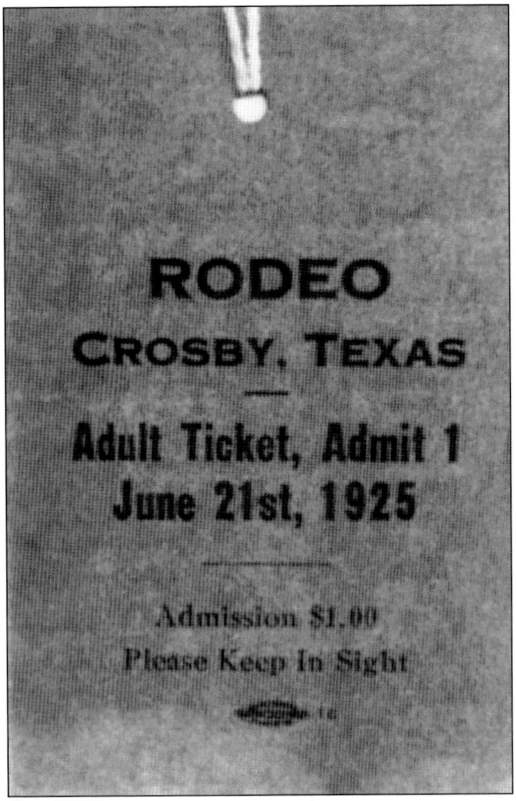

The Crosby Chamber of Commerce established the Crosby Fair & Rodeo in 1923. Below is a photograph of the first rodeo parade in October 1923, marching south down Main Street over the railroad tracks, past the Dunks general store. The 1924 fair was canceled because of a local quarantine for hoof and mouth disease. A ticket from the 1925 rodeo is shown at left. The rodeo continued until the late 1930s. In 1937, the Crosby Roping Club was created and began holding riding and roping competitions after the fair was discontinued. In 1947, the Crosby Future Farmers of America established a poultry show and auction. In 1951, it joined with the Crosby Roping Club and held a combined event that grew into today's Crosby Fair & Rodeo.

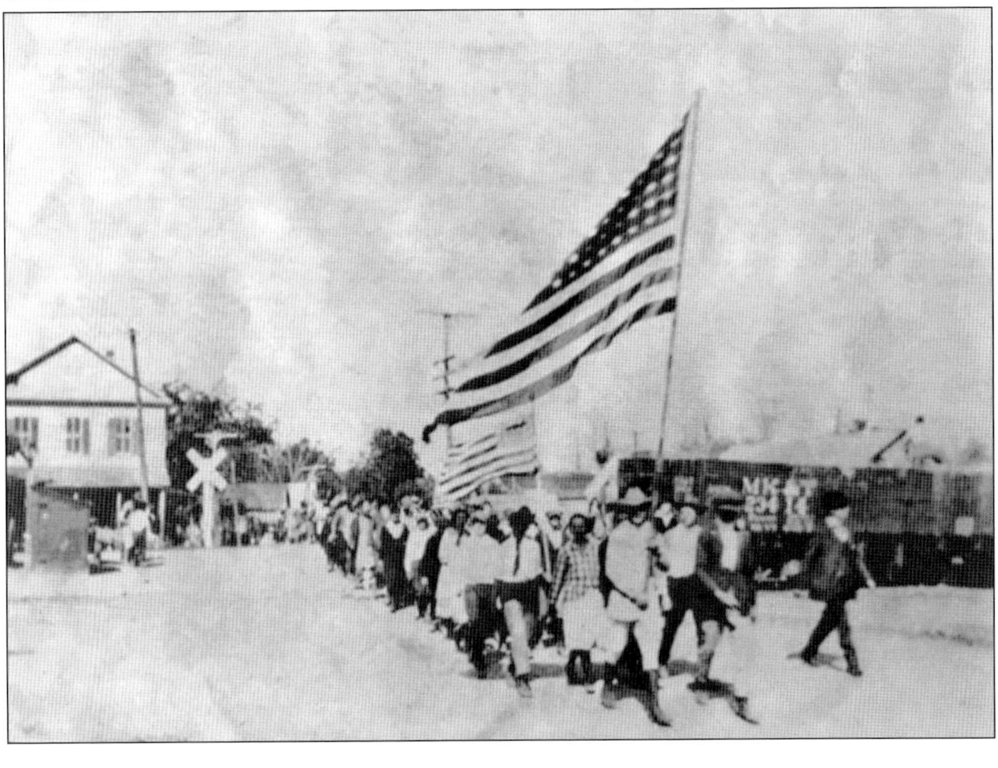

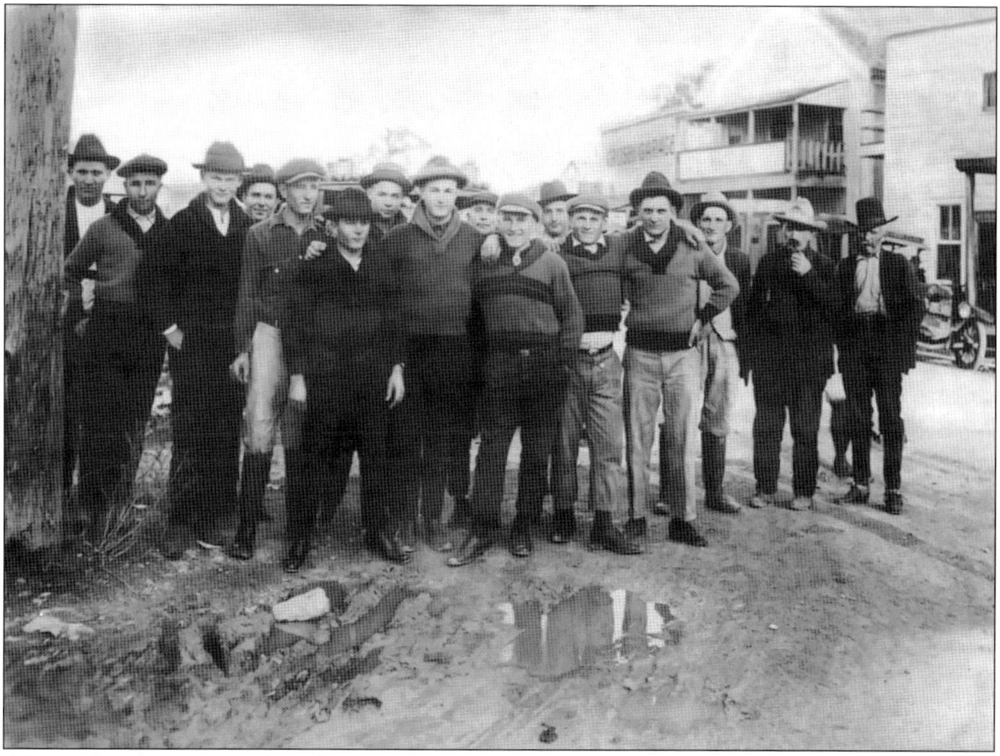

Above, Czech men stand at the corner of Kernohan and Main Streets in 1923. In unknown order are ? Hargrave, ? Sonka, Adolph Dlouhy, Frank Slovacek, Joe Kratky, John Kratky, Pete Kristynik, Ed Jasek Sr., Charlie Franta, Charlie Marek, ? Kelarek, another ? Kelarek, John Strocek, Ben Kristynik, Frank Strocek, and Ted Sonka. The photograph below was taken in 1925 of the same corner. It was taken from Main Street looking down Kernohan Street. The Crosby Garage and Crosby Café are in the background. (Above, courtesy of Ron Shanks; below, courtesy of Lisa Duncan.)

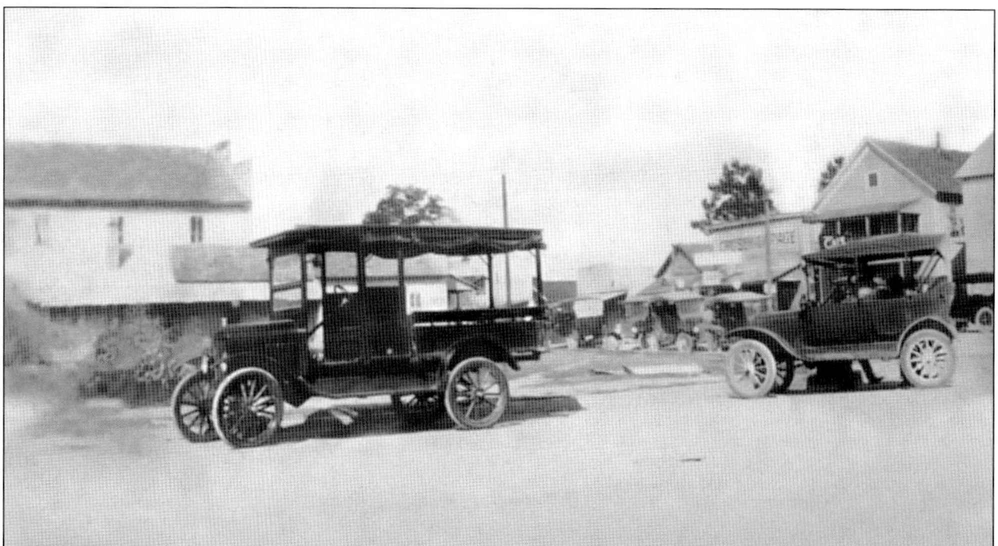

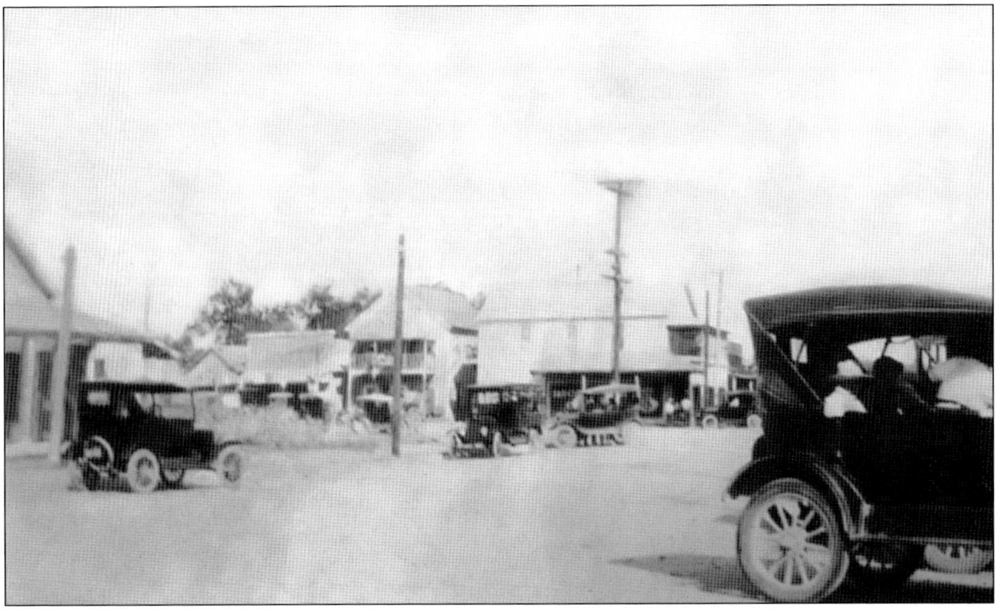

Here are a couple more views of a busy downtown Crosby looking south at the intersection of Main and Kernohan Streets in 1925. Abe Aron's dry goods store is the large two-story building at center above. To the left is the Crosby Hotel and Café (also a two-story building). Next is the Crosby Garage, followed by Hilliard's meat market. The cars in the foreground are parked in front of Larson's drugstore. By 1925, a number of Crosby's residents owned a car, and Saturday was the day everyone drove to town. (Both, courtesy of Lisa Duncan.)

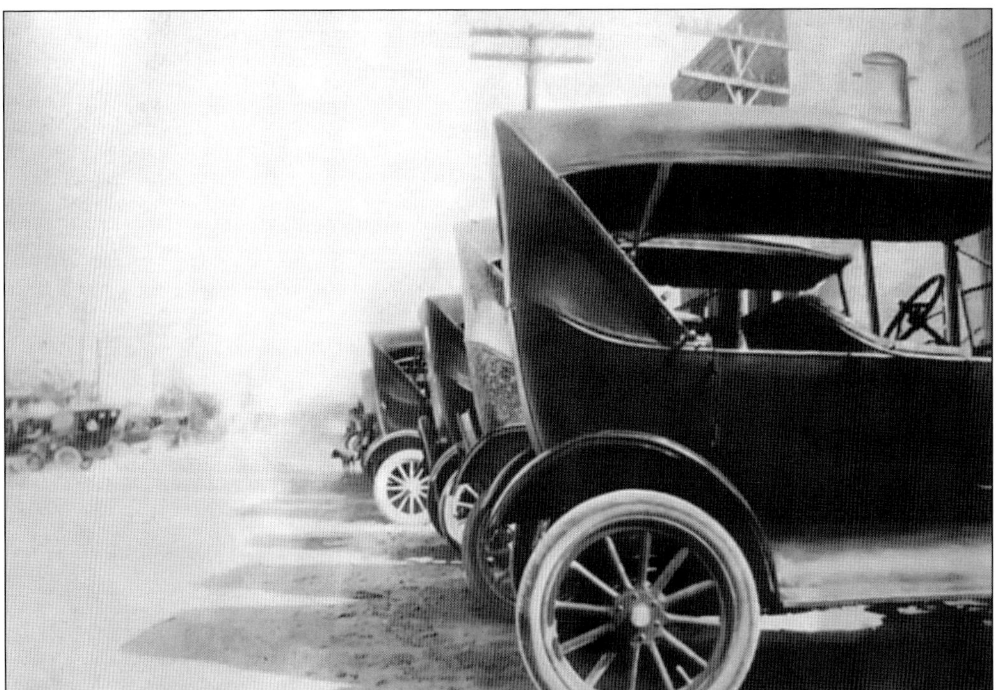

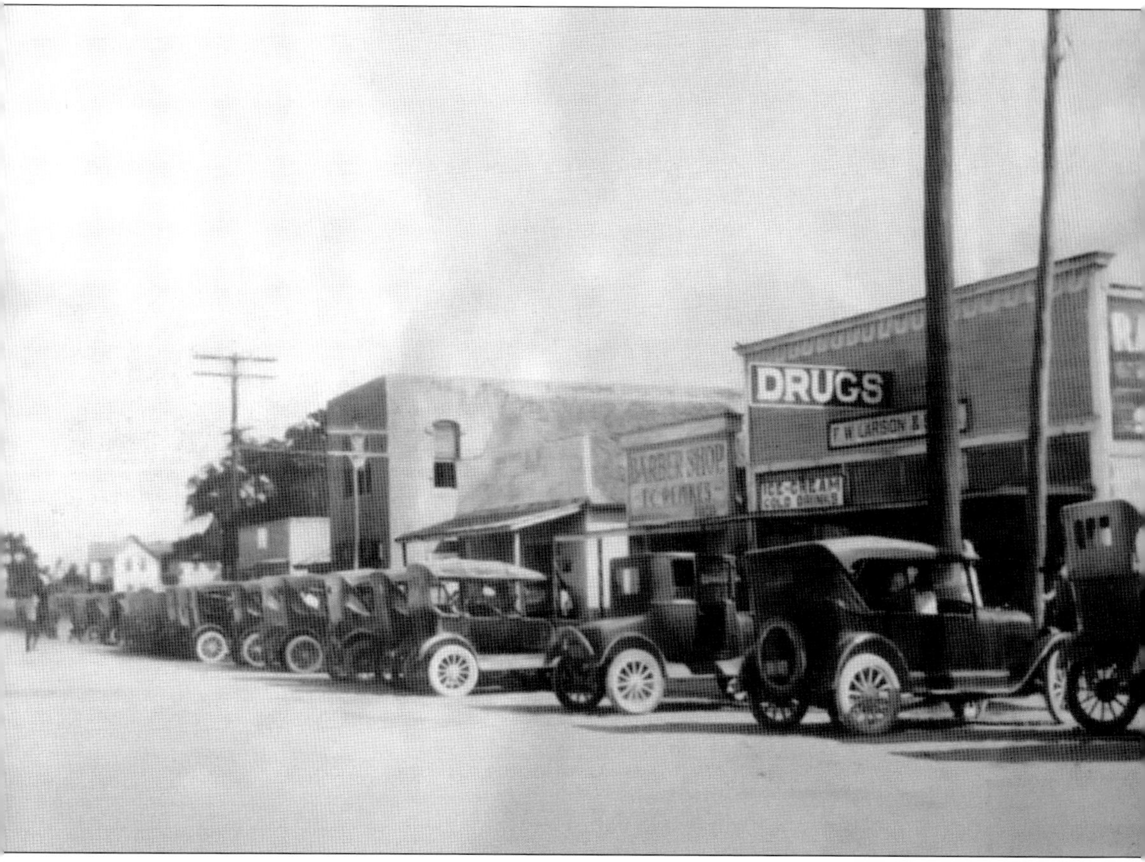

The buildings in this photograph are, from front (right) to back, F.W. Larson & Sons drugstore, T.C. Remke's barber shop, Cozy Confectionery, Crosby State Bank, and the Ford dealership. The large white structure in the distance is the Lynch boardinghouse. The owner of the barbershop was T.C. "Thad" Remke, who came to Crosby in 1914. He worked at this location for over 35 years. He said that when he got here, only three people in the town had cars, and two of them were doctors. He added that he, like most of the other people in town, hauled buckets of water from the train depot because that was the only water well in town. (Courtesy of Lisa Duncan.)

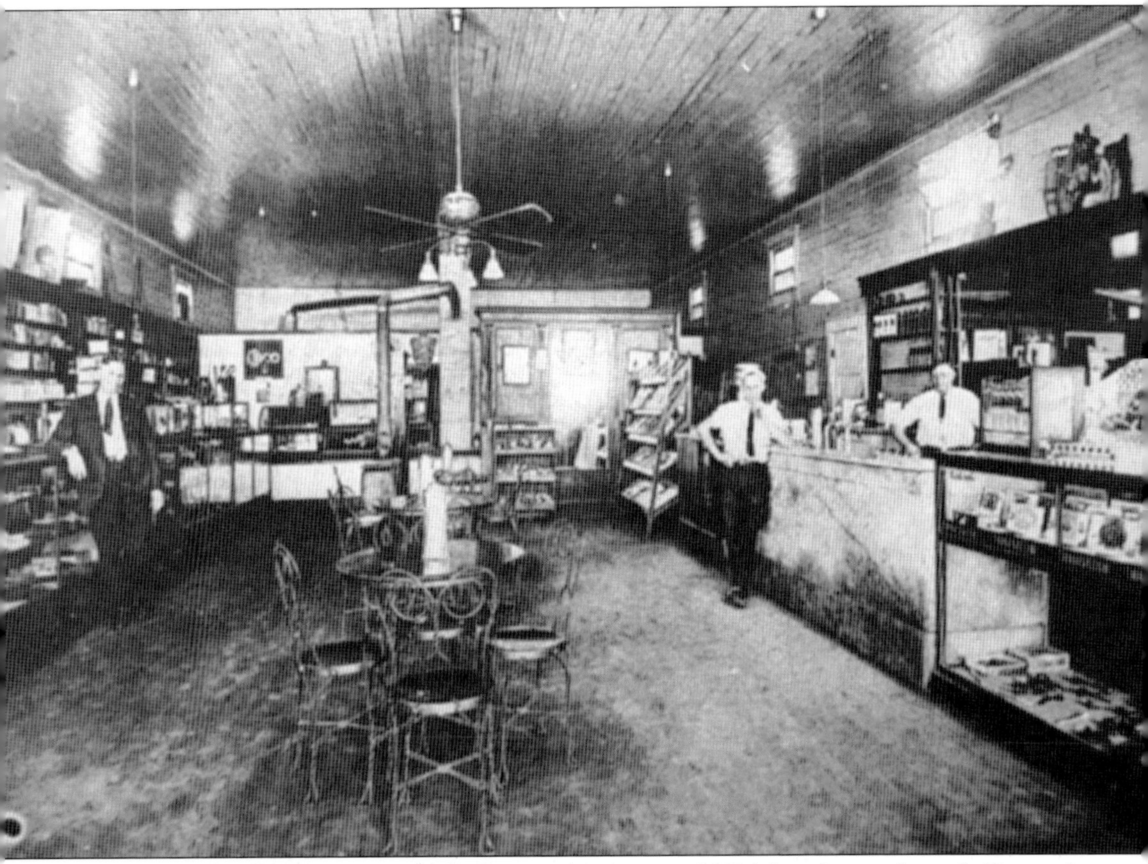

Here is a c. 1920 interior view of the Larson drugstore at 5623 Main Street, formerly Ramsey's drugstore. It sold tobacco products, magazines, candy, snacks, soft drinks, ice cream, and some groceries. It was comparable to a modern-day convenience store that catered to train passengers. From left to right are Frank W. Larson and his sons Leroy and Ernest. Later in life, Leroy became a watch repairman, but he remained a bachelor his entire life. Ernest died in 1944 from an accidental gunshot wound. (Courtesy of Lisa Duncan.)

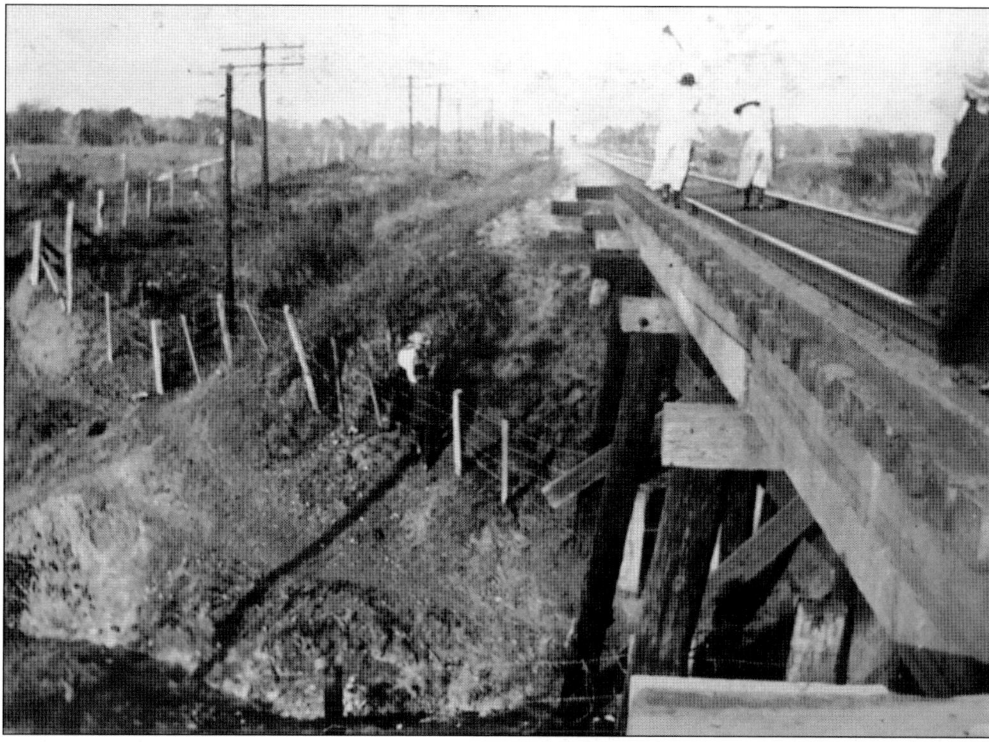

Local dentist Dr. Millard Goodwin had an untimely death on the railroad bridge above. He was accidentally shot by a 21-year-old Western Union messenger named Prince Albert Dunks (right). Dunks tripped while chasing a burglary suspect in 1909 and accidentally shot the dentist in the head. Dr. Goodwin was killed almost immediately. However, in a twist of fate, Dunks saved the life of a motorist who was trapped beneath his overturned car in 1914. He was the son of local store owner R.E. "Heinan" Dunks and worked as a Western Union dispatcher and later for the Southern Pacific Railroad. He also operated a shoe repair store next to his father's business. Prince Albert Dunks was a very capable young man who could make or repair almost anything. (Above, courtesy of the McKinney family; right, courtesy of the Newton family.)

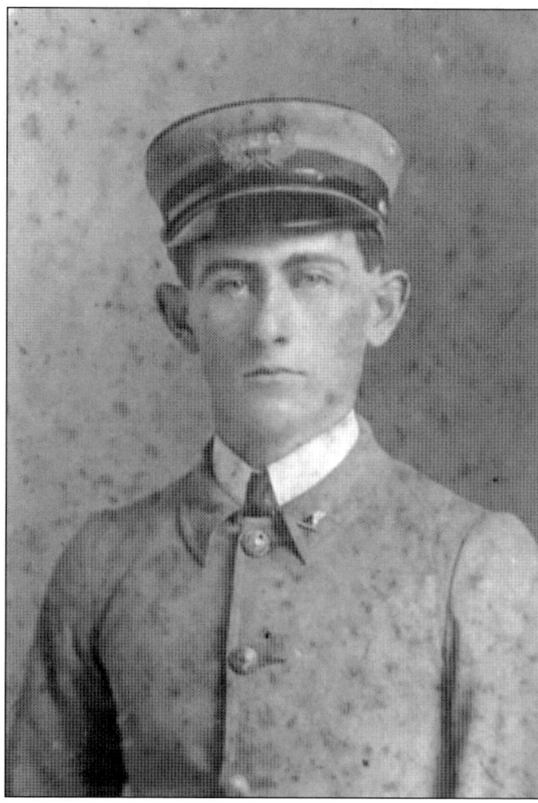

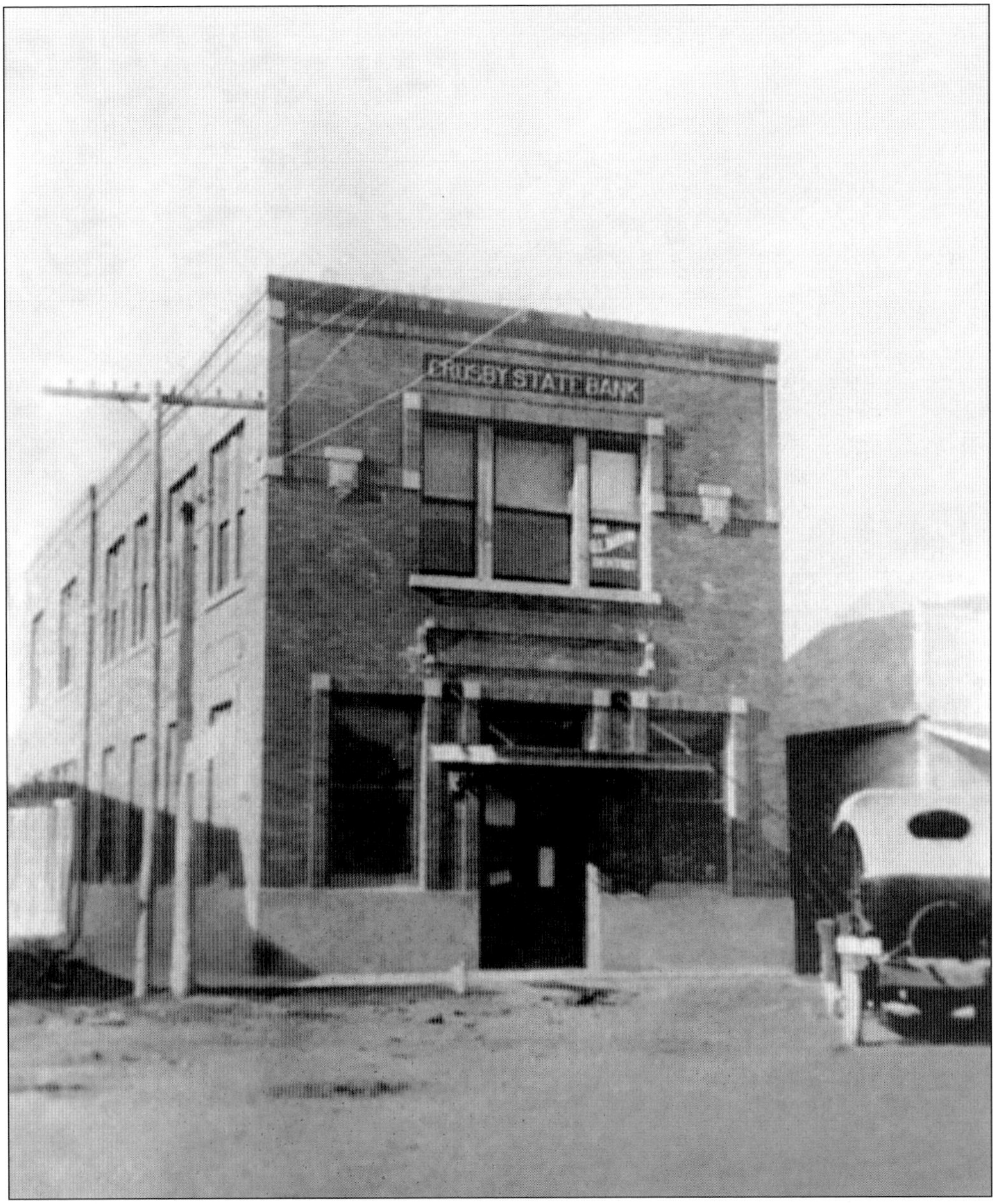

Pictured here is the Crosby State Bank in 1925, with Dr. O.Z. Barton's dentist office upstairs. Barton replaced Dr. Goodwin after he was accidentally killed. The space above the bank was used for a number of things over the years. Two spaces were rented out over time. The front was usually occupied with a more permanent tenant. The rear was used for parties, beauty contests, dances, and more, like in 1917 after the first Czech Bazaar. The bazaar was held just a hundred feet away on Kernohan Street. Afterward, attendees used the upstairs of the bank to dance the night away. The upstairs also served as a land office, an insurance agency, a newspaper publishing office, and lastly, the law offices of Leroy Anderson.

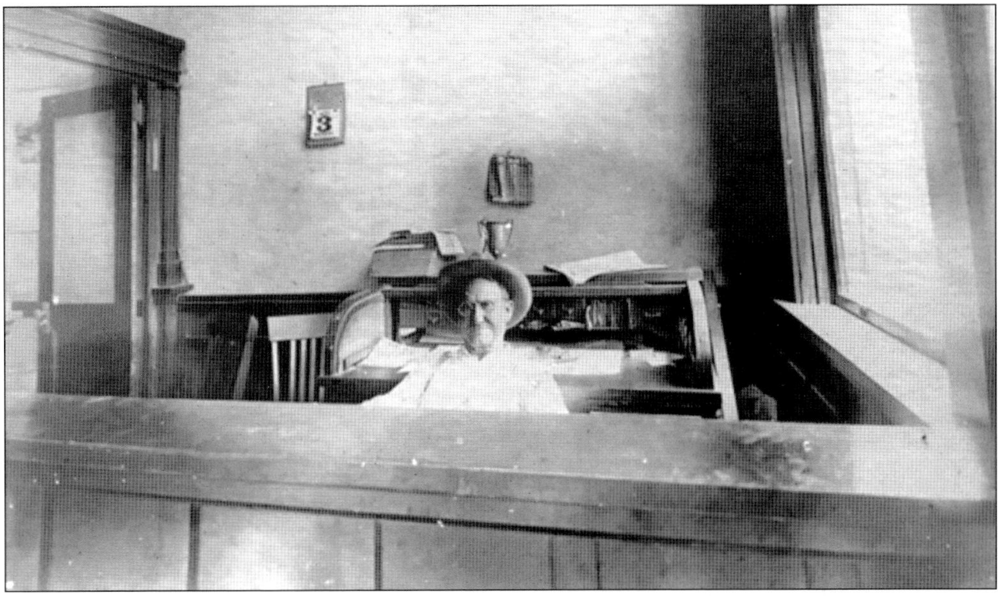

The bank president's desk was to the right when walking in the front door. This photograph was taken on May 3, 1926, of bank president John T. Hare at his desk. The back half of the bank was the post office. An outdoor staircase led to the offices upstairs. (Courtesy of the Hare family.)

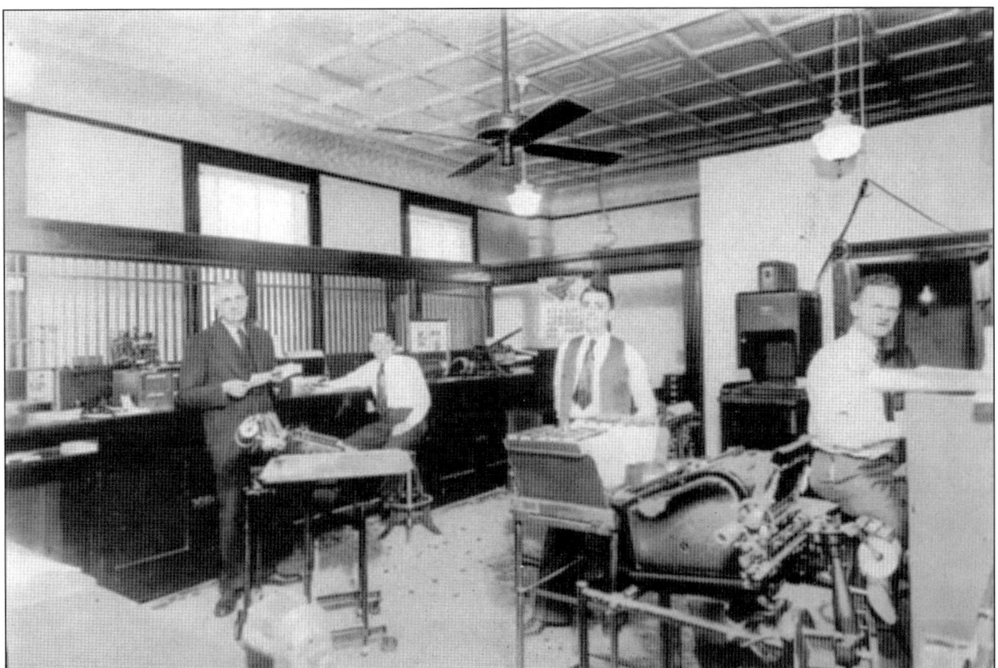

Pictured here is the bank teller's cage of the Crosby State Bank with four employees. From left to right are C.A. Fortner, Arnold H. Garbs, James Ewell, and Othello Hare. Garbs became bank president in 1964. Three years later, he was taken hostage in the town's first bank robbery. (Courtesy of the Hare family.)

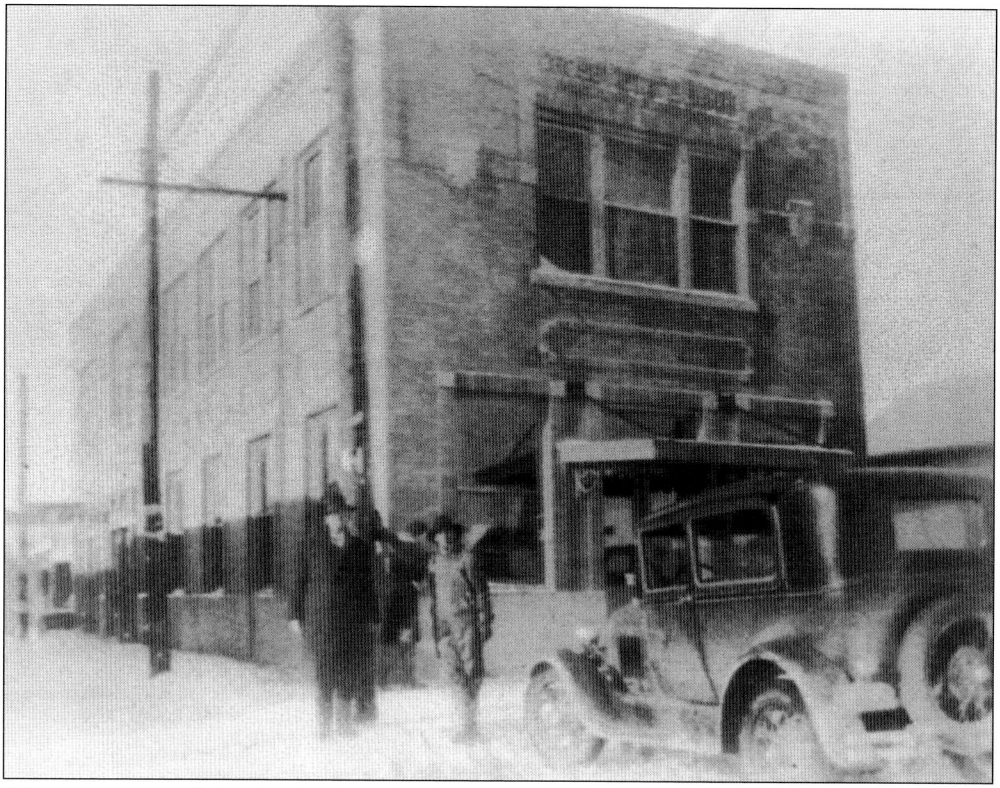

Above is a view of the Crosby State Bank in the 1920s. In 1918, the US Coast and Geodetic Survey placed a benchmark on the bank's façade. It established the exact elevation of that spot at 48.14 feet above sea level. Below is Marguerite Nelson Peterson inside the teller cage doing bank filings in the 1920s. C.A. Fortner is seated at the desk behind her. (Both, courtesy of the Peterson family.)

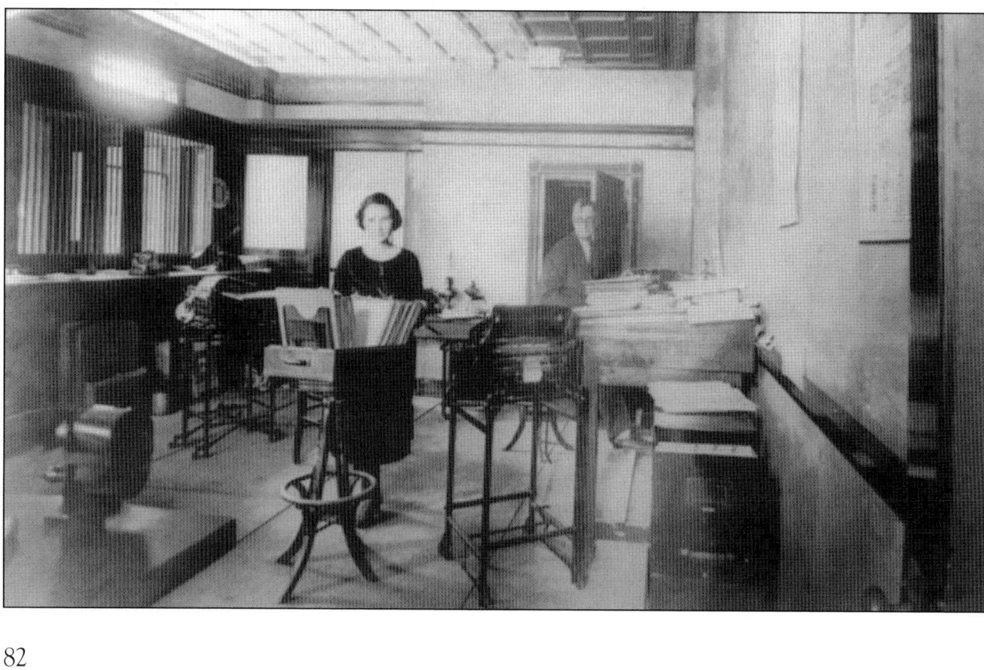

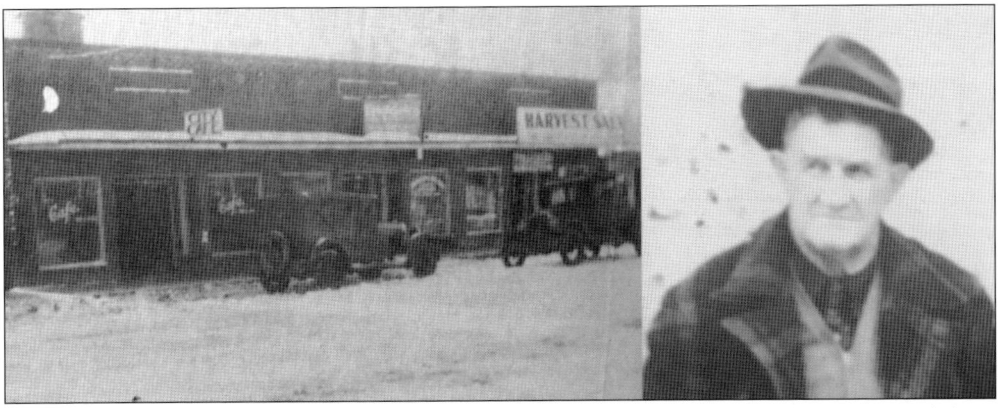

In 1926, Charles Wilson (pictured at right) erected the building pictured at left. It housed three rental spaces at 116, 118, and 120 Kernohan Street. Philip Gerson's department store occupied the space at 116. It was holding a harvest sale at the time. Swanson & Wilson General Contractors were at 118. The City Café occupied the third space. This photograph is from the late 1920s, and a recent snowfall covers the ground. Theodore "Mike" Reidland's water tower is the dark structure visible above the building at left. It remained the primary water source for downtown until the Crosby Municipal Utility District bought the water service in the 1970s. (Courtesy of the Swanson family.)

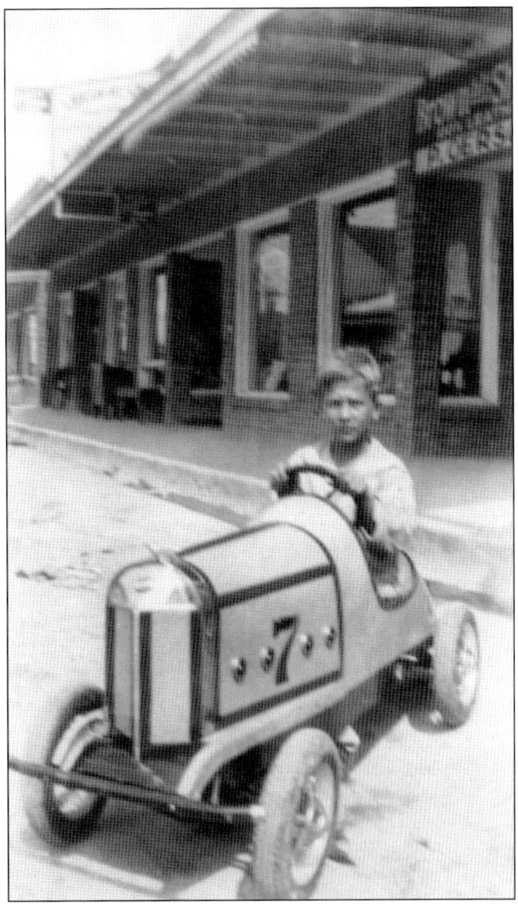

Pictured here is Alvin Stasney in his pedal car in front of the building seen above in the late 1920s. (Courtesy of the Stasney family.)

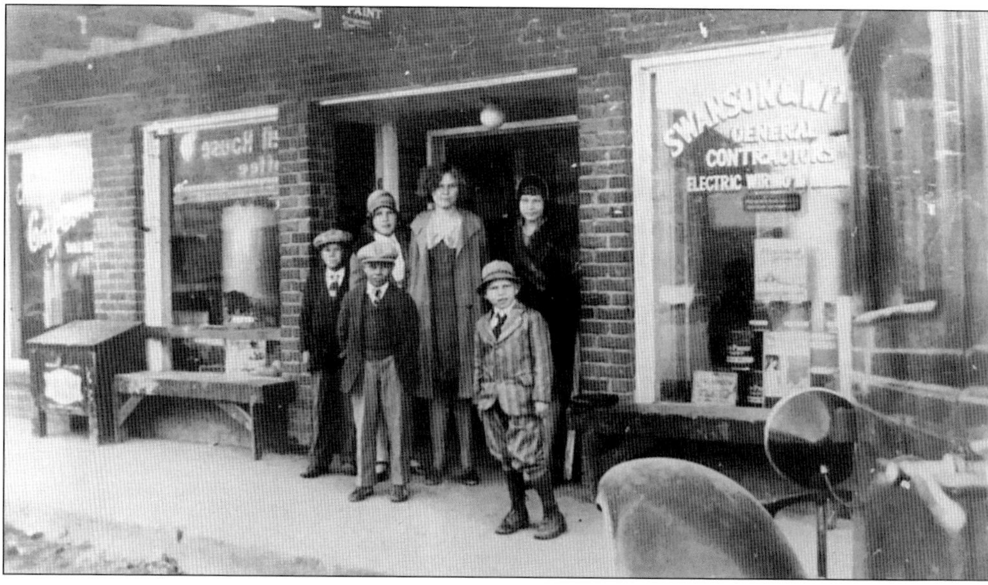

Once the building was complete, Charles's son Art and his partner C.A. Swanson opened a business called Swanson & Wilson General Contractors. Their store was the middle portion of the building. The company did plumbing and electrical work. The partners went their separate ways around 1928; Swanson continued with plumbing and wiring, and Wilson opened a hardware store at this same location. Members of the Swanson family are pictured above around 1926. Below is the interior of the Swanson & Wilson General Contractors store at 118 Kernohan Street in the late 1920s. (Both, courtesy of the Swanson family.)

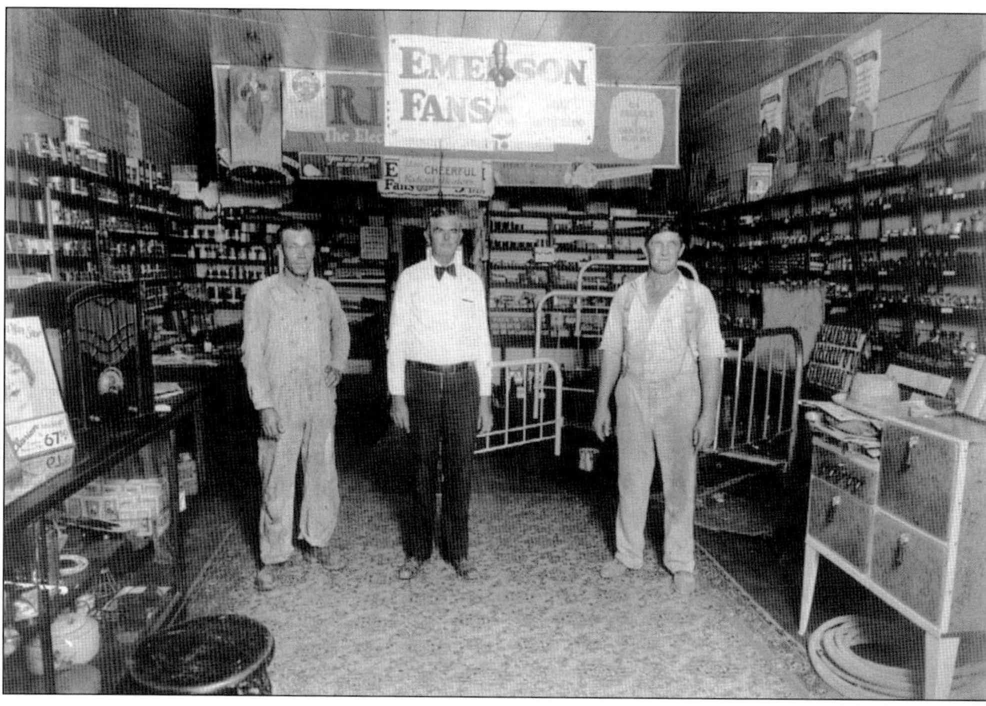

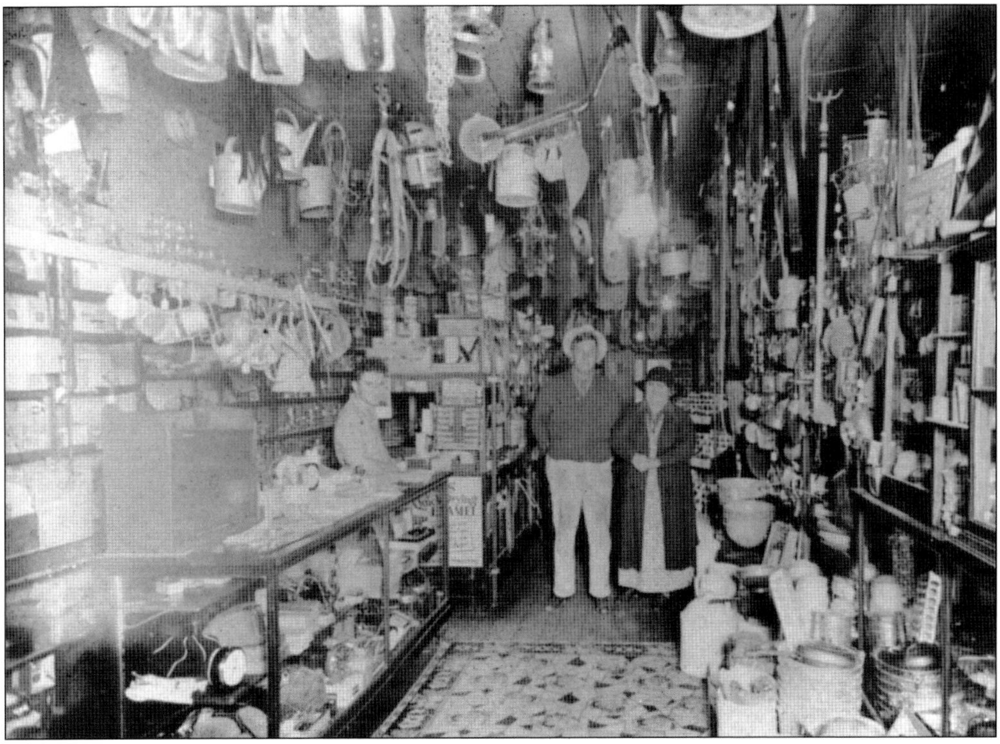

After his partnership with C.A. Swanson dissolved, Art Wilson and his wife, Alice, opened a hardware store. This is an interior photograph of the Wilson Hardware Store at 118 Kernohan Street taken around 1928. Pictured are Art and Alice Wilson and an unidentified employee. In the 1940s, it became Gentry's Hardware. In the 1950s, it was the Meigs Hardware Store. By the 1960s, it was the Gentry & Meigs Hardware Store after Sammie Gentry joined forces with John Meigs. After they retired in the 1970s, it was purchased by Vernon Hord, who eventually moved the business to 5419 Main Street, where it was Crosby Newport Hardware. Today, it is Crosby Ace Hardware. (Both, courtesy of the Swanson family.)

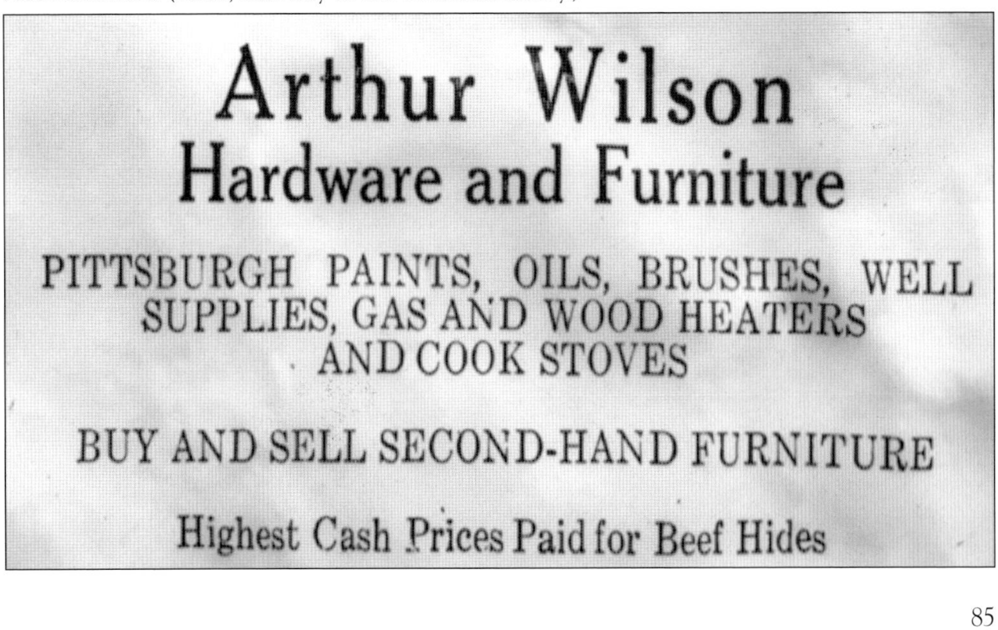

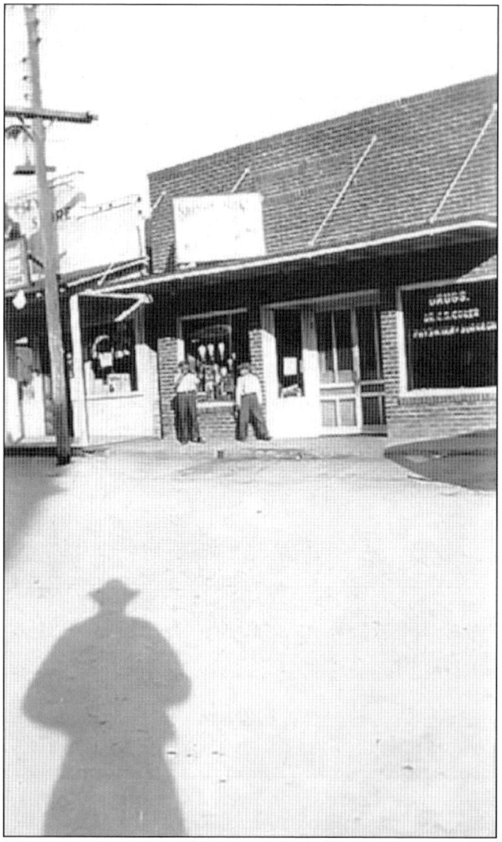

The photograph below was taken around 1926 from the top of a railroad structure north of the 100 block of Kernohan Street looking south. The buildings in the foreground are, from left to right, Crosby Theater, the Dewees and Larquet store, Krenek ice house (small brick building), and the Texas Mercantile Company. On the opposite side of the street was Frank Kulak's bakery, Nelson's drugstore, and the City Café, among others. Behind them is the Reidland water tower. This was the wooden one, which was eventually replaced with a steel one. The shadow in the picture at left was cast by C.A. Swanson as he took the photograph. He had moved his plumbing and wiring business into the brick building pictured. Swanson took many of the photographs in this book. (Both, courtesy of the Swanson family.)

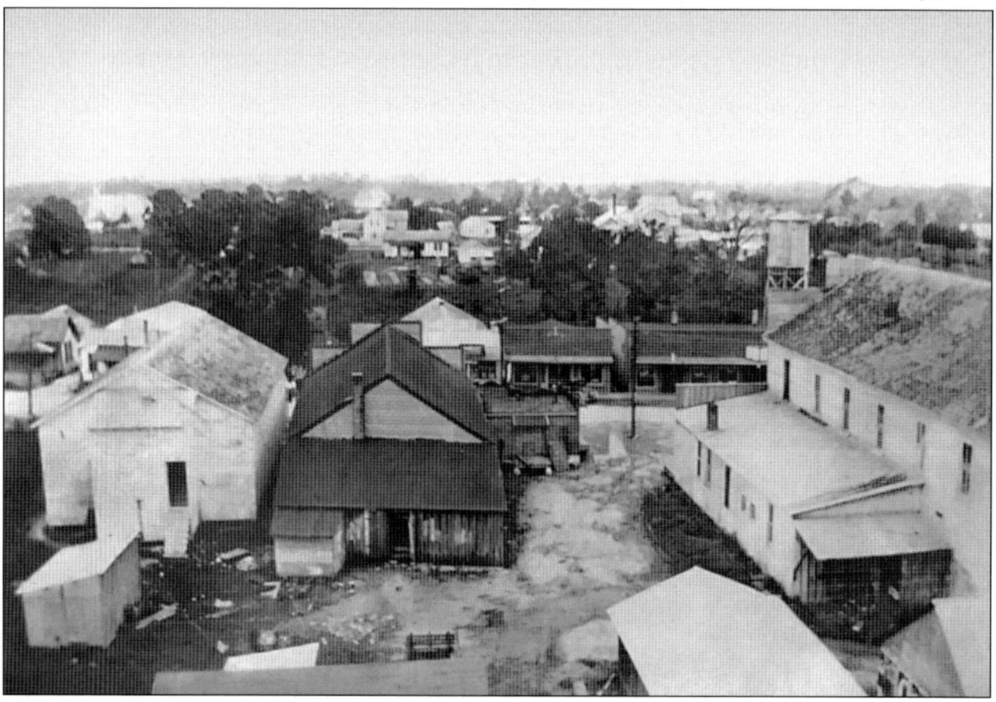

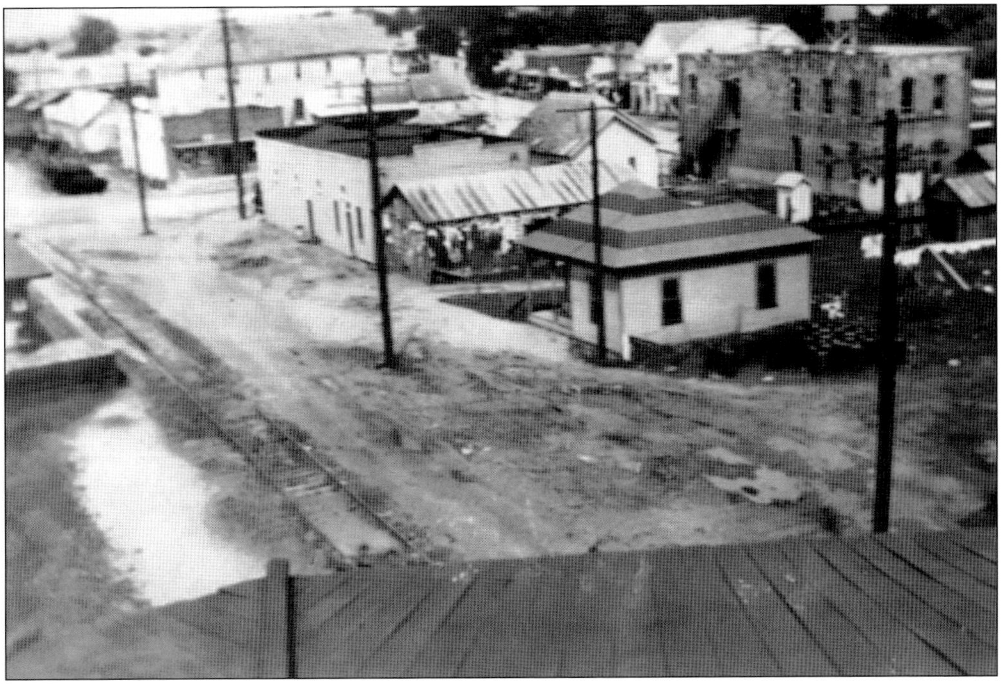

These photographs were both taken from atop the railroad water tower around 1929. Local photographers often climbed up on the railroad water tower to get an aerial perspective of the town. C.A. Swanson took these two images. Above, a portion of the water tower roof can be seen. This water tower was used to fill the boilers on steam-powered trains. The town also had a water tower for drinking water. It is visible below, in the background behind the Crosby State Bank. (Both, courtesy of the Swanson family.)

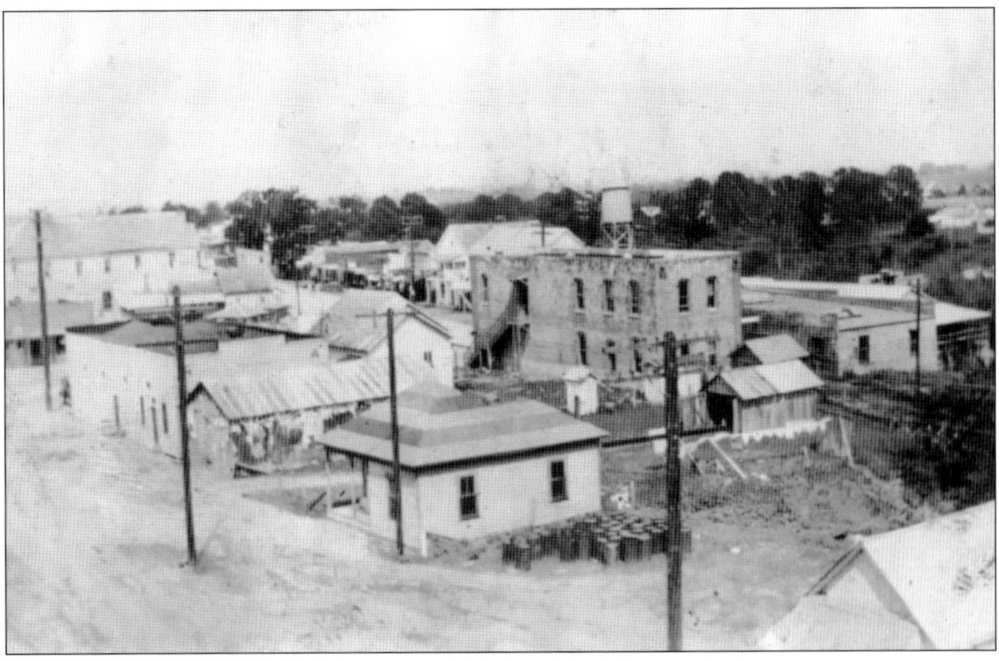

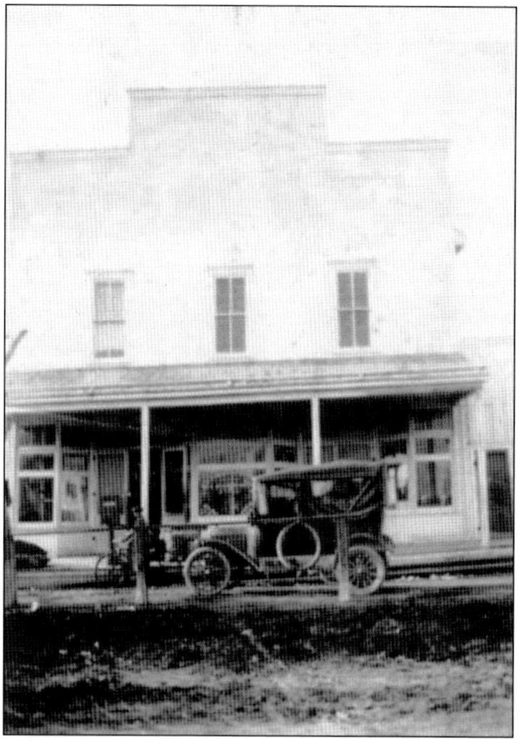

In the late 1920s, the Crosby Mercantile Company purchased the Texas Mercantile Company from William Truxaw. It operated both stores until the mid-1930s. At that time, the original Crosby Mercantile Company store was closed, and the name Crosby Cash Store was adopted. It was the second general store to be named the Crosby Cash Store. A store owned by R.C.J. Kenning and his wife, Anna, on Runneburg Road, was the first. This one was a general store offering everything from coffins to fresh vegetables. It was in the 100 block of Kernohan Street in the old Texas Mercantile Store building. The telephone exchange was in the white structure on the side, seen below. The post office was at far right. (Both, courtesy of the Harris family.)

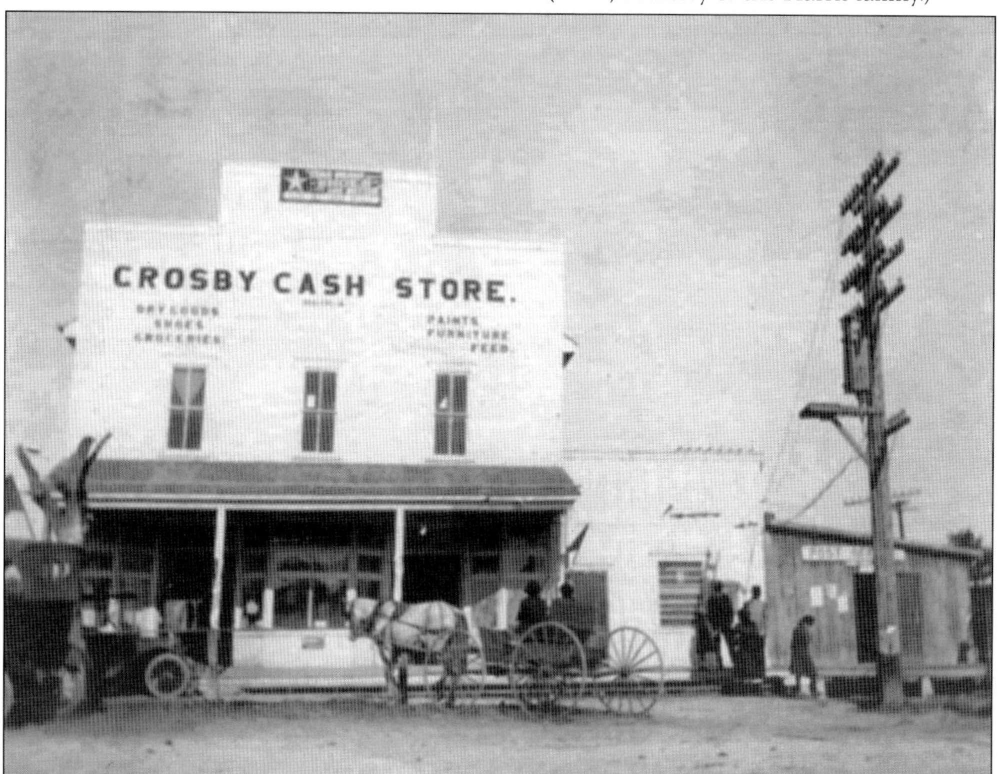

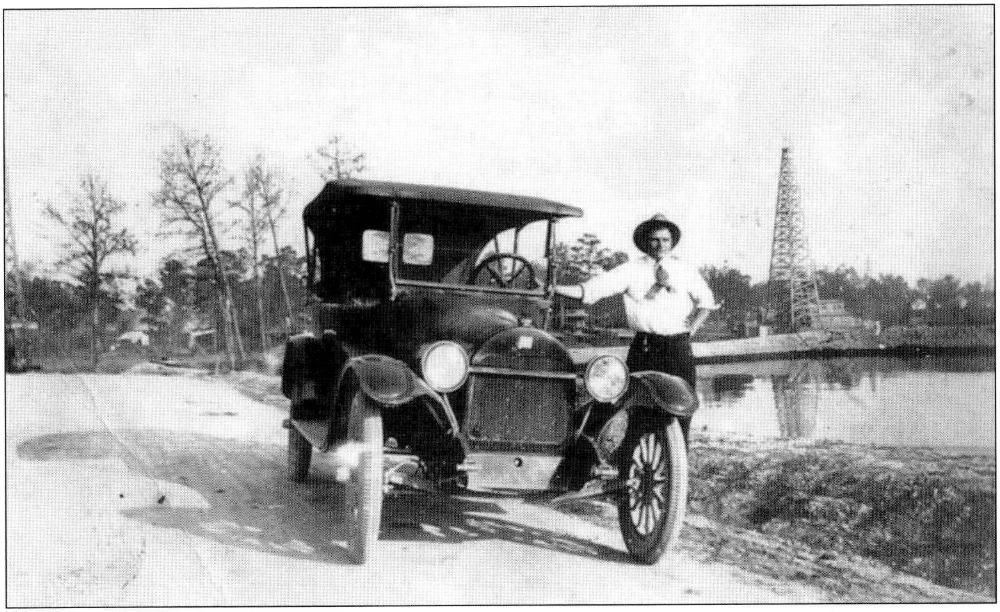

Millie Zadrapa married Joseph Stasney in 1920, shortly after he returned from World War I. They had their first child in 1921, named Alvin. Two more sons, Gordan and Odell, were born in 1923. Joseph (pictured above) was a farmer and worked in the local oil fields. Unfortunately, he committed suicide in 1925, leaving Millie to raise the three boys alone during the height of the Great Depression. Their three young sons are pictured below. She opened the Crosby Café, which she ran until all of her sons returned home from World War II in 1945. (Both, courtesy of the Stasney family.)

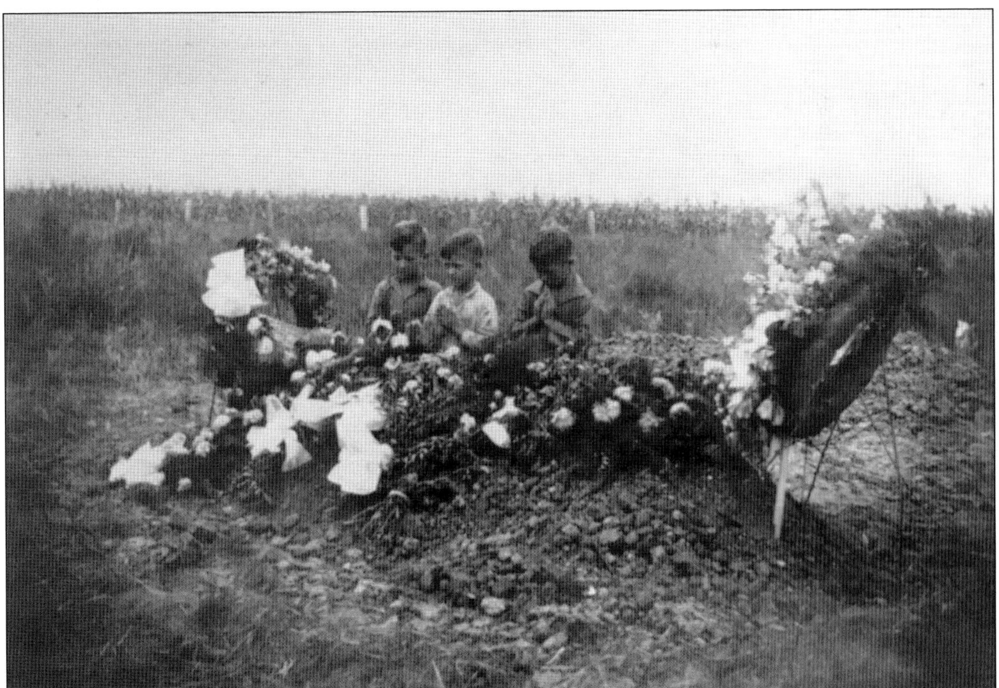

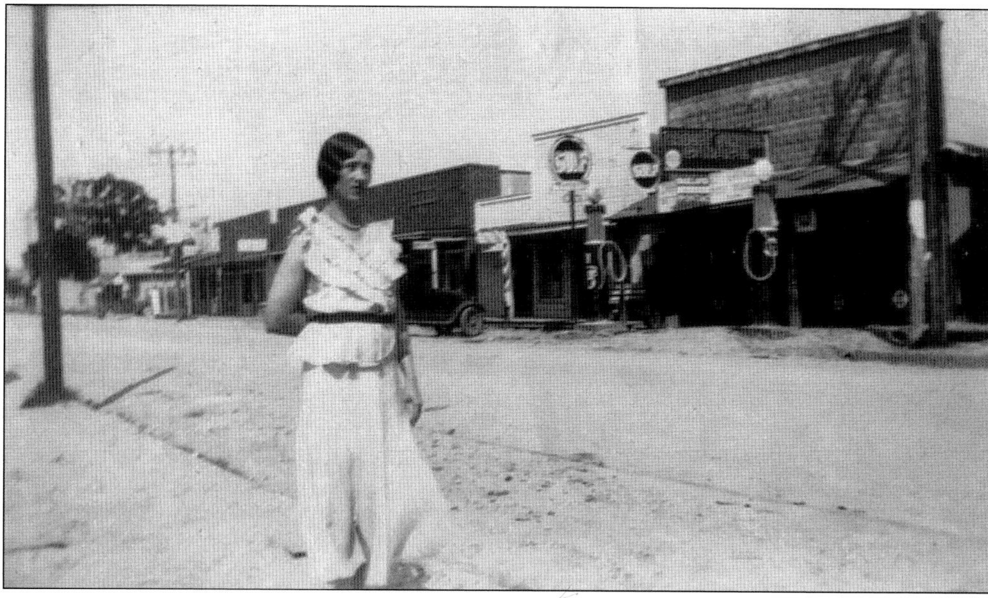

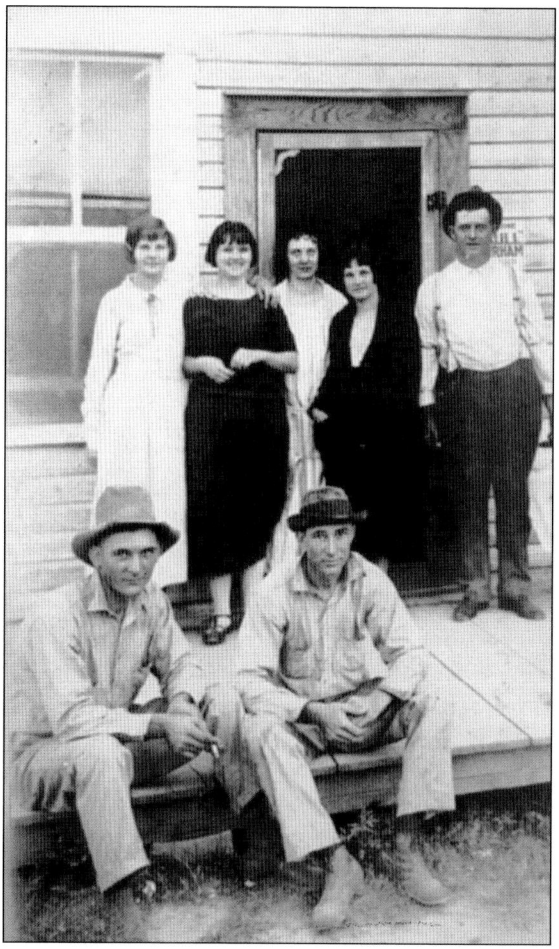

Above, Millie Stasney stands in front of the stores along Kernohan Street. Her café is across the street from where she is standing. At left, a group of friends are seated on the porch in front of the Crosby Café. Frank Slovacek is seated at left. His sister Christina Slovacek Lord is standing second from left. The Crosby Café was one of the most popular in town and was a fixture for two decades. Millie Stasney prided herself on her home-cooked foods and fresh pies. (Both, courtesy of the Stasney family.)

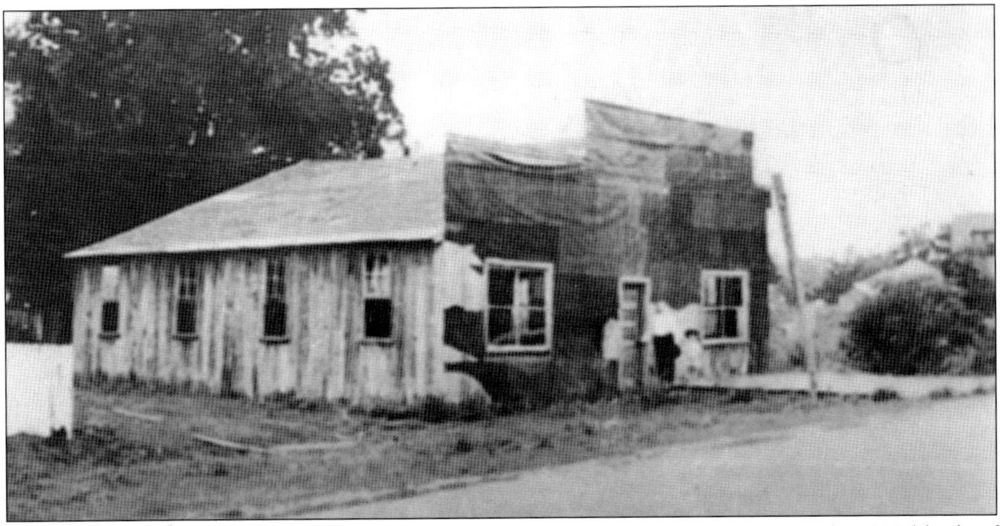

The J.D.H. Garage was owned by Joel C. Harvey, a wheelwright. It was in the 600 block of Runneburg Road and later served as the first building for the First Baptist Church, which is still at this location. Crosby had a number of other gas stations and car repair businesses. (Courtesy of Klaus Duda.)

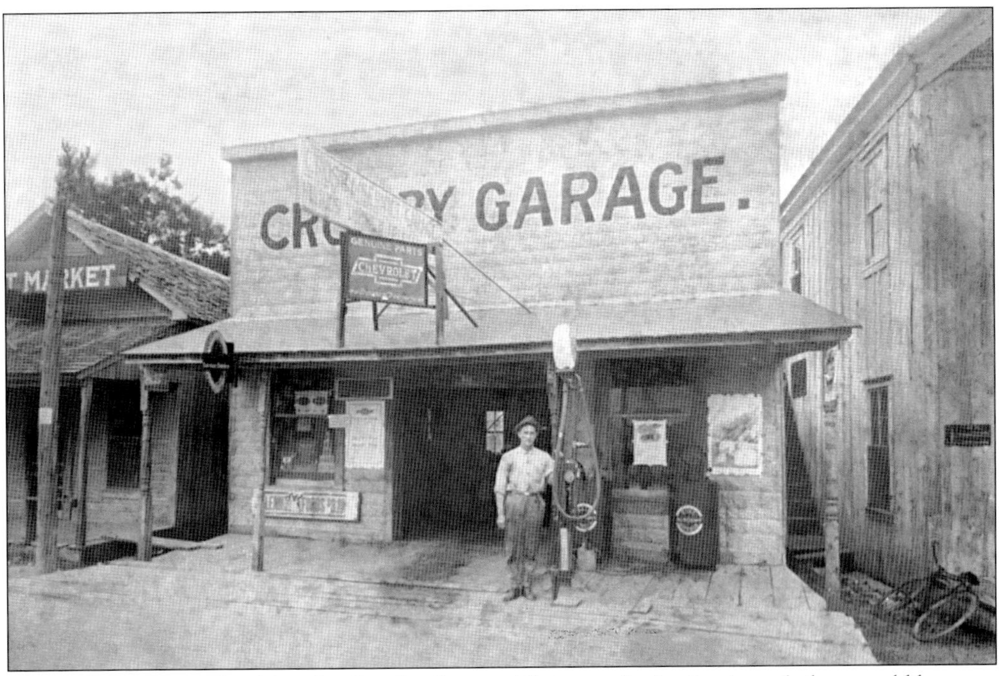

Pictured here around 1922 is the Crosby Garage. This was the beginning of what would become Ramsey Chevrolet. The building belonged to August Sirocka, but the business belonged to Harry Terry Harvey, who is standing out front. Hilliard's meat market is to the left. On the right is the Crosby Café and Hotel. (Courtesy of Klaus Duda.)

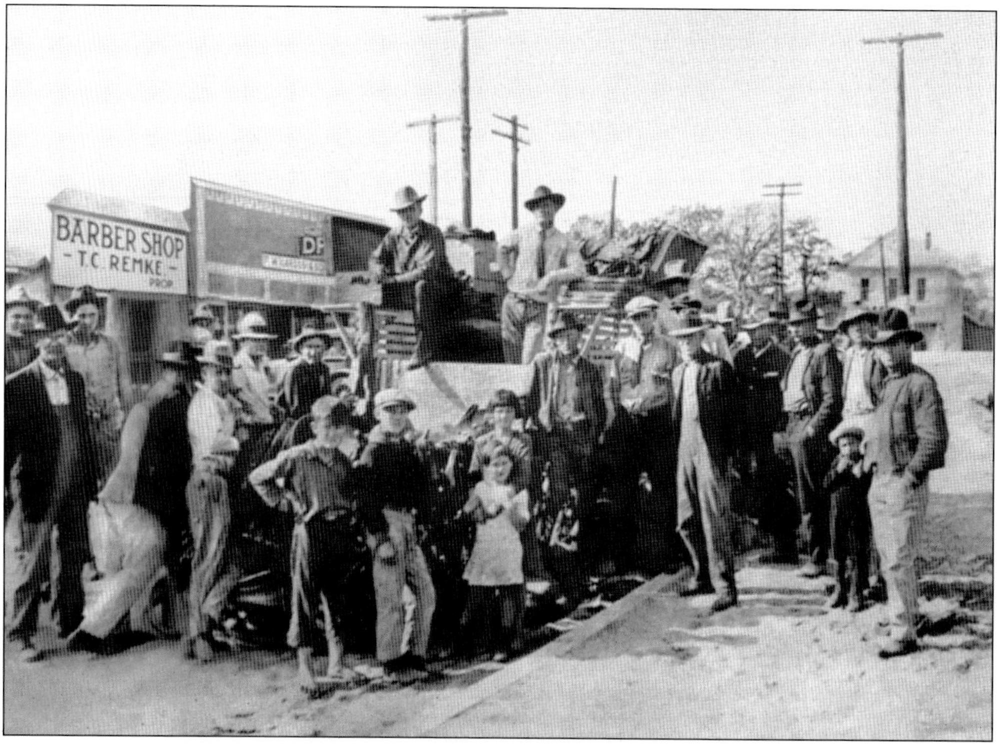

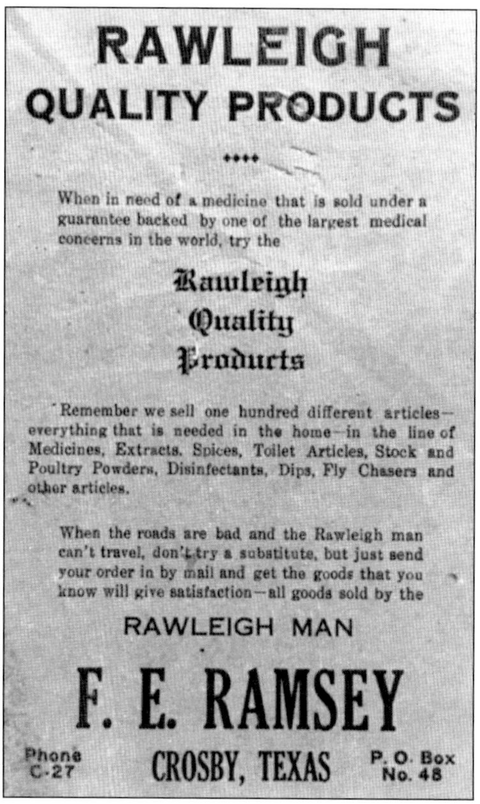
RAWLEIGH
QUALITY PRODUCTS

When in need of a medicine that is sold under a guarantee backed by one of the largest medical concerns in the world, try the

Rawleigh Quality Products

Remember we sell one hundred different articles—everything that is needed in the home—in the line of Medicines, Extracts, Spices, Toilet Articles, Stock and Poultry Powders, Disinfectants, Dips, Fly Chasers and other articles.

When the roads are bad and the Rawleigh man can't travel, don't try a substitute, but just send your order in by mail and get the goods that you know will give satisfaction—all goods sold by the

RAWLEIGH MAN

F. E. RAMSEY

Phone C-27 CROSBY, TEXAS P. O. Box No. 48

Pictured above is a traveling army surplus salesman parked on Main Street in December 1925. Locals surround the wagon, looking for good bargains on their Christmas shopping. In the background is T.C. Remke's barber shop, Larson's drugstore, and the Sampson Masonic Lodge, which was on the other side of the railroad tracks. Many early entrepreneurs began as traveling salesmen. Fred Ramsey began selling household items as a Rawleigh Company salesman around 1918. His ad is pictured at left. Ramsey later established the O.S.T. Garage and Chevrolet dealership. (Above, courtesy of the Prochazka family; left, courtesy of Sheryl Shaw.)

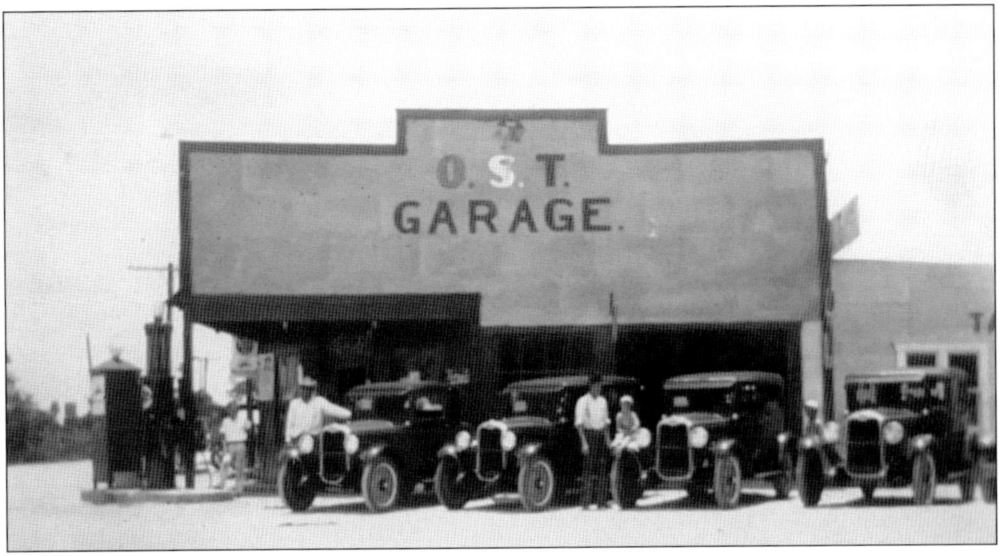

Fred Ramsey and his brother Charles came to Crosby in 1898 from Missouri. Charles opened Ramsey's drugstore in 1904. Fred built the O.S.T. Garage (above) in 1927. It was named after the Old Spanish Trail, which ran in front. It was at the corner of Kernohan and First Streets. Charles Ramsey started the business in 1923 when he purchased Harry Harvey's garage at the corner of Kernohan and Main Streets. It was the first Chevrolet dealership in Crosby. Below is an interior view of the O.S.T. Chevrolet dealership service area. (Both, courtesy of the Ramsey family.)

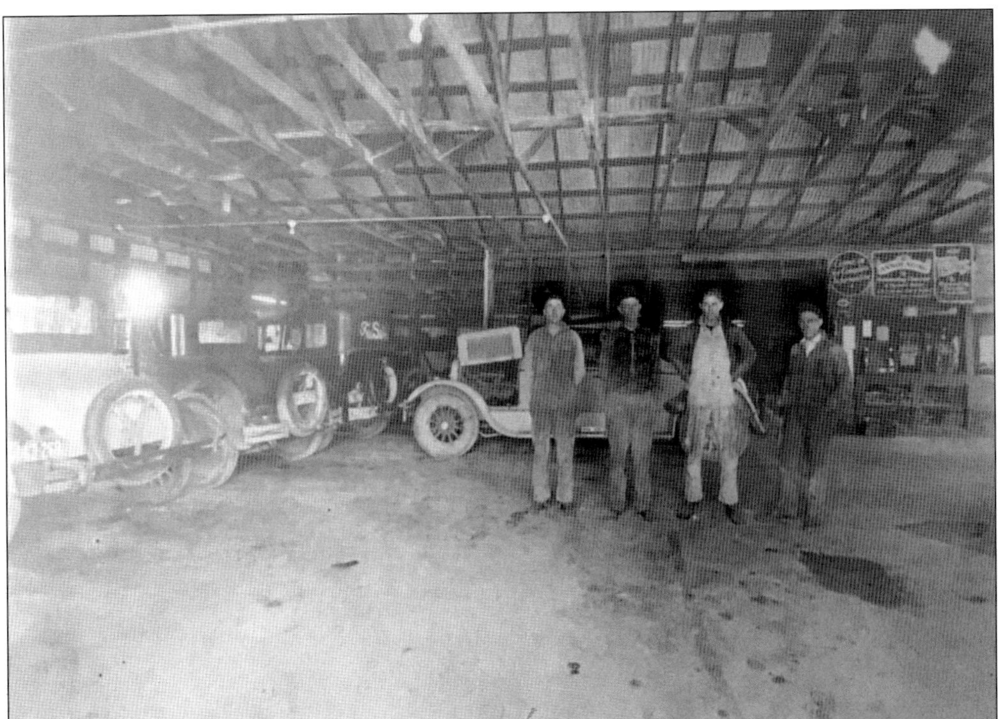

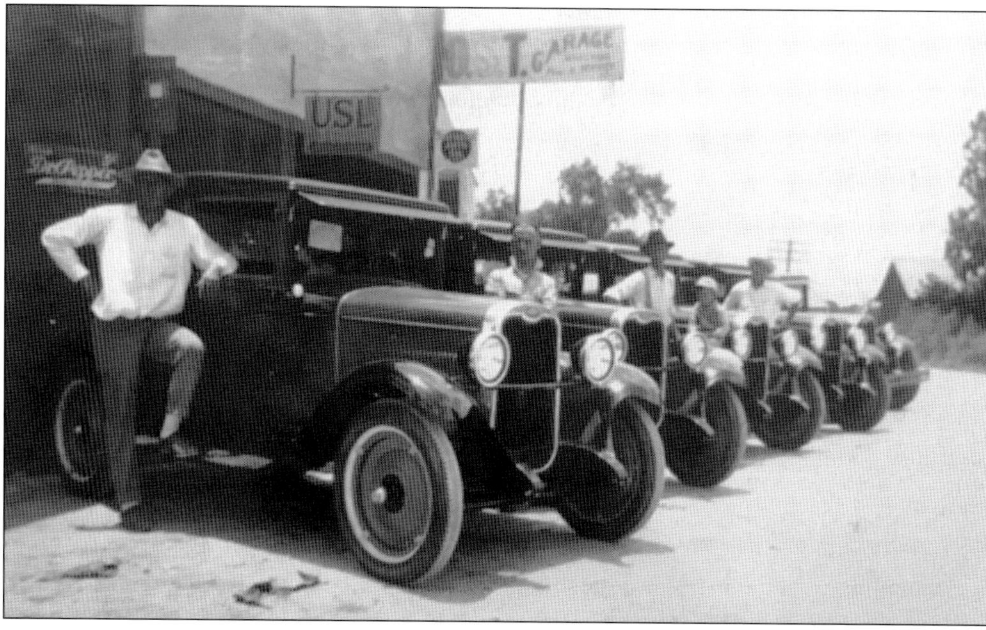

Above is the O.S.T. Garage in 1928. It offered a full range of auto services, including a gas station, along with selling cars. This photograph shows the year's new lineup of Chevrolet cars. Fred Ramsey and his sons operated the business from this location until 1950, when they moved to 5418 Main Street. In the 1950s, they changed the name to Ramsey Chevrolet. The business continued into the 1980s. Pictured below from left to right are Theo Ramsey, Ramon Ramsey, Fred Ramsey (owner), and Harry Dietrich. (Both, courtesy of the Ramsey family.)

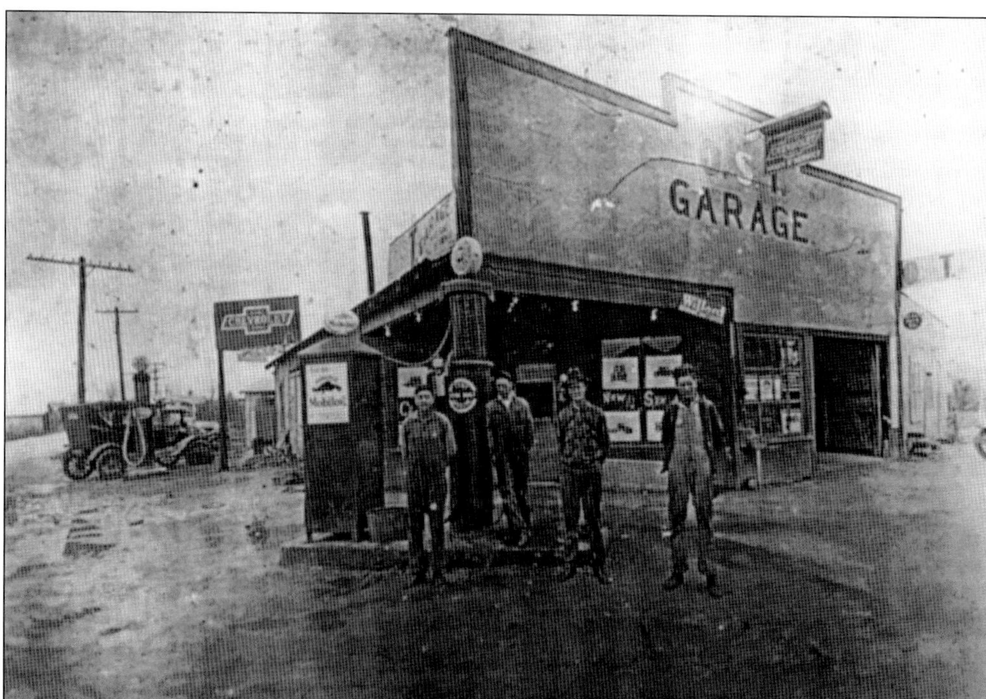

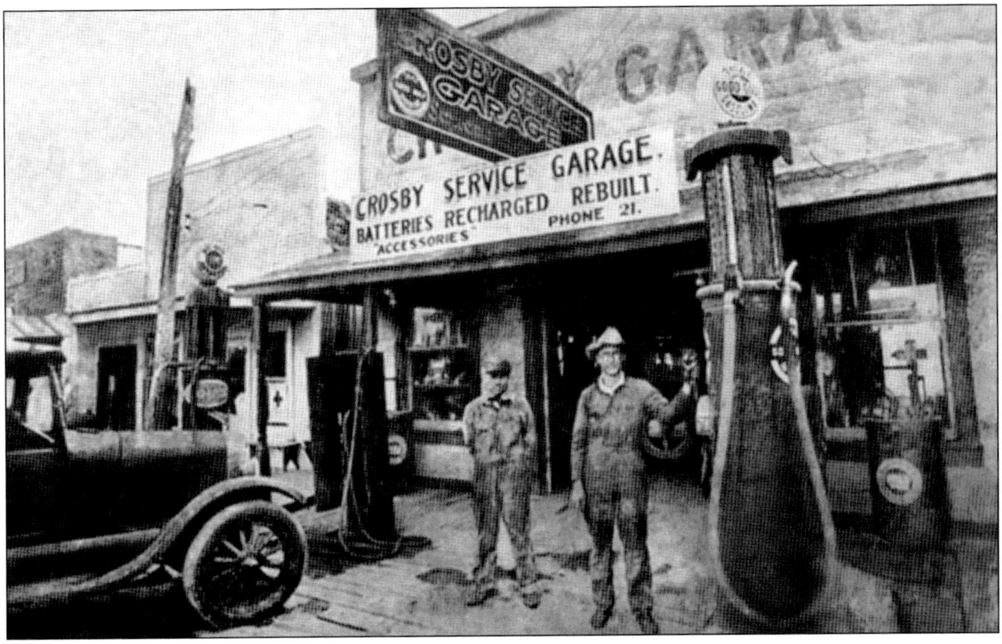

Above is the Crosby Service Garage in 1928. In that era, most places that sold gas also sold batteries and did engine repairs. This garage was originally owned by Harry Harvey, who sold it to Fred Ramsey. Ramsey then sold it to Charles J. Garbs, who is pictured at right with his son Arnold. Arnold Garbs eventually became president of the Crosby State Bank. Pictured below is the Farmers Service Station that sat at the "Y" intersection of Main and First Streets in 1921, where Danny's Station is now. (Both, courtesy of Klaus Duda.)

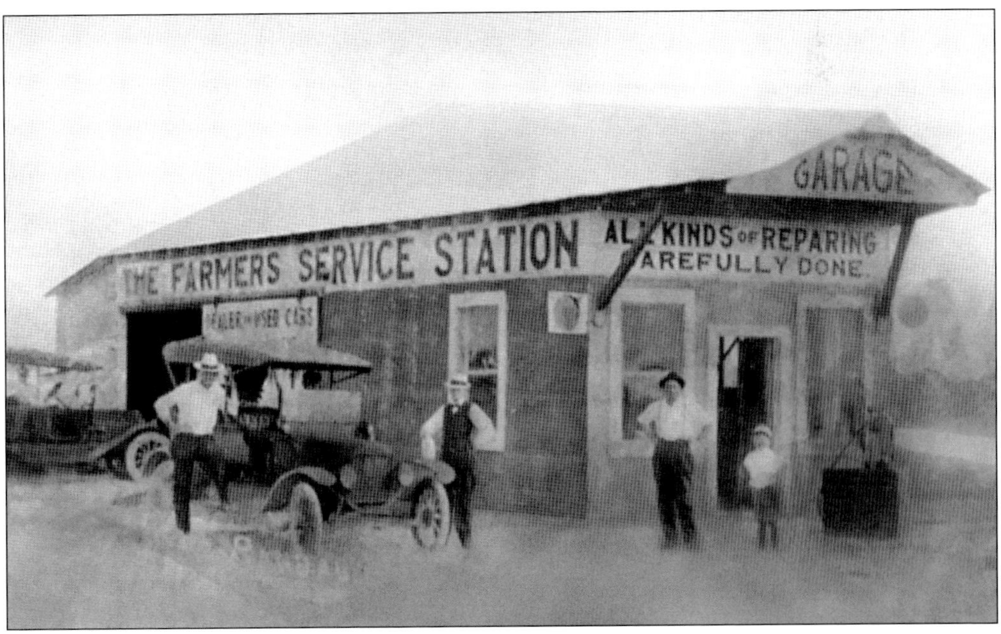

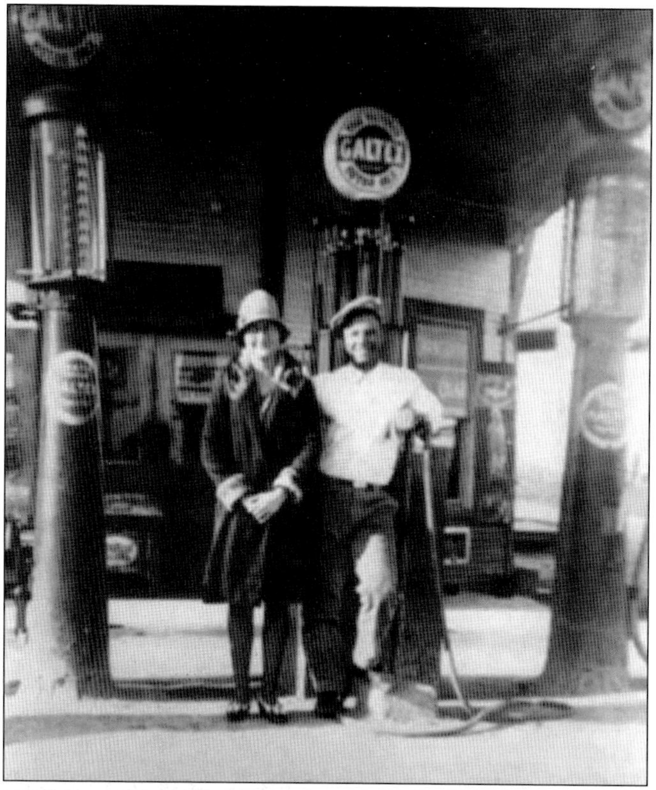

After the Farmers Service Station closed, it was taken over by Herman and Katie Dunks. They are pictured standing next to the pumps in front of Dunk's Service Station in 1927 shortly after it opened. This station was also at the "Y" intersection of First and Main Streets. (Courtesy of the Dunks family.)

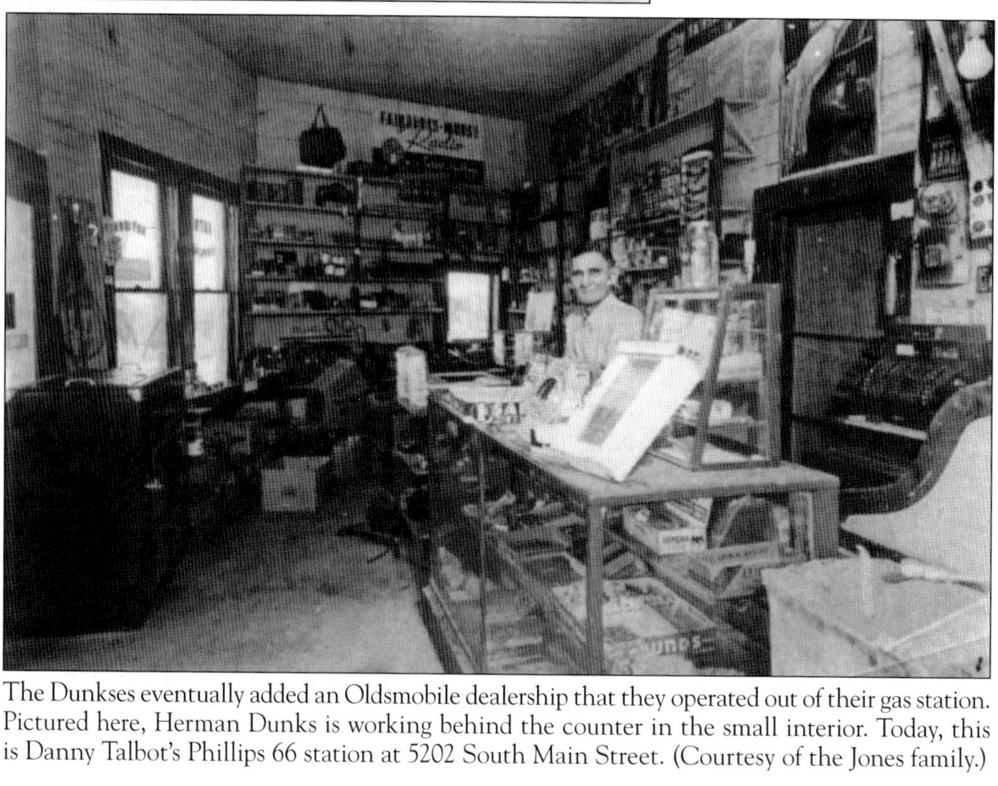

The Dunkses eventually added an Oldsmobile dealership that they operated out of their gas station. Pictured here, Herman Dunks is working behind the counter in the small interior. Today, this is Danny Talbot's Phillips 66 station at 5202 South Main Street. (Courtesy of the Jones family.)

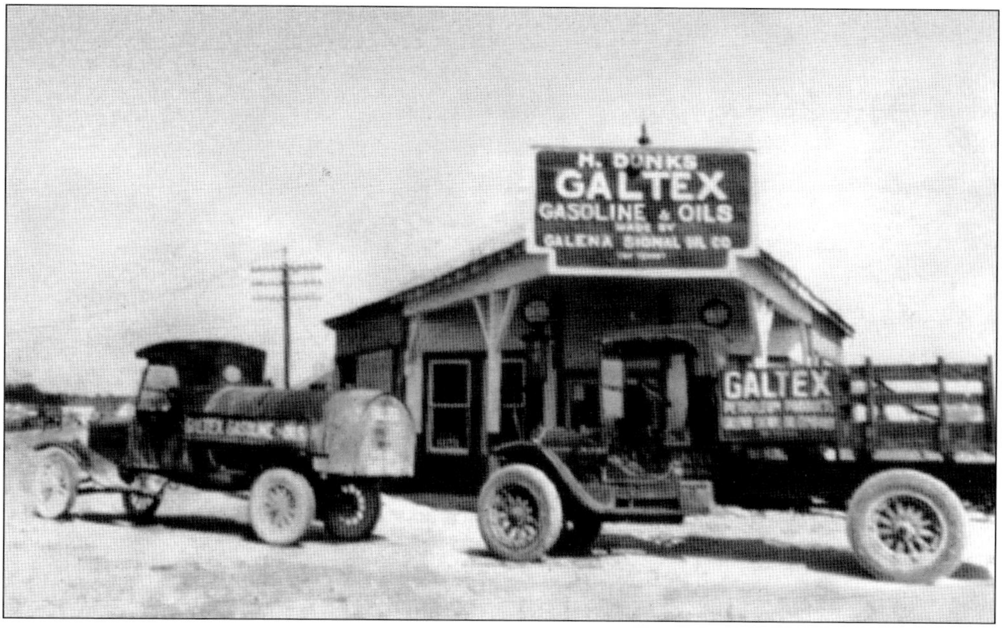

Pictured above are Galtex delivery trucks bringing fuel to the Dunks gas station. Galtex was an oil company based in Galveston, Texas, that was owned by the Sealy family. They were in partnership with the Texas Oil Company (Texaco). Ultimately, Galtex became a division of the Deyo Oil Company of Binghamton, New York. The two companies split in December 1924. The location of this gas station has led to a number of car crashes over the years. In 1934, Ben Hargrave lost control of his car and ran into the building. The damaged building is seen below. (Above, courtesy of the Wyatt family; below, courtesy of the Duda family.)

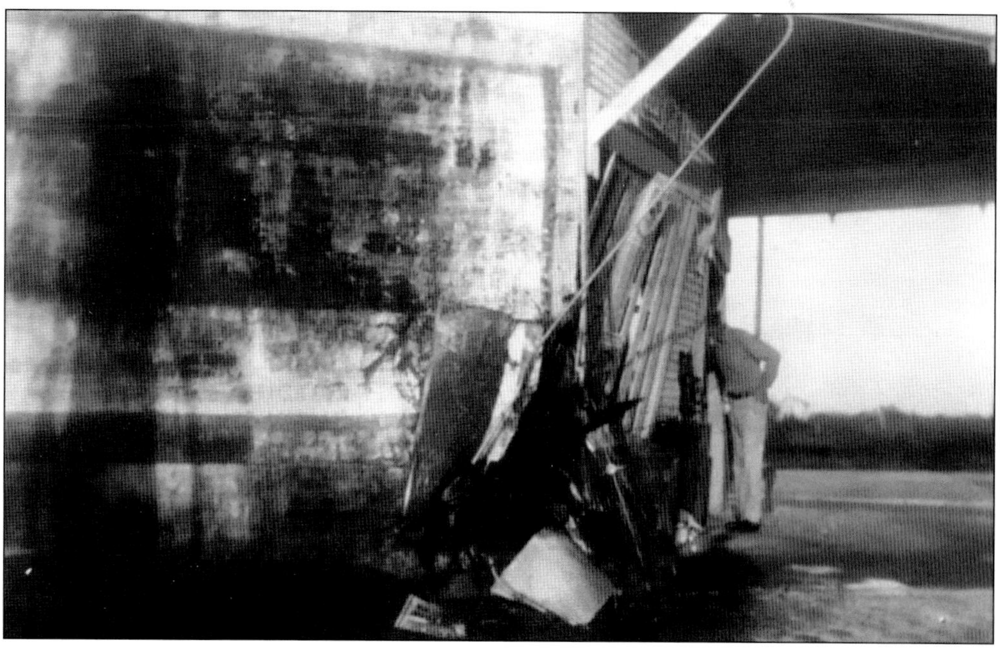

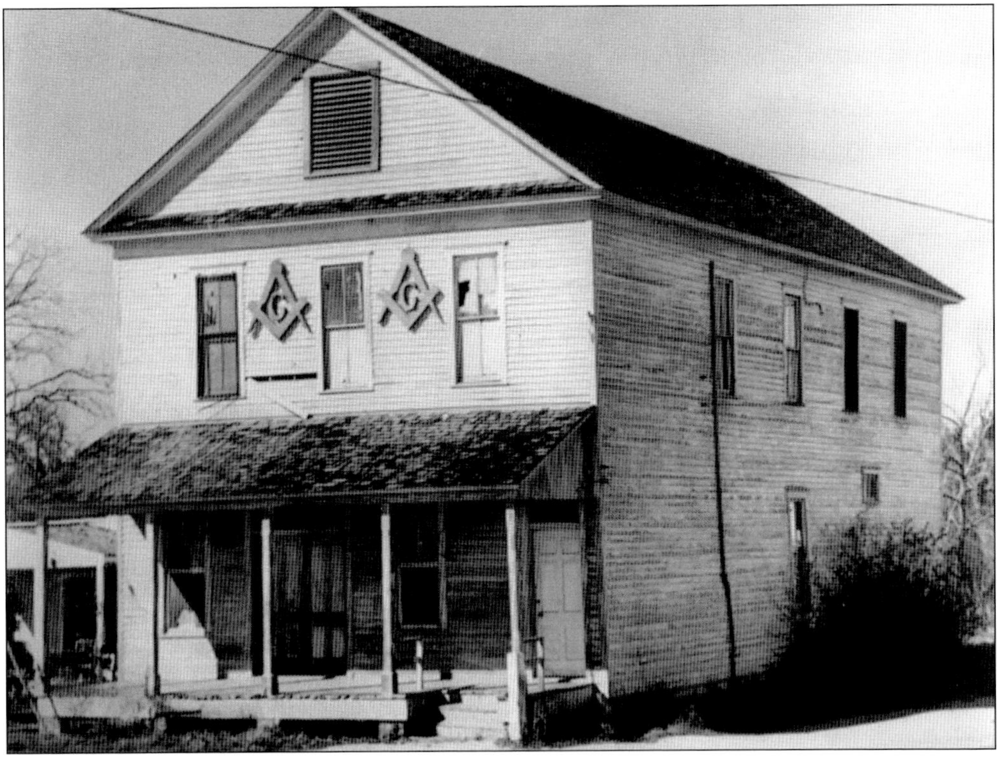

Above is a 1922 photograph of the Sampson Masonic Lodge. It was built in 1901, with general store lease space on the first floor. It was just north of the railroad tracks on the corner of Main and Jackson Bayou Streets. Below is a New Year's Eve celebration possibly held in the upstairs of the lodge. Early Crosby residents would often use one of the schoolhouses for celebrations. Another option for parties in the wintertime was to move all of the furniture to another part of the house and clear out a large space in the living room or parlor to dance. (Both, courtesy of Klaus Duda.)

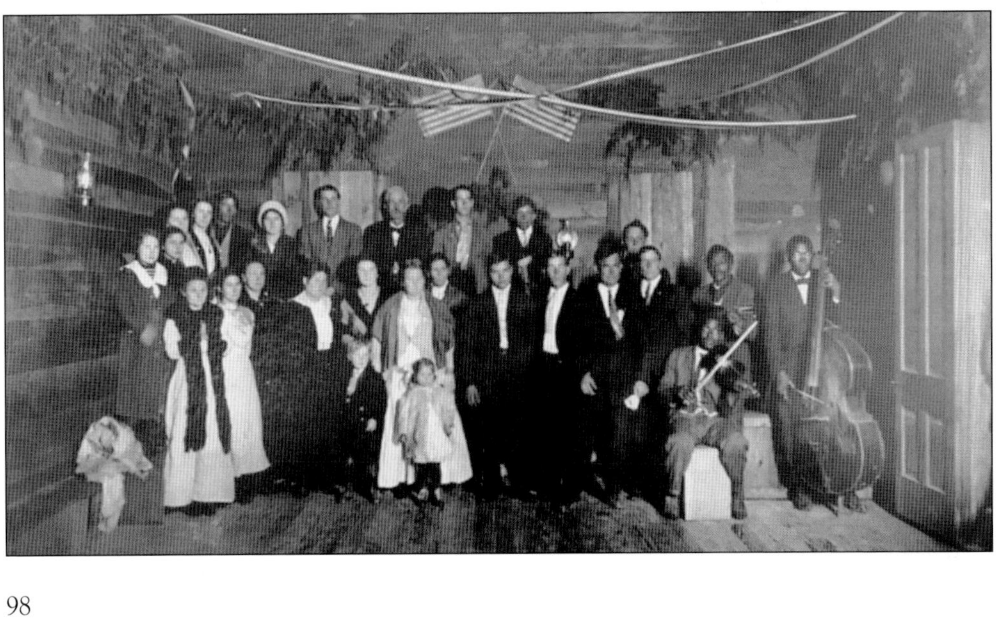

Crosby had an amateur baseball team as early as 1904. By 1913, the town had its own ballpark. This c. 1914 photograph shows the local ballpark. By 1922, the Crosby team was known as the Giants. They played against surrounding towns and several company teams from Houston. (Courtesy of the Keller family.)

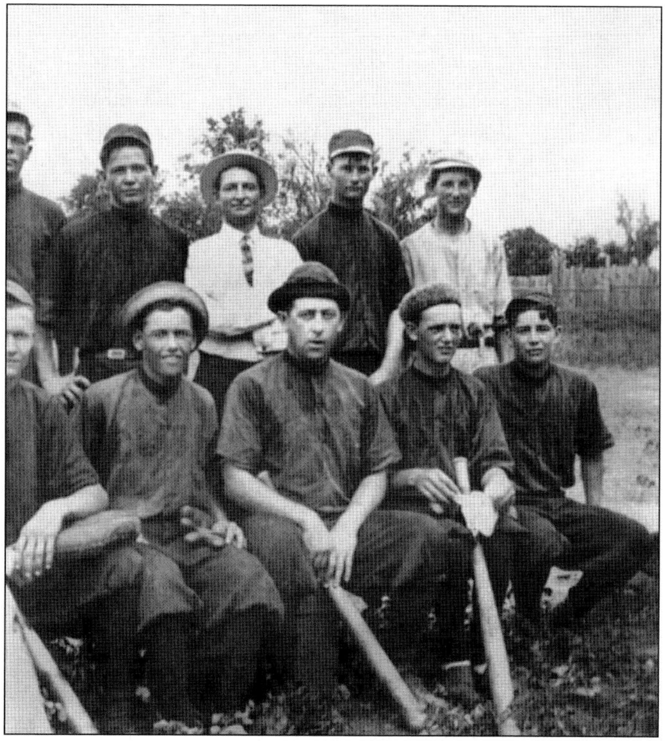

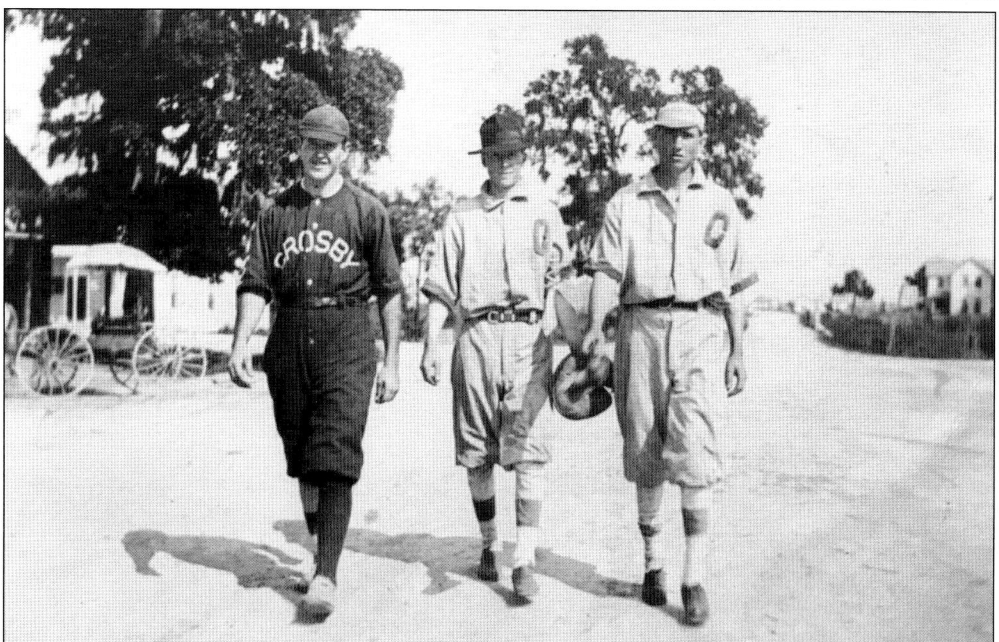

From left to right, Ollie Henson, Homer Lord, and Jim Gibson head for the Crosby train depot to play a baseball game in Liberty in 1918. The first of several professional athletes to grow up in Crosby came from this early team. In 1914, Louis Reidland played professional baseball for the Belton Braves, a minor league team that was part of the Middle Texas League. (Courtesy of the Lord family.)

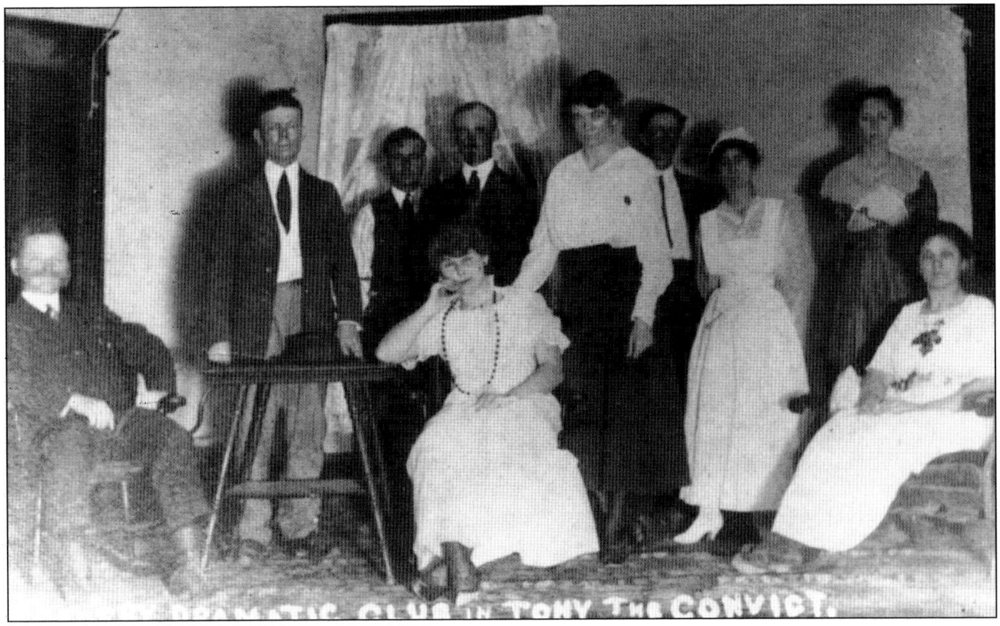

From 1915 to 1917, residents formed the Crosby Dramatic Club. The club put on a number of plays in the Crosby High School auditorium to entertain the community. In 1918, the community got its first movie theater, which quickly filled the town's thirst for entertainment. In 1911, a commercial advocacy club was organized. Its role was to try to lure new businesses to the area. In 1923, the fledgling group established the first Crosby Fair & Rodeo. In 1924, the Crosby Chamber of Commerce was formally organized. Pictured below are members of the 1925 chamber of commerce. (Both, courtesy of the Evans family.)

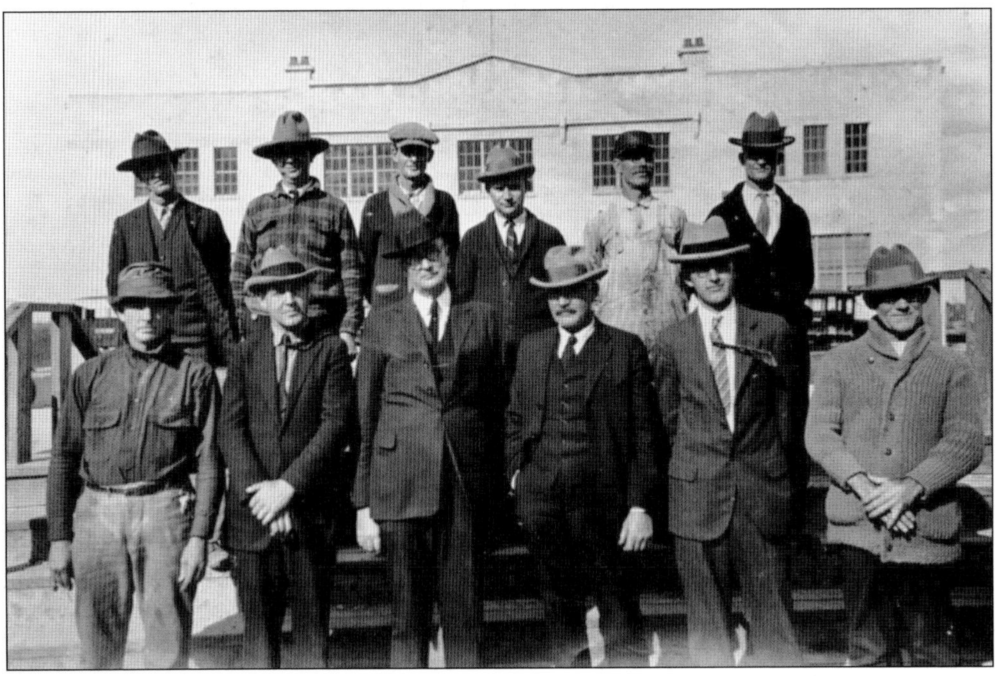

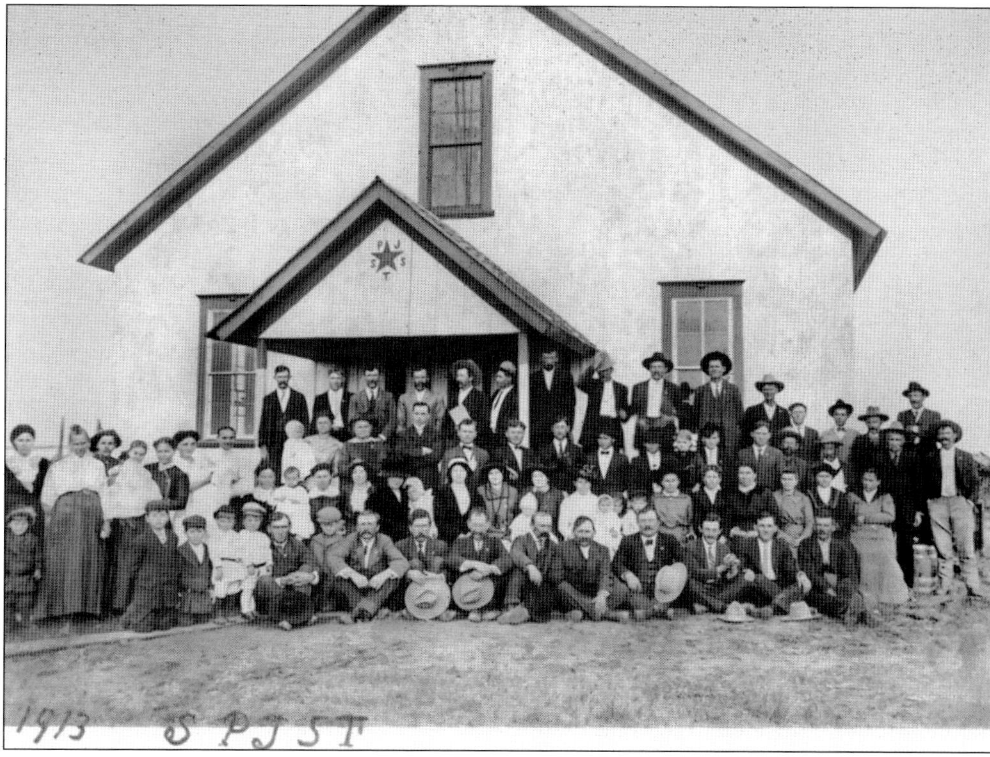

The Slovanske Podporujici Jednoty Statu Texas Lodge No. 91 (also known as the Bohemian Hall) is pictured above. The hall was used for meetings as well as Czech parties, wedding receptions, and weekend dances, usually on Sundays after church. The Crosby Orchestra would play traditional Czech songs with an occasional American patriotic song. It was the central gathering place for Czech families in the community. Many of the original founding families are pictured in this 1913 photograph. The image below is from July 4, 1916. Members are pictured behind the hall under a homemade, mule-powered merry-go-round provided by Joseph Stasney.

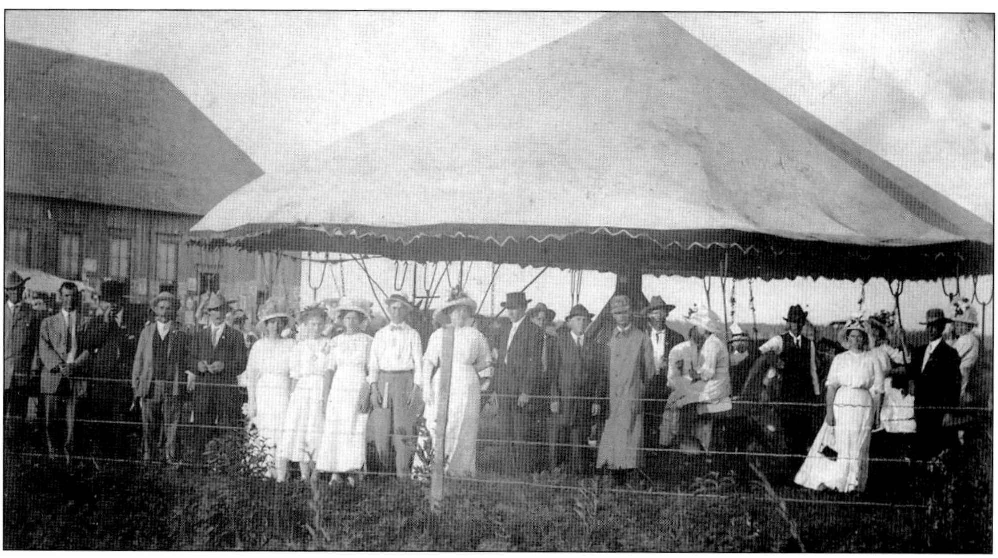

The Old Bohemian Hall

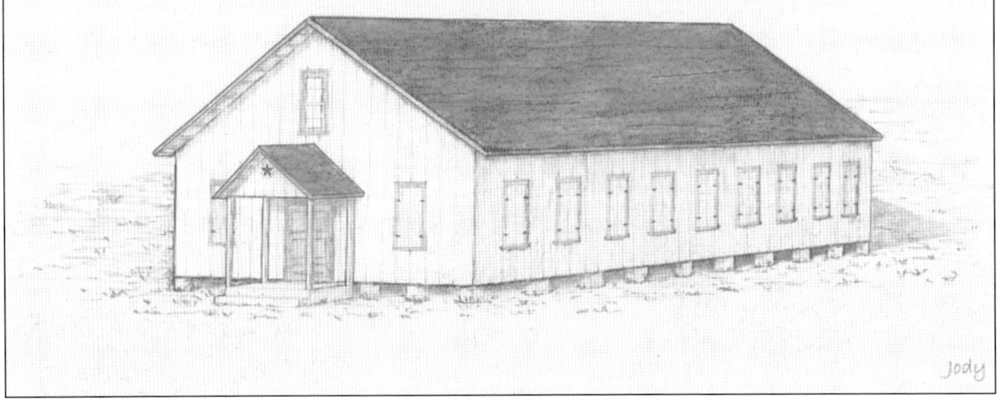

The Slovanske Podporujici Jednoty Statu Texas was an insurance cooperative, made up of the Czech families in Texas. Its name in English is Slavonic Benevolent Order of the State of Texas. The first hall in Crosby was called Bohemian Hall, and is how Bohemian Hall Road got its name. It was in the 14000 block of Bohemian Hall Road on a portion that is now called the Old Road. Below are several members of the Slovanske Podporujici Jednoty Statu Texas in a c. 1928 photograph of the hall. Around 1930, a second hall was built in Crosby at 6613 FM 2100, called Magnolia Hall. (Above, author drawing; below, courtesy of the Marek family.)

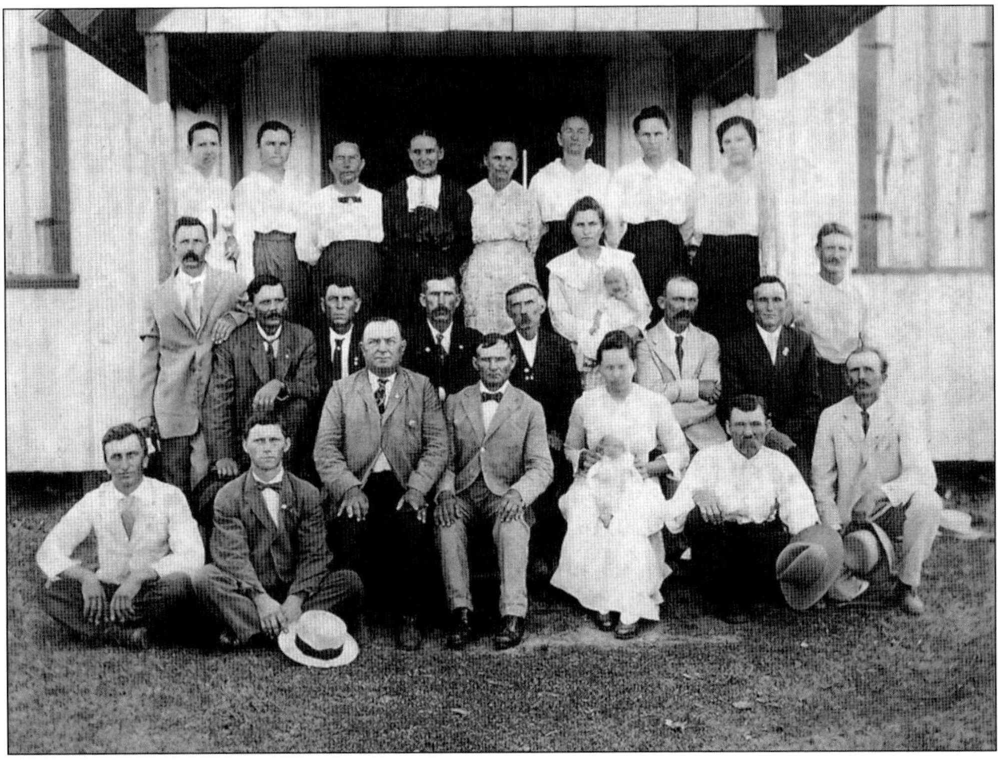

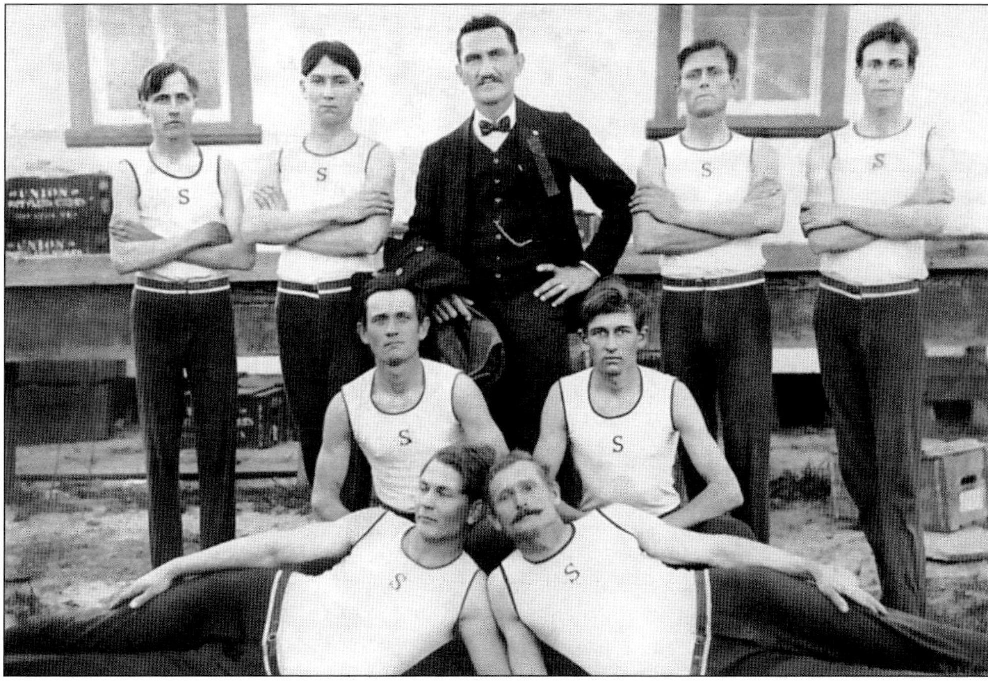

Czech performers from various communities often performed at the Crosby Bohemian Hall. Pictured above are the Sokols (also known as the Falcons), a group of Czech gymnasts who traveled to Crosby to perform around 1915. The Sokols were a Slavic gymnastic society that originated in Prague in 1862. They are pictured here next to the Crosby Bohemian Hall. The famous Baca Band from Fayetteville and the Crosby Czech Band (below) accompanied them on many occasions when they performed in the various Czech communities in and around Houston. The manager of the 20-piece Crosby Band was local resident Steven Kelarek. (Above, courtesy of the Stasney family; below, courtesy of the Holy family.)

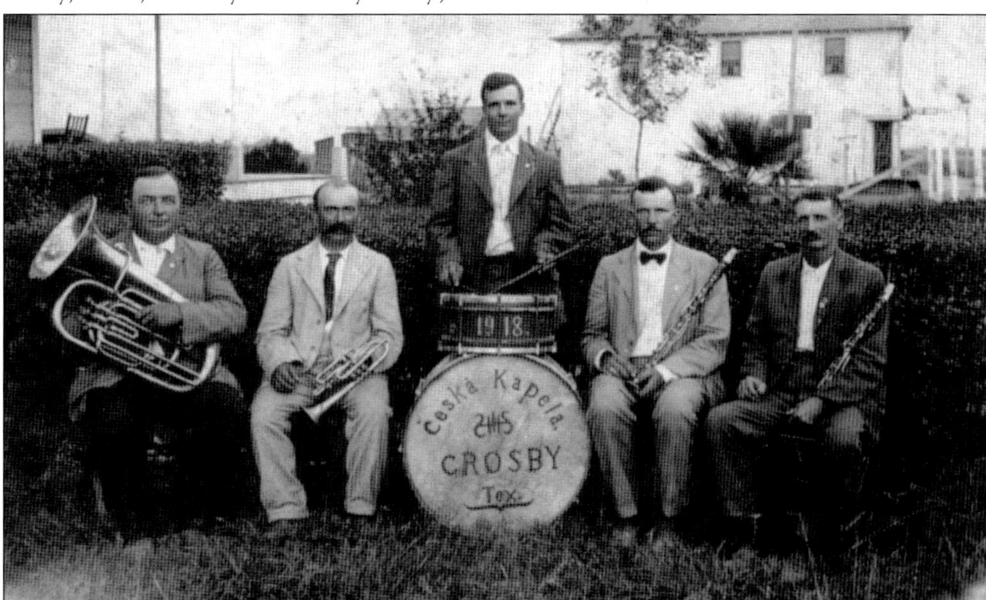

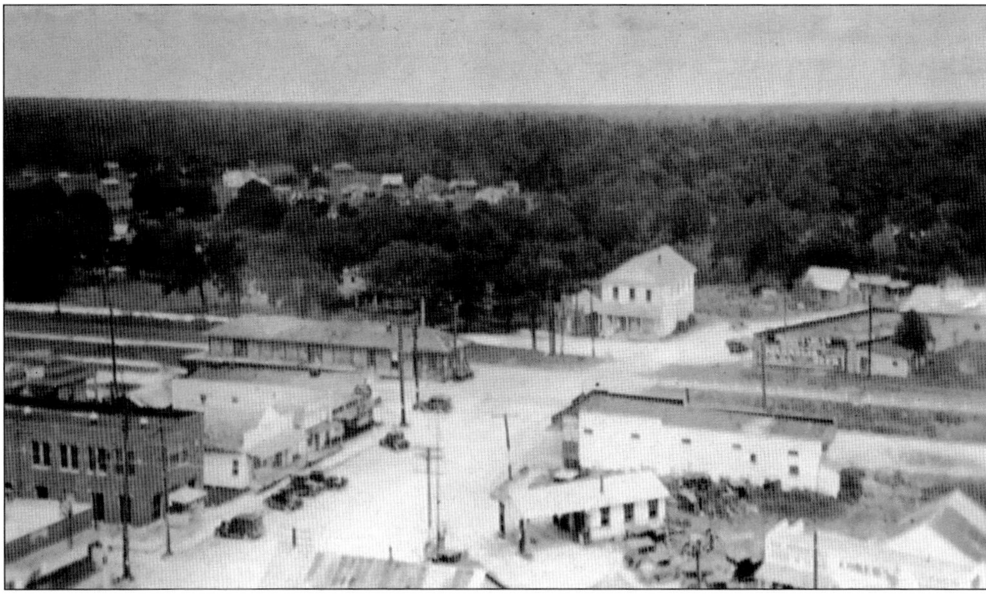

Richard Ramsey took these photographs from Reidland's water tower in 1929. The gas station on the corner of Kernohan and Main Streets was the Joe Sirocka service station. He originally had a saloon at this location but was forced to close it during Prohibition. The long white building behind the service station is Lady Hare's Food Market. The two-story white building in the background housed the Masonic lodge upstairs and a government canning facility below during the Depression. Prince Albert Dunks's shoe store is next to it. Across the street is the Shadowland Lounge. The train depot can also be seen in the background. The Shipula blacksmith shop is at far right.

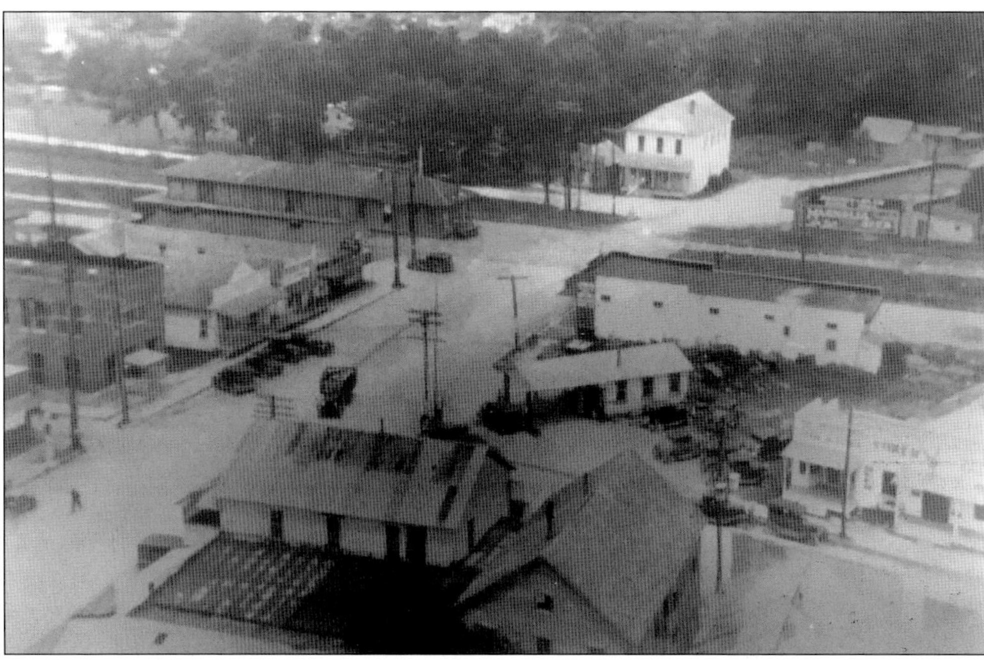

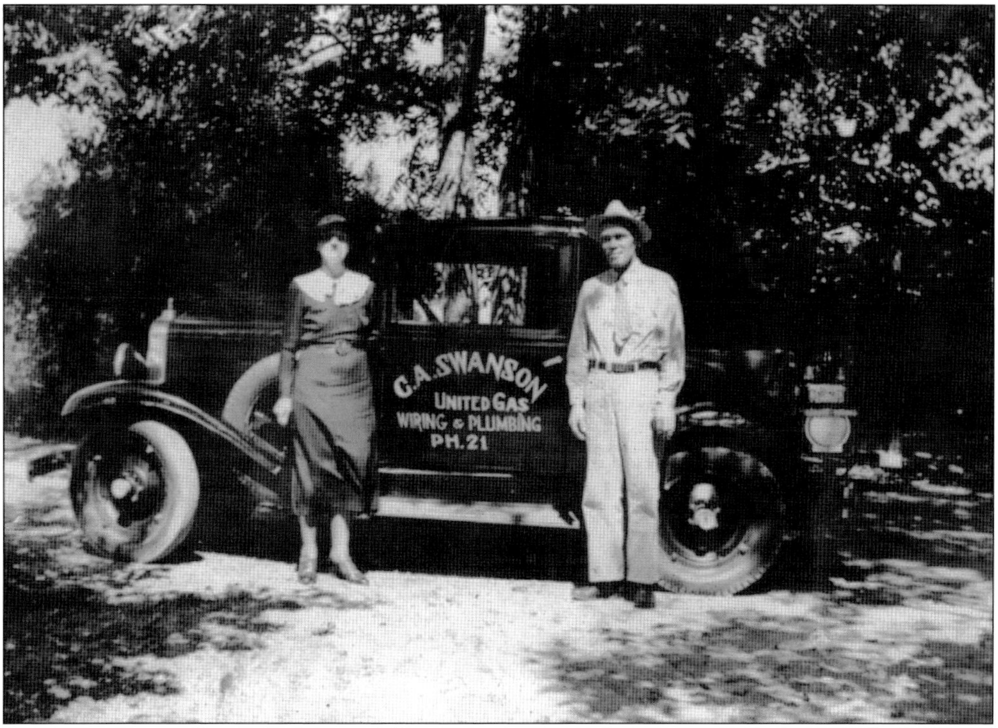

C.A. Swanson owned a wiring and plumbing business that began in the late 1920s. In the following years, he would wire and plumb many of the early buildings in Crosby that had been built without either. In the fall of 1929, when Crosby began receiving its first gas service lines from the United Gas Company, Swanson used a roman candle to ignite the gas line flare at the community celebration that heralded the event. The following year, he began serving his customers in the 1929 Chevrolet above. Posing with him is his wife, Victoria. Below is the Victor Lostak fuel depot. (Above, courtesy of the Swanson family; below, courtesy of the Lostak family.)

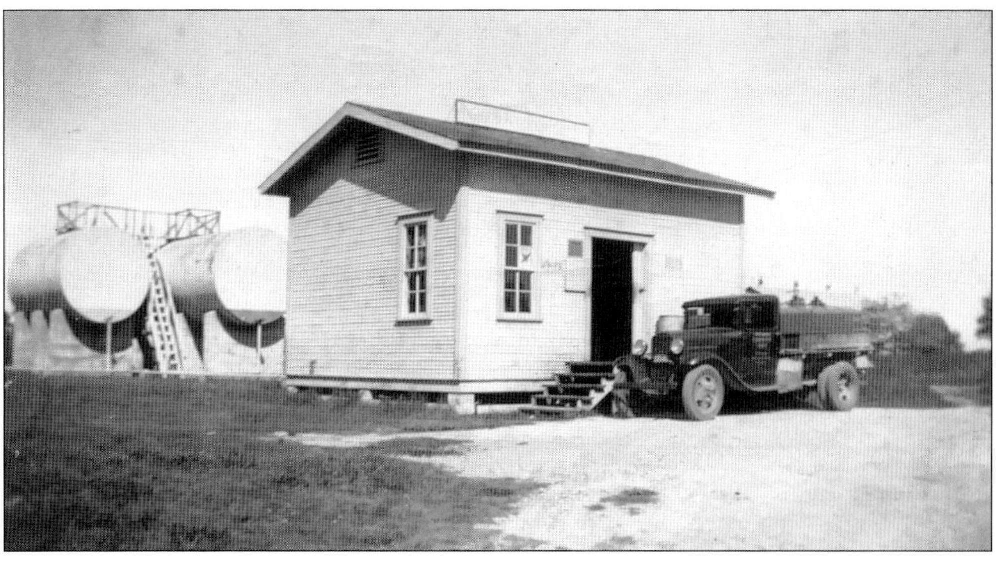

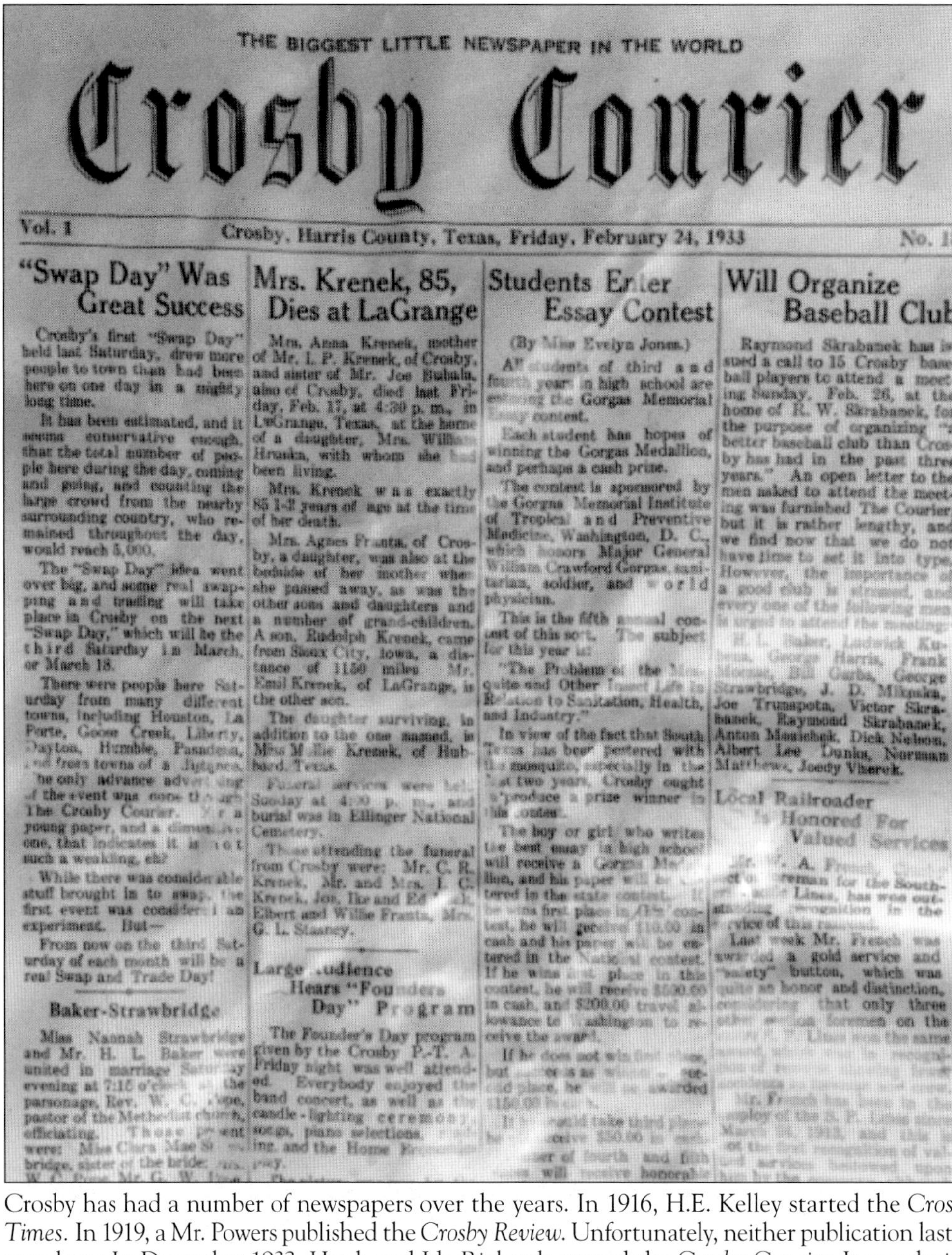

THE BIGGEST LITTLE NEWSPAPER IN THE WORLD

Crosby Courier

Vol. 1 | Crosby, Harris County, Texas, Friday, February 24, 1933 | No. 18

"Swap Day" Was Great Success

Crosby's first "Swap Day" held last Saturday, drew more people to town than had been here on one day in a mighty long time.

It has been estimated, and it seems conservative enough, that the total number of people here during the day, coming and going, and counting the large crowd from the nearby surrounding country, who remained throughout the day, would reach 5,000.

The "Swap Day" idea went over big, and some real swapping and trading will take place in Crosby on the next "Swap Day," which will be the third Saturday in March, or March 18.

There were people here Saturday from many different towns, including Houston, La Porte, Goose Creek, Liberty, Dayton, Humble, Pasadena, and from towns of a distance. The only advance advertising of the event was done through The Crosby Courier. [illegible] a young paper, and a diminutive one, that indicates it is not such a weakling, eh?

While there was considerable stuff brought in to swap, the first event was considered an experiment. But—

From now on the third Saturday of each month will be a real Swap and Trade Day!

Baker-Strawbridge

Miss Nannah Strawbridge and Mr. H. L. Baker were united in marriage Saturday evening at 7:15 o'clock at the parsonage, Rev. W. C. Pope, pastor of the Methodist church, officiating. Those present were: Miss Clara Mae Strawbridge, sister of the bride; [illegible]

Mrs. Krenek, 85, Dies at LaGrange

Mrs. Anna Krenek, mother of Mr. L. P. Krenek, of Crosby, and sister of Mr. Joe Bubala, also of Crosby, died last Friday, Feb. 17, at 4:30 p. m., in LaGrange, Texas, at the home of a daughter, Mrs. William Hrabka, with whom she had been living.

Mrs. Krenek was exactly 85 1-2 years of age at the time of her death.

Mrs. Agnes Frantz, of Crosby, a daughter, was also at the bedside of her mother when she passed away, as was the other sons and daughters and a number of grand-children. A son, Rudolph Krenek, came from Sioux City, Iowa, a distance of 1150 miles. Mr. Emil Krenek, of LaGrange, is the other son.

The daughter surviving, in addition to the one named, is Miss Mollie Krenek, of Hubbard, Texas.

Funeral services were held Sunday at 4:00 p. m., and burial was in Ellinger National Cemetery.

Those attending the funeral from Crosby were: Mr. C. R. Krenek, Mr. and Mrs. L. C. Krenek, Joe, Ike and Ed [illegible], Elbert and Willie Frantz, Mrs. G. L. Stasney.

Large Audience Hears "Founders Day" Program

The Founder's Day program given by the Crosby P.-T. A. Friday night was well attended. Everybody enjoyed the band concert, as well as the candle-lighting ceremony, songs, piano selections, [illegible] ing, and the Home [illegible] [illegible]

Students Enter Essay Contest

(By Miss Evelyn Jones.)

All students of third and fourth year in high school are entering the Gorgas Memorial Essay contest.

Each student has hopes of winning the Gorgas Medallion, and perhaps a cash prize.

The contest is sponsored by the Gorgas Memorial Institute of Tropical and Preventive Medicine, Washington, D. C., which honors Major General William Crawford Gorgas, sanitarian, soldier, and world physician.

This is the fifth annual contest of this sort. The subject for this year is:

"The Problem of the Mosquito and Other Insect Life in Relation to Sanitation, Health, and Industry."

In view of the fact that South Texas has been pestered with the mosquito, especially in the last two years, Crosby ought to produce a prize winner in this contest.

The boy or girl who writes the best essay in high school will receive a Gorgas Medallion, and his paper will be entered in the state contest. If he wins first place in this contest, he will receive $10.00 in cash and his paper will be entered in the National contest. If he wins first place in this contest, he will receive $500.00 in cash, and $200.00 travel allowance to Washington to receive the award.

If he does not win first place, but [illegible] is he [illegible] second place, he [illegible] awarded $150.00 [illegible]

[illegible]

Will Organize Baseball Club

Raymond Skrabanek has issued a call to 15 Crosby baseball players to attend a meeting Sunday, Feb. 26, at the home of R. W. Skrabanek, for the purpose of organizing "a better baseball club than Crosby has had in the past three years." An open letter to the men asked to attend the meeting was furnished The Courier, but it is rather lengthy, and we find now that we do not have time to set it into type. However, the importance of a good club is stressed, and every one of the following men is urged to attend the meeting:

H. L. Baker, Ludwick Kubena, George Harris, Frank Moerae, Bill Garba, George Strawbridge, J. D. Mikeska, Joe Trumpota, Victor Skrabanek, Raymond Skrabanek, Anton Mouchek, Dick Nelson, Albert Lee Danks, Norman Matthews, Joedy Vheruk.

Local Railroader Is Honored For Valued Services

Mr. W. A. French, [illegible] section foreman for the Southern Pacific Lines, has won outstanding recognition in the service of this railroad.

Last week Mr. French was awarded a gold service and "safety" button, which was quite an honor and distinction, considering that only three other section foremen on the [illegible] Lines won the same [illegible]

Mr. French has been in the employ of the S. P. Lines since March [illegible] [illegible]

Crosby has had a number of newspapers over the years. In 1916, H.E. Kelley started the *Crosby Times*. In 1919, a Mr. Powers published the *Crosby Review*. Unfortunately, neither publication lasted very long. In December 1932, Hank and Ida Richards started the *Crosby Courier*. It was during the Great Depression, and the bank had a space upstairs that was not being rented at the time. The couple exchanged free advertisements for rent. Hank started a free ad column for people to trade what they had for things they needed. It was a big hit. In fact, so many items came across his desk to trade that he soon convinced local merchants to organize a trade day one Saturday of each month. (Courtesy of the Swanson family.)

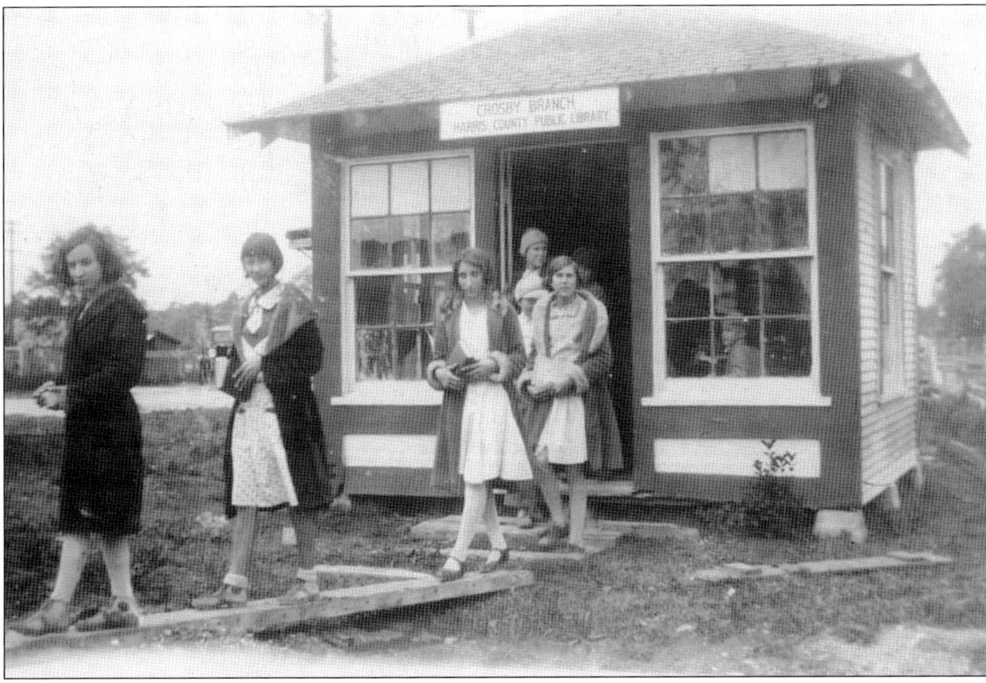

The Crosby branch of the Harris County Public Library opened for business on January 5, 1930. J.J. Orsag provided a small lot, and Oscar Reidland donated a nine- by twelve-foot building. Florence Nelson helped raise funds to remodel the building, and Albert Nelson did the carpentry and painting. Prior to an actual building, the community's small collection of books had been housed in the township school during the school year and at the post office during the summer months. The building was in the 200 block of Kernohan Street, and Imogene Vaughan served as its first librarian. Unfortunately, she died in 1932 at age 28. (Both, courtesy of Harris County.)

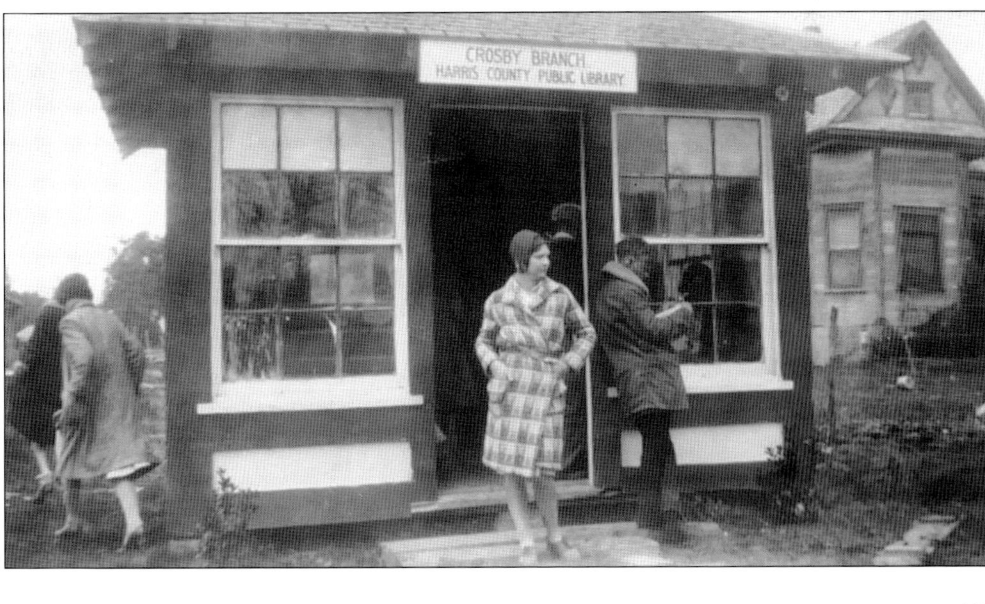

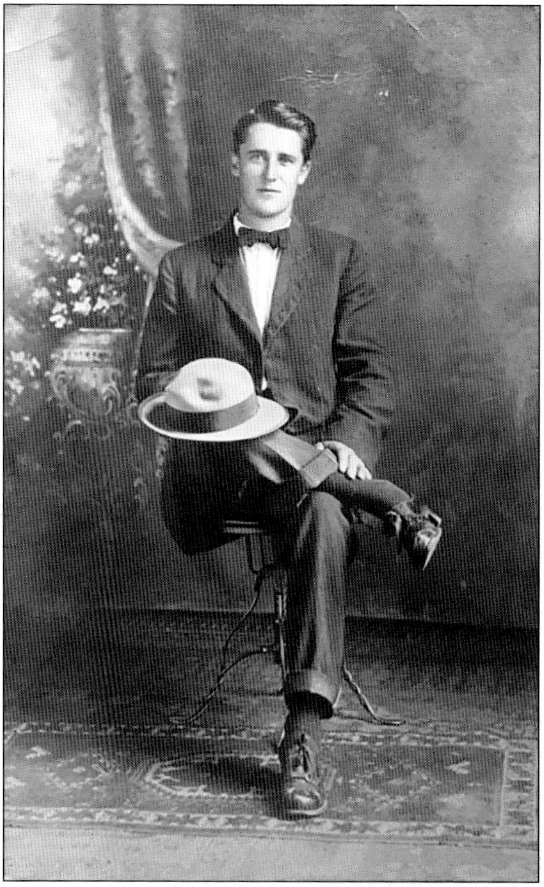

Sim Bergdahl was injured as a young man when he jumped out of a hayloft and landed on a pitchfork. It stuck into his calf, and he remained somewhat crippled for the rest of his life. He originally worked as a clerk at the Texas Mercantile Company. In the 1930s, he opened his own dry goods store next door at 127 Kernohan Street in the old Dewees & Larquet grocery store building. He sold clothes, shoes, hats, and miscellaneous items, as seen below. Bergdahl ran the store until his death in 1965. (Both, courtesy of the Kubin family.)

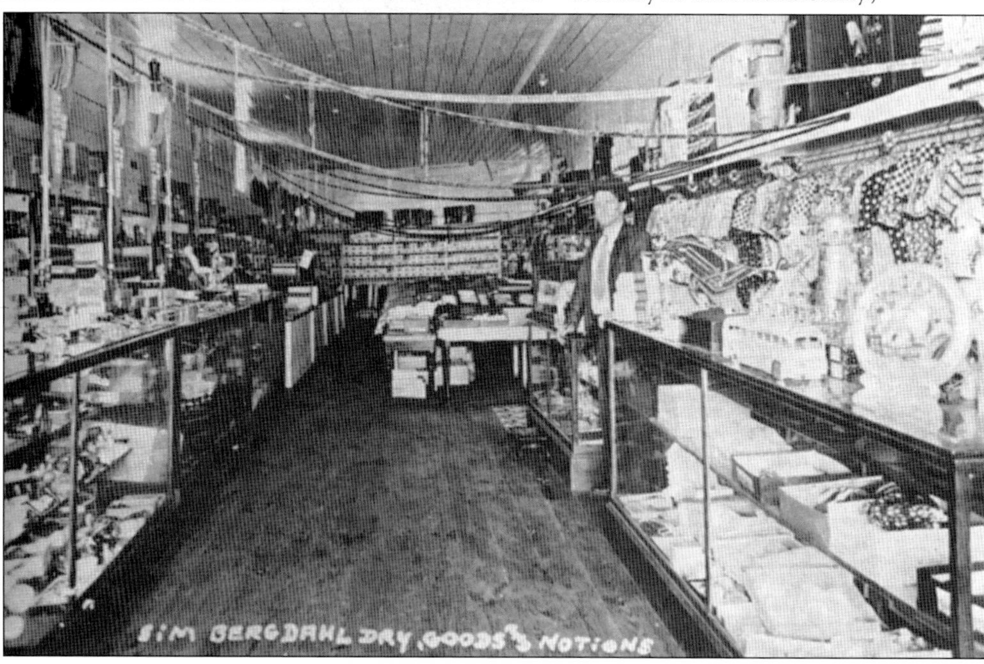

Five

Early Homes and Farms

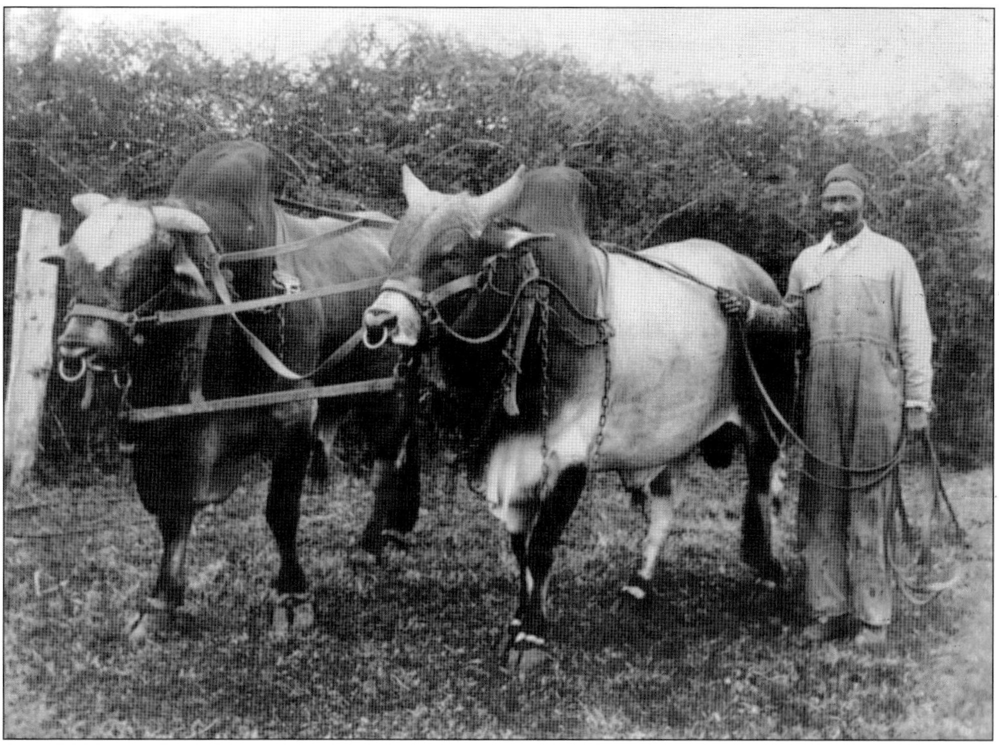

This is thought to be Mack I. Eagleton holding the reins to some early imported Brahma bulls. They were brought to Crosby because they were not as sickened by mosquito bites as European breeds. Ultimately, they were crossbred with the more docile and tastier European breeds, like Angus and Herefords. (Courtesy of Cecil Newton.)

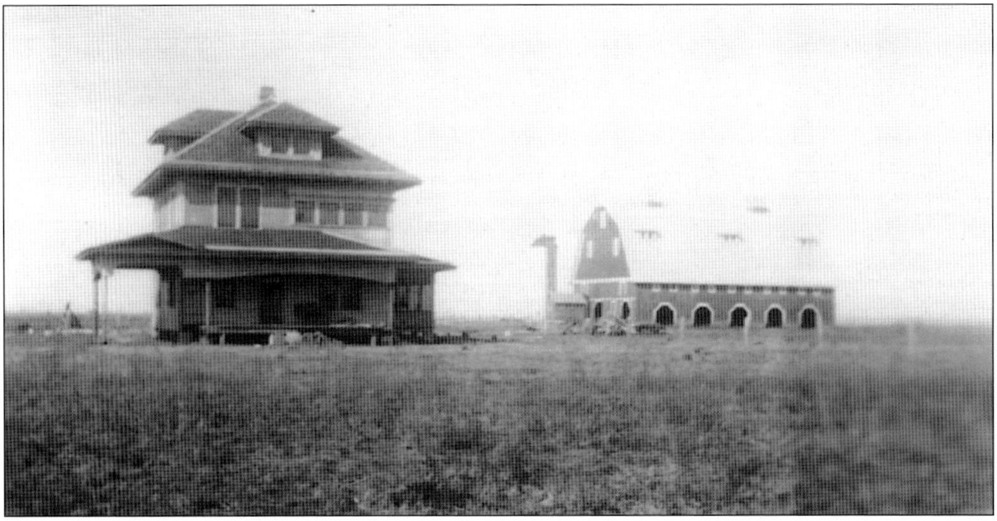

Roy Fleming built the incredible barn seen in these photographs in 1918. Two years later, he built the family home, seen at left above. The farm was on Runneburg Road near where it intersects Lindstrom Road. The barn may have been the largest in Texas at the time, requiring over 100,000 board feet of lumber. The family came from Illinois, where large barns were a necessity for farm animals to survive the long winters. Having a large barn enabled the northerners to house and feed their cattle throughout the winter without having to deal with the snow. Shortly after the family arrived here, Crosby had some unusually heavy snowfall and accumulation. The newcomers might have thought it was normal. A windstorm finally blew down the five-story structure in the late 1980s. (Both, courtesy of the Fleming family.)

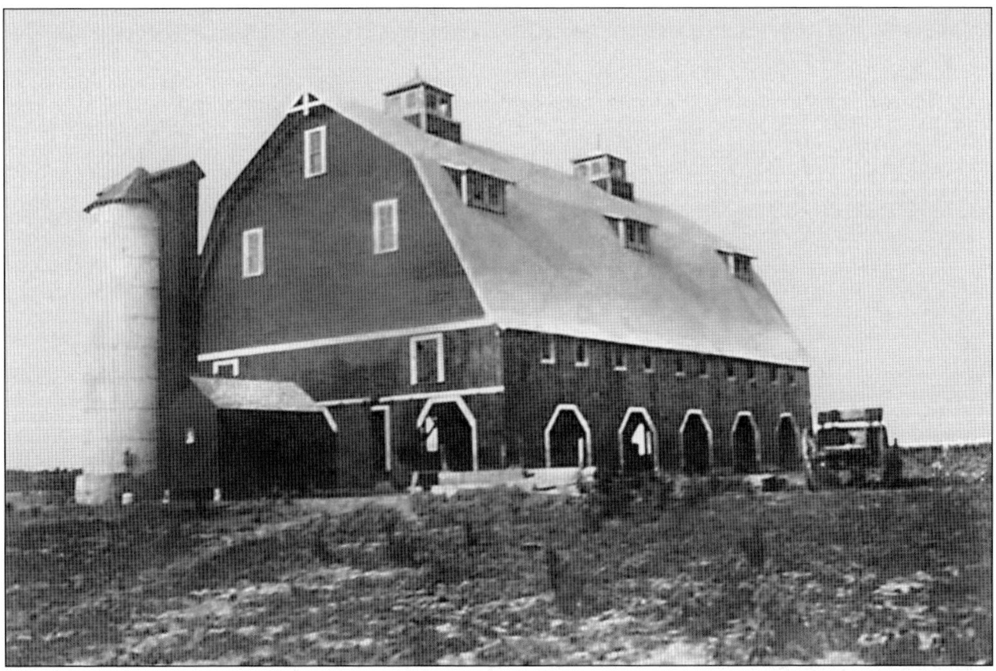

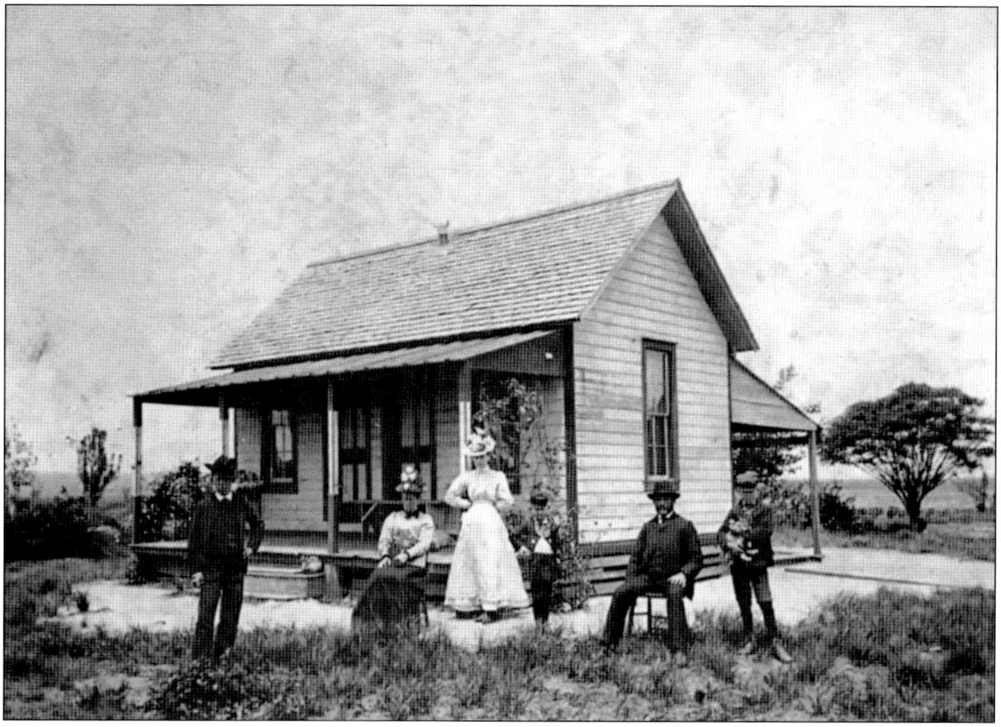

The Pira farmhouse, pictured above in 1903, was on Crosby Dayton Road north of the railroad tracks on land directly behind the baseball park. The Pira family built the home in 1896. From left to right are Walter, Marie, Lydia, Dave, Claus, and Adolph Pira. The C.A. Lindstrom family home is pictured below in 1918. It was on property at the intersection of Runneburg and Bohemian Hall Roads. C.A. and his wife, Hilda, later built a new home at the corner of Lindstrom and Runneburg Roads. It was built by their son Fredolph, a brick mason. (Above, courtesy of Klaus Duda; below, courtesy of Lisa Duncan.)

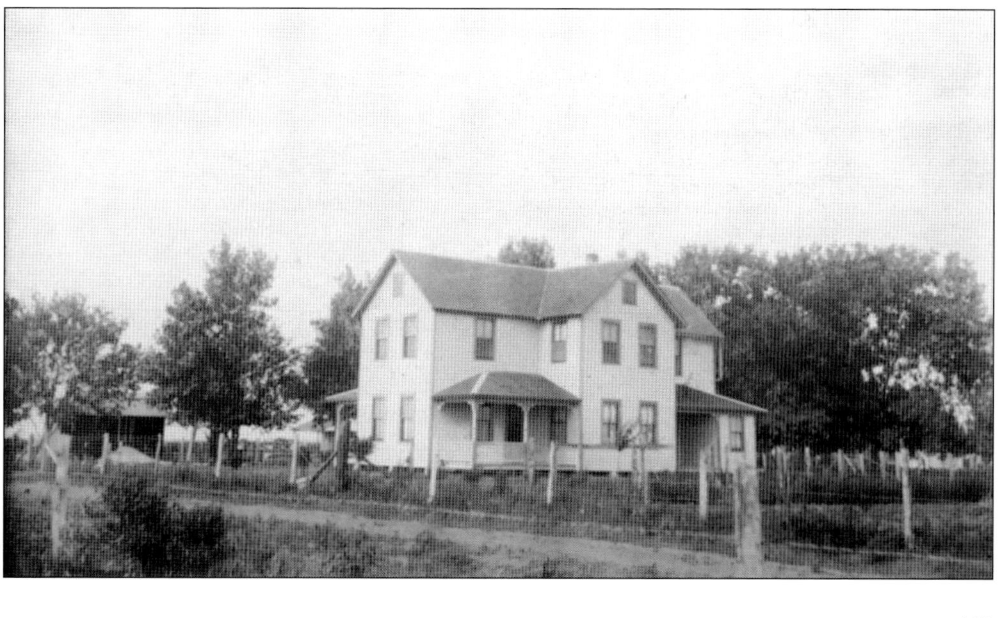

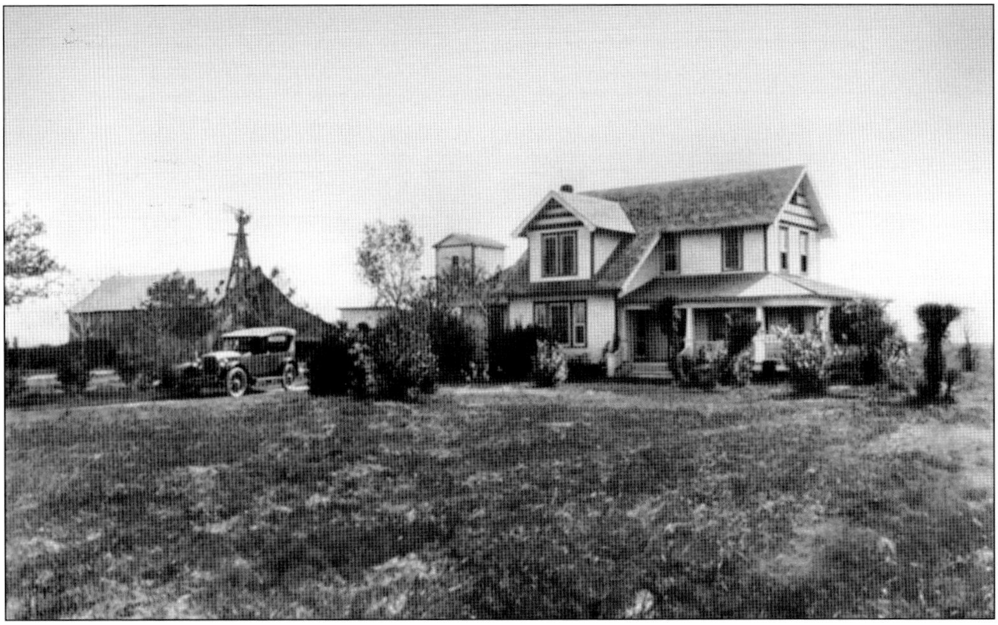

Pictured above is the Swan Runneberg farmhouse in 1916. It was on Runneburg Road on land where US 90 is now. Runneberg came to Baytown with an Illinois neighbor in 1908 to check on the neighbor's property in the Baytown area. He became interested in the area and bought 320 acres in Crosby for $5,280. Below is the Lulu and John T. Hare Sr. home in 1925. The Hares also moved to Crosby around 1908 from the Lynchburg area. John's father Captain Hare was held in very high regard by many of the town elders because most had served under him during the Civil War. John and Lulu owned a very large ranching operation consisting of several thousand acres on the north edge of downtown Crosby. (Above, courtesy of the Evans family; below, courtesy of the Hare family.)

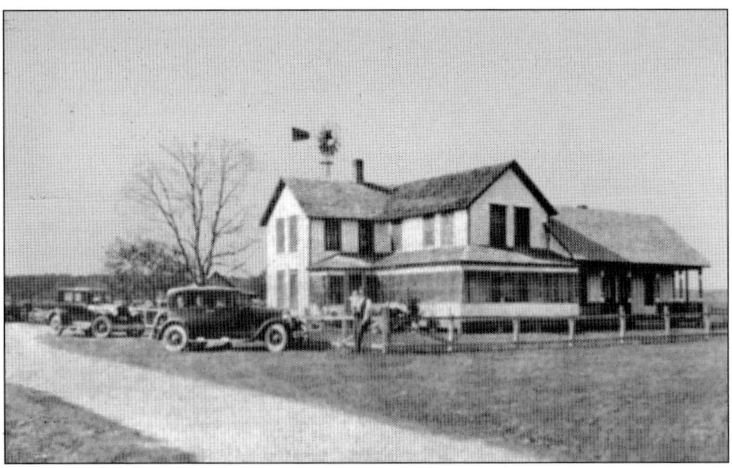

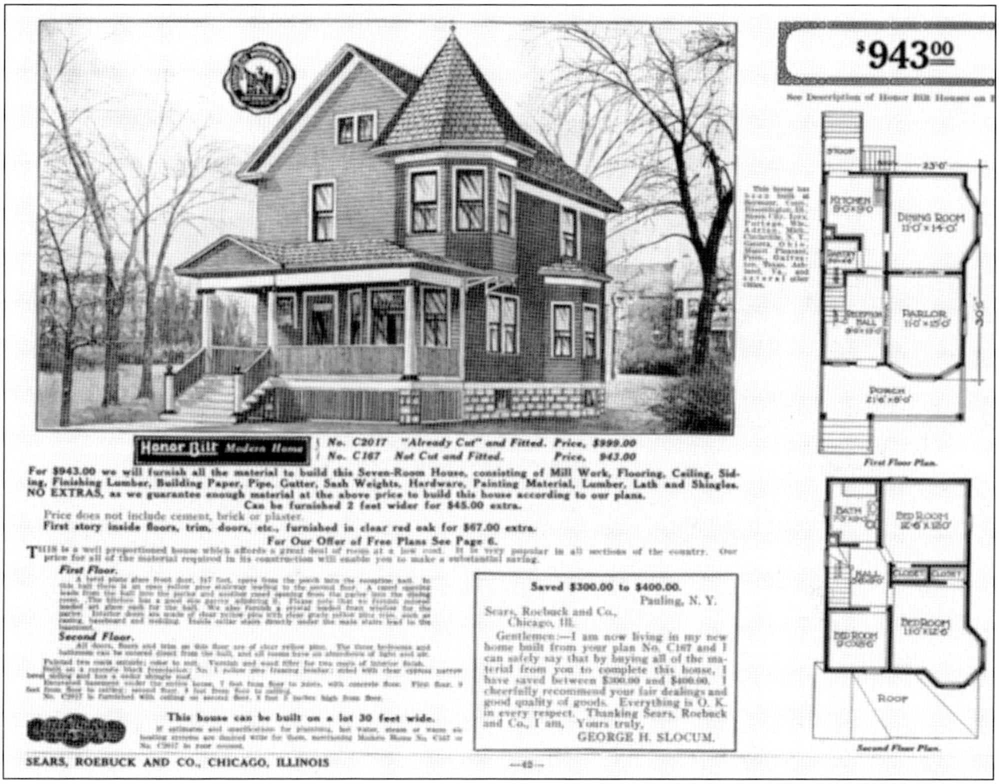

$943.00

Honor Bilt Modern Home — No. C2017 "Already Cut" and Fitted. Price, $999.00 / No. C167 Not Cut and Fitted. Price, 943.00

For $943.00 we will furnish all the material to build this Seven-Room House, consisting of Mill Work, Flooring, Ceiling, Siding, Finishing Lumber, Building Paper, Pipe, Gutter, Sash Weights, Hardware, Painting Material, Lumber, Lath and Shingles. NO EXTRAS, as we guarantee enough material at the above price to build this house according to our plans.

Can be furnished 2 feet wider for $45.00 extra.

Price does not include cement, brick or plaster.

First story inside floors, trim, doors, etc., furnished in clear red oak for $67.00 extra.

For Our Offer of Free Plans See Page 6.

THIS is a well proportioned house which affords a great deal of room at a low cost. It is very popular in all sections of the country. Our price for all of the material required in its construction will enable you to make a substantial saving.

First Floor.

Second Floor.

This house can be built on a lot 30 feet wide.

Saved $300.00 to $400.00.

Pauling, N. Y.

Sears, Roebuck and Co.,
Chicago, Ill.

Gentlemen:—I am now living in my new home built from your plan No. C167 and I can safely say that by buying all of the material from you to complete this house, I have saved between $300.00 and $400.00. I cheerfully recommend your fair dealings and good quality of goods. Everything is O. K. in every respect. Thanking Sears, Roebuck and Co., I am, Yours truly,

GEORGE H. SLOCUM.

SEARS, ROEBUCK AND CO., CHICAGO, ILLINOIS —42—

This is the Elroy and Minnie Cook Home at 1310 Hare-Cook Road. It was a Sears, Roebuck and Company mail-order home. All the construction material was delivered to Crosby by train in 1911. Sears homes were not low-end homes; at the time, Sears used its purchasing power to buy material for less and passed on the savings to the customer. Many of the homes had oak floors, cypress siding, and cedar shingles with fancy trim and upgradable options. Sears sold somewhere between 70,000 and 75,000 of these catalog homes between 1908 and 1940.

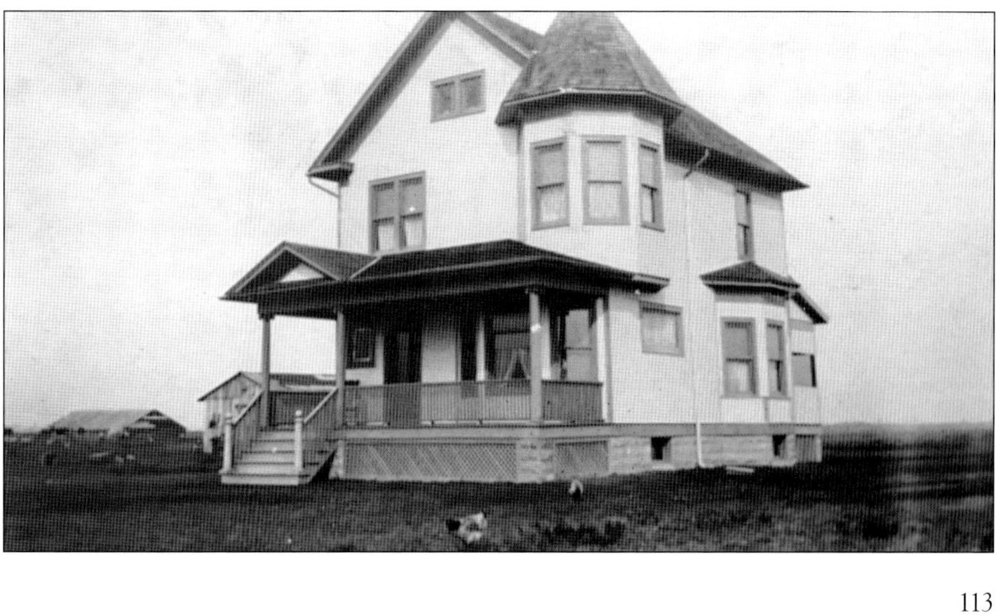

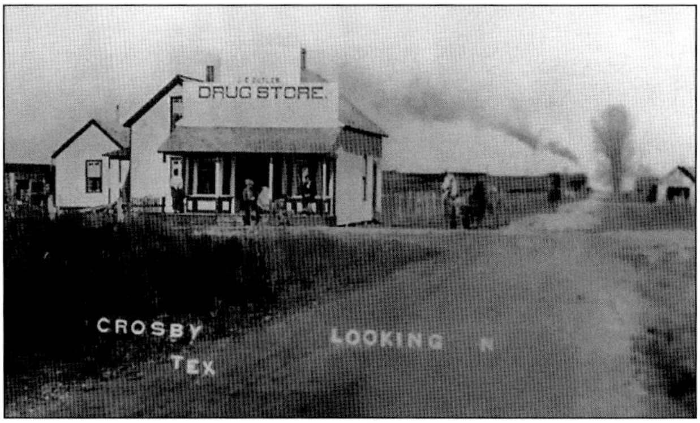

Dr. Cutler's original office was on Main Street between Ramsey's confectionery and the Sirocka Saloon. His home was above his office. That may have been why he relocated here on what is now the northwest corner of Kernohan and First Streets. Behind Dr. Cutler's office is a home that was probably already built when he moved there. (Courtesy of the Duda family.)

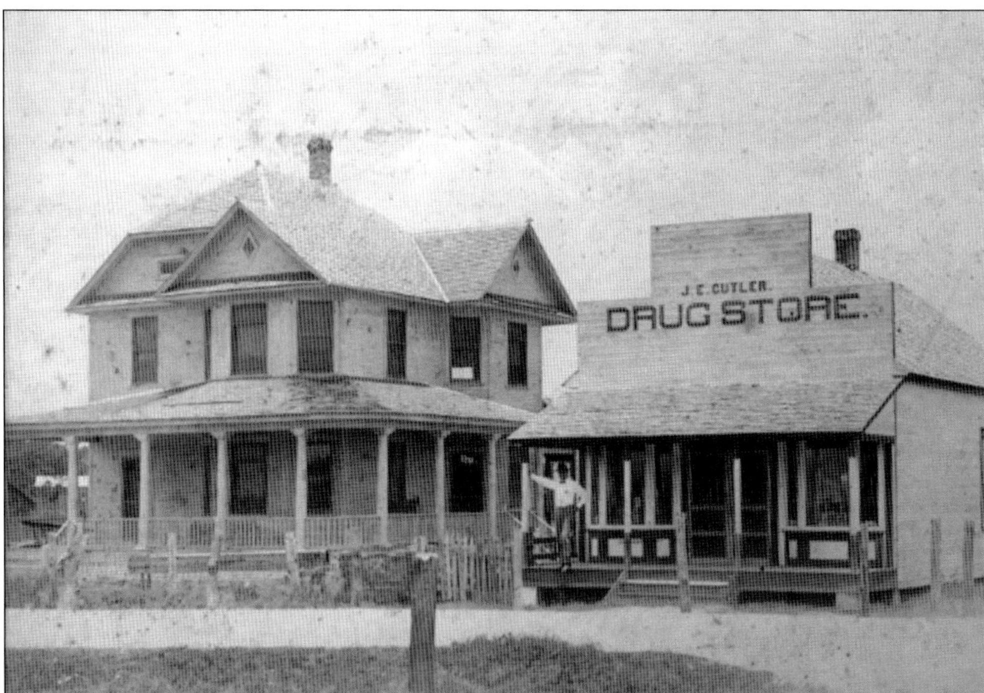

The small building Dr. Cutler used as his office may have earlier been used by the railroad as an engineering office. It was originally at 5623 Main Street. (Courtesy of the Cutler family.)

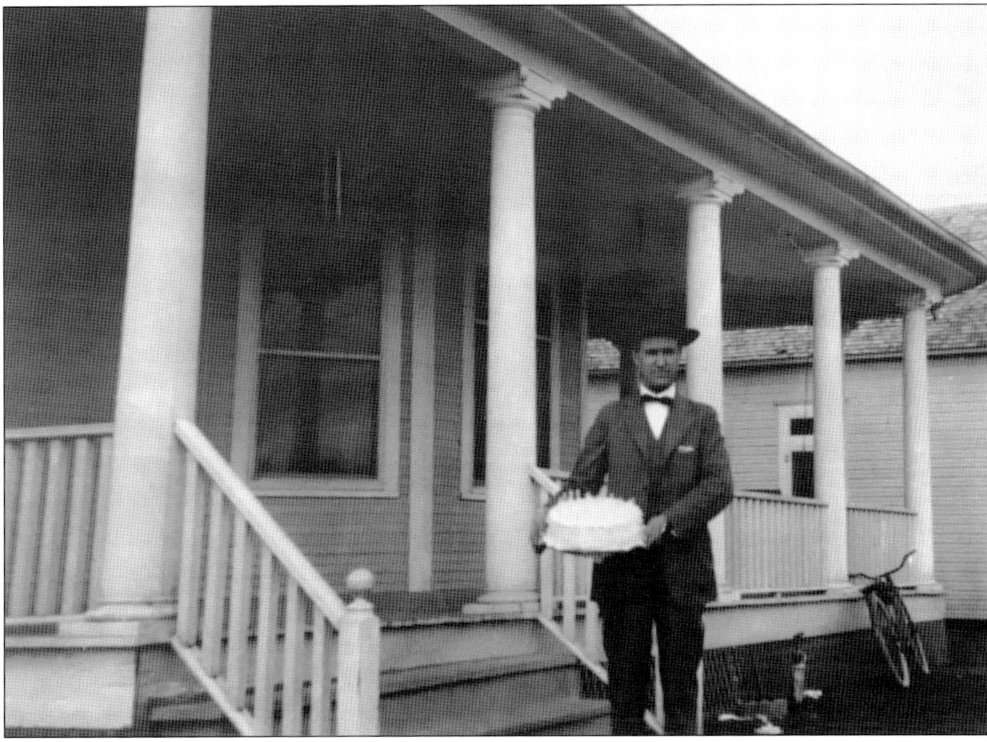

In 1915, after selling the original house that was on the property, Dr. Cutler built one of the nicer homes in Crosby at the same location. It is still located at 423 Kernohan Street. Dr. Cutler opened the first medical practice in Crosby. He delivered most of the babies born in Crosby during a 26-year span. Many were named after him and his wife, Alleen, who served as his nurse. He also served as the Harris County health officer from 1908–1910 and served as the secretary of the local Masonic organization. He had his signature applied to the raised portion on his medicine bottles (pictured below), which were sold in his drugstore. Cutler died in 1929. (Above, courtesy of the Cutler family; below, courtesy of the Duda family.)

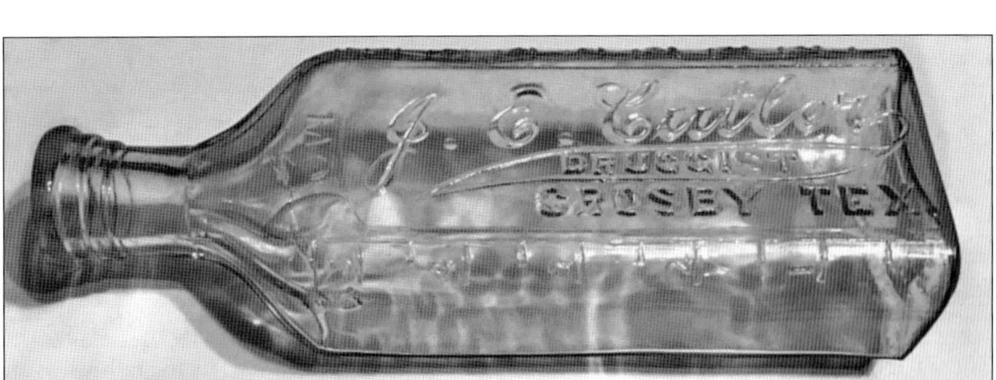

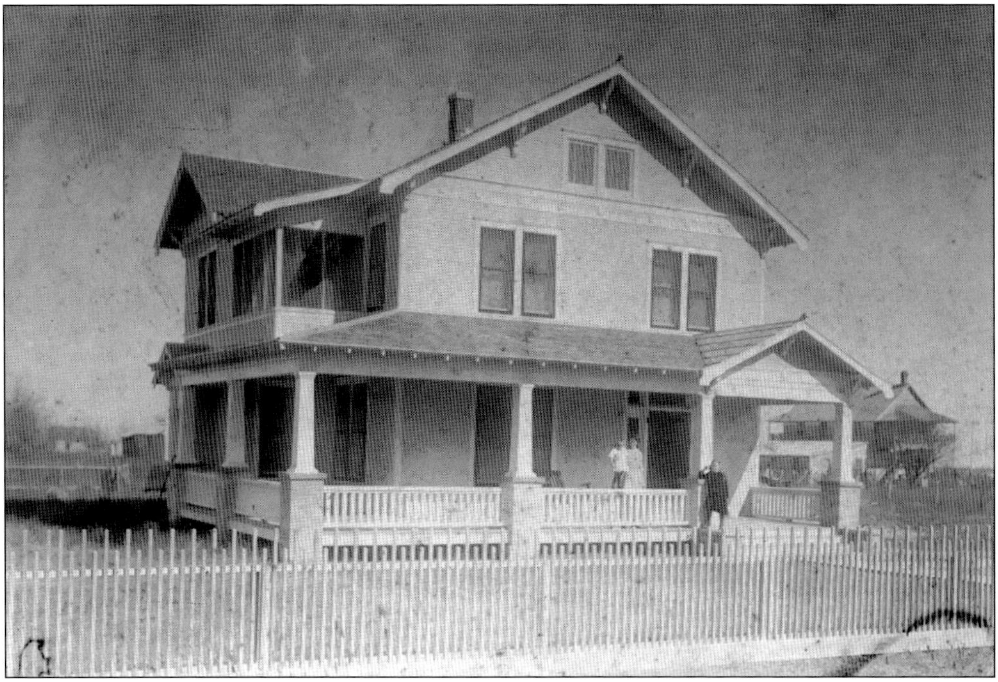

Above is the Theodore and Mary Anderson home, built in 1930 at 503 Kernohan Street on the northeast corner of the intersection with First Street. The Crosby Cash Store is in the background. Below is the David and Hulda Reidland home at 5702 Crosby Dayton Road. The Crosby School is in the background. The photograph was taken in 1913, the same year the house was built. It was bought by R.C.J. Kenning and his wife, Anna, a couple of years later. Both Mary and Anna were daughters of Lars Nelson, who lived across the street. (Both, courtesy of the Barrett family.)

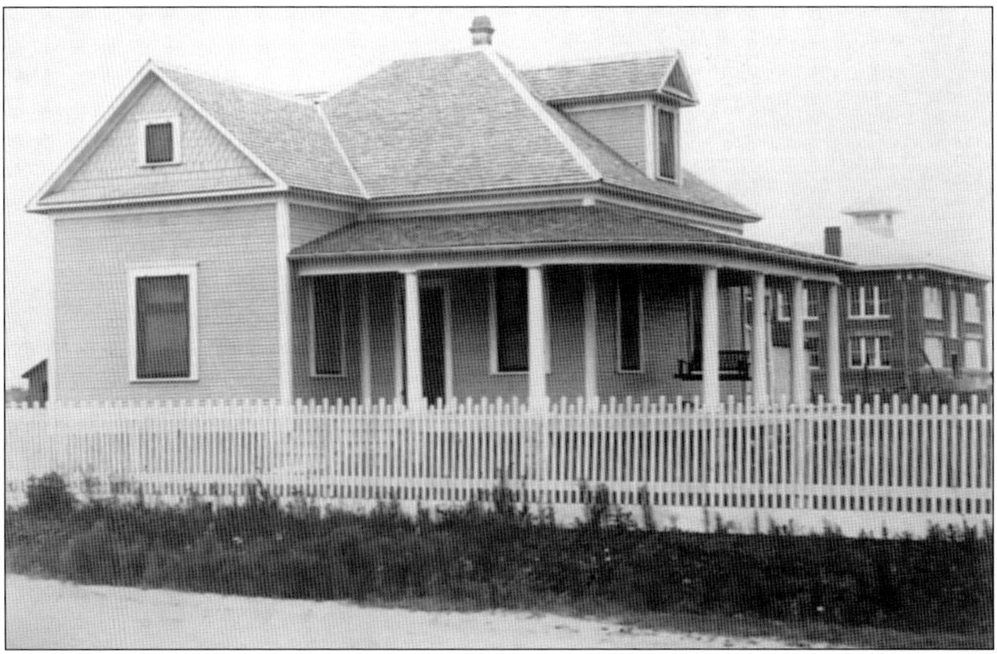

Six

Churches and Schools

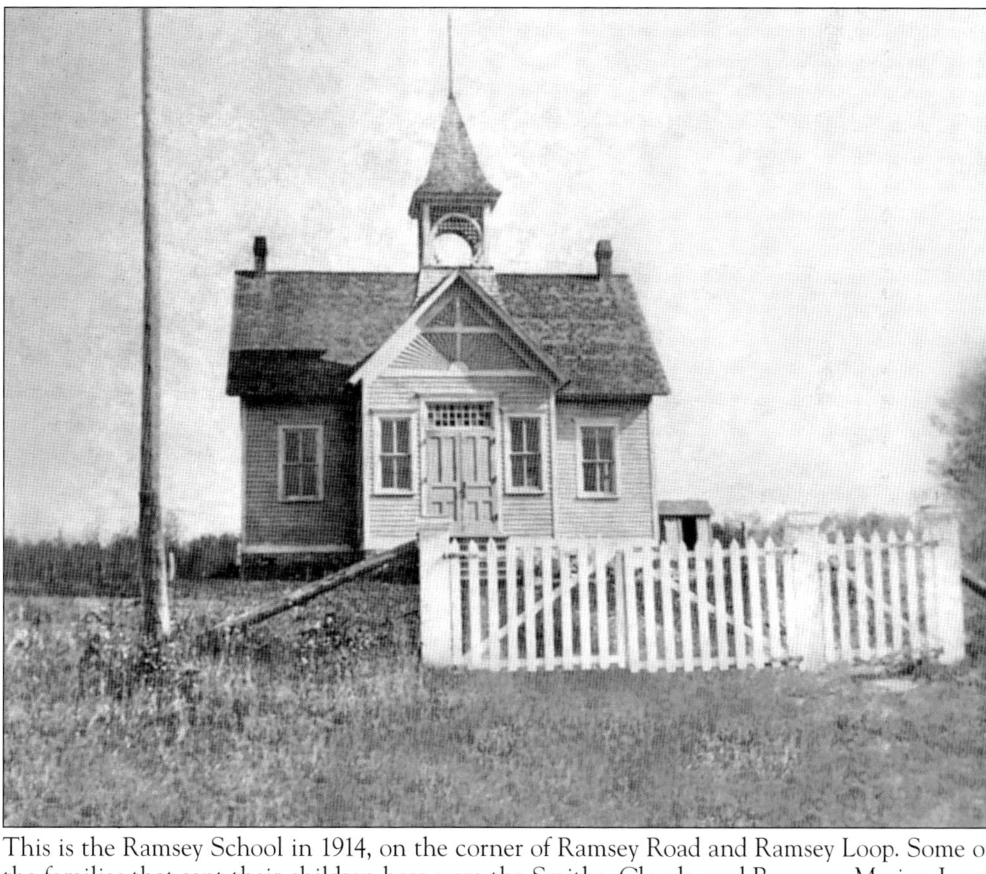

This is the Ramsey School in 1914, on the corner of Ramsey Road and Ramsey Loop. Some of the families that sent their children here were the Smiths, Clouds, and Ramseys. Marion Jones was the school's first teacher. It was closed in 1924 when the district built a new high school and established a centralized grammar school. (Courtesy of the Blomstrom family.)

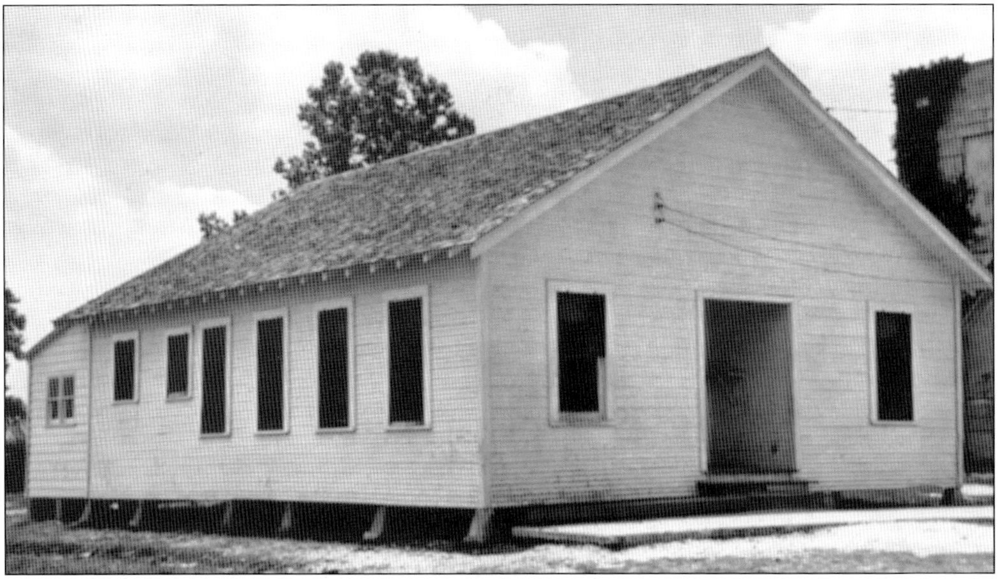

This is the Crosby Township School that was built in 1897. It served as both a school and a church. It was at 602 Kernohan Street. Prior to this, there was a private school in a log cabin on Live Oak Street, built in 1892. Two other Crosby schools were built in the late 1890s. Students at the Crosby Township School filled their water jugs at the Crosby Mercantile Company a block away. Below are students of the Township School in 1909. Beginning in 1929, this building served as the Crosby Church of Christ until 1940, when the Crosby PTA acquired the old building and relocated it next to the 1910 school building and used it as the first school cafeteria. (Both, courtesy of the Swanson family.)

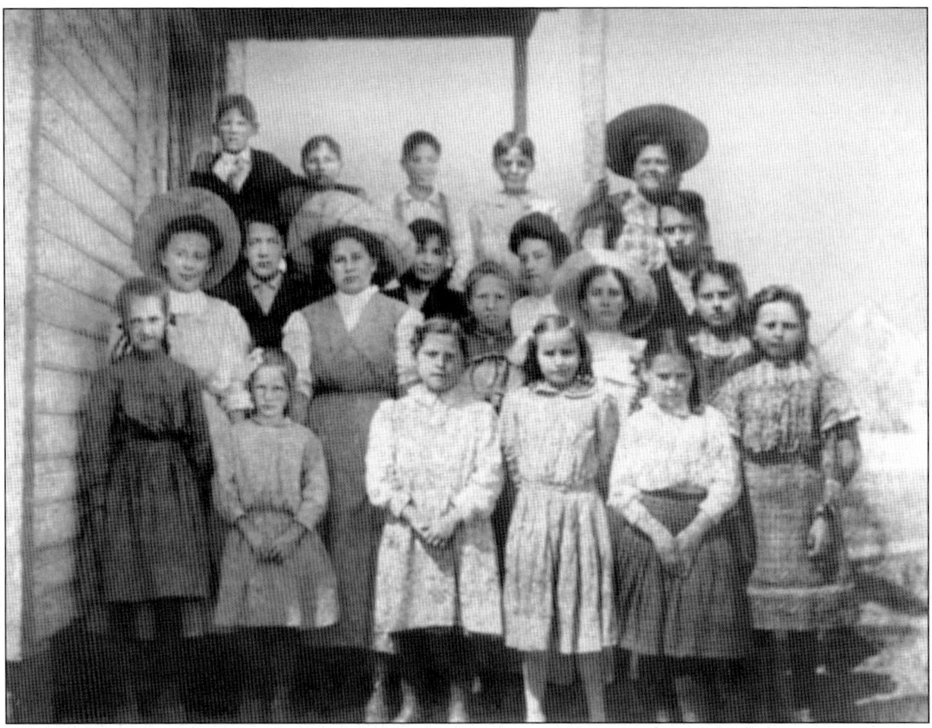

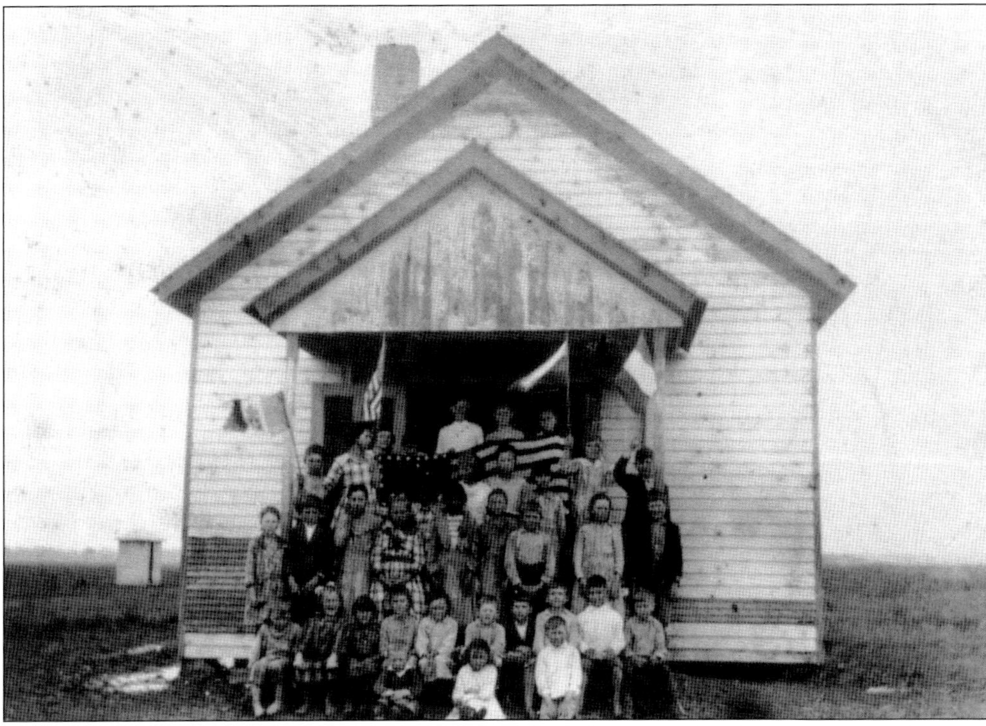

Beginning in 1897, the community built a number of single-room schoolhouses to serve the widespread community. There were 13 different one-room schools in the surrounding area, including Adlong, Barrett, Clawson, Gum Gully, Elena, Friendship, Kenning-Wilson, Krenek, Ramsey, Shiloh, Township, Ulrich, and White Settlement. Above is the Krenek schoolhouse in 1915, at the corner of Krenek and Bohemian Hall Roads. Below is the Krenek schoolhouse in 1924. The teacher was Gladys Beard, and the approximately 40 students were taught in the single classroom. The small building sitting behind the schoolhouse is the lone outhouse that all the students used.

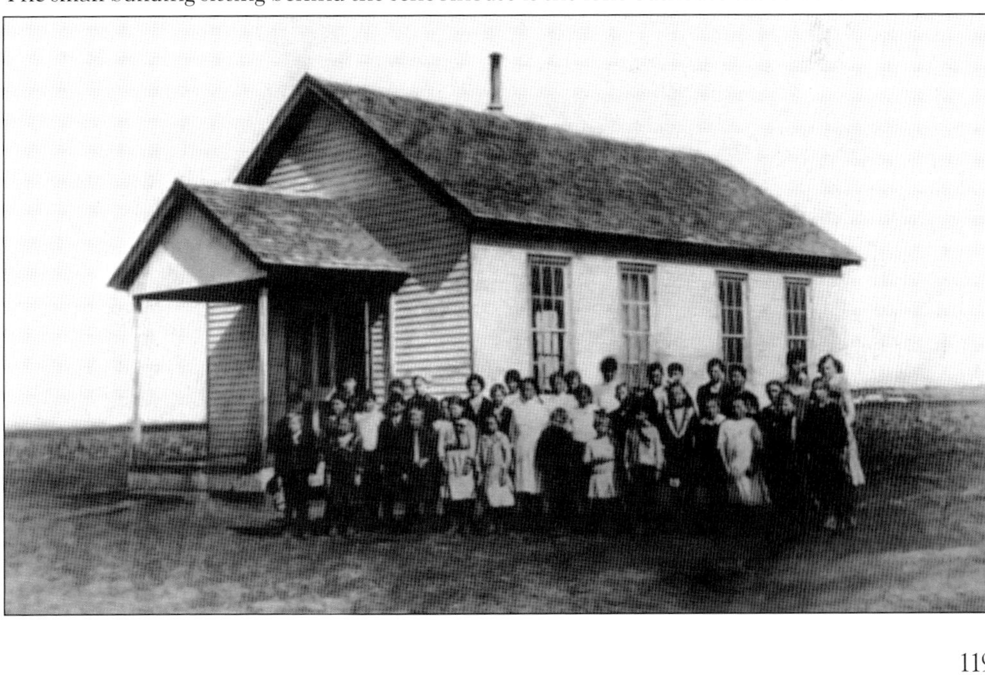

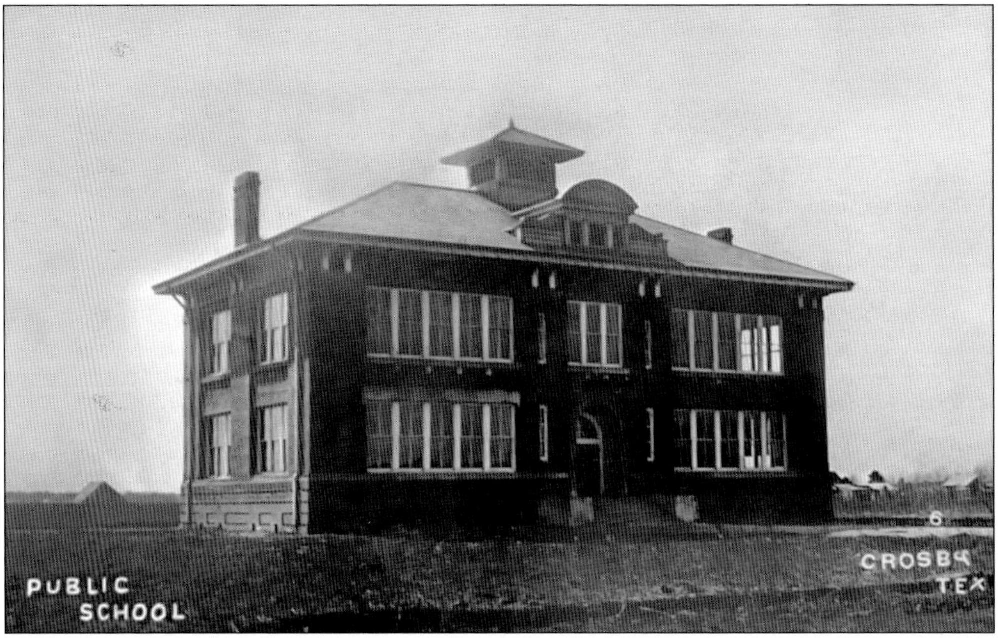

In 1910, Harris County built a centrally located school in Crosby at the corner of Runnerburg Road and Pecan Street, which is pictured here. Crosby residents were very proud of their new $10,000 brick schoolhouse. It was near the 1897 Township School and began offering additional grades. The eight classrooms served students from first grade all the way through high school. However, in the early years, high school stopped at the ninth grade. Over time, it increased to include the 10th grade, then 11th, and finally 12th grade. (Above, courtesy of the Newton family; below, courtesy of the Keller family.)

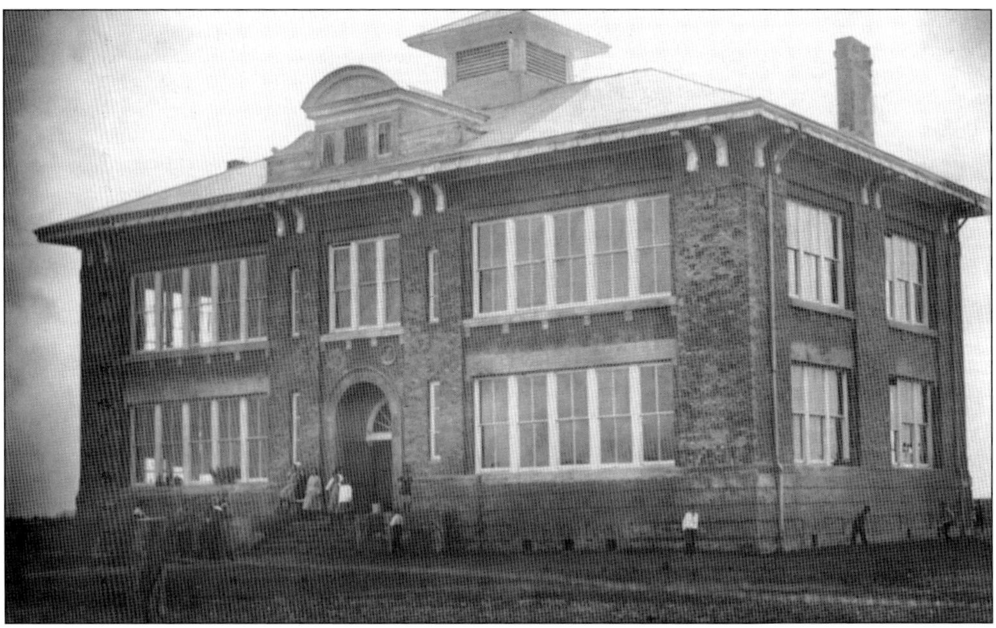

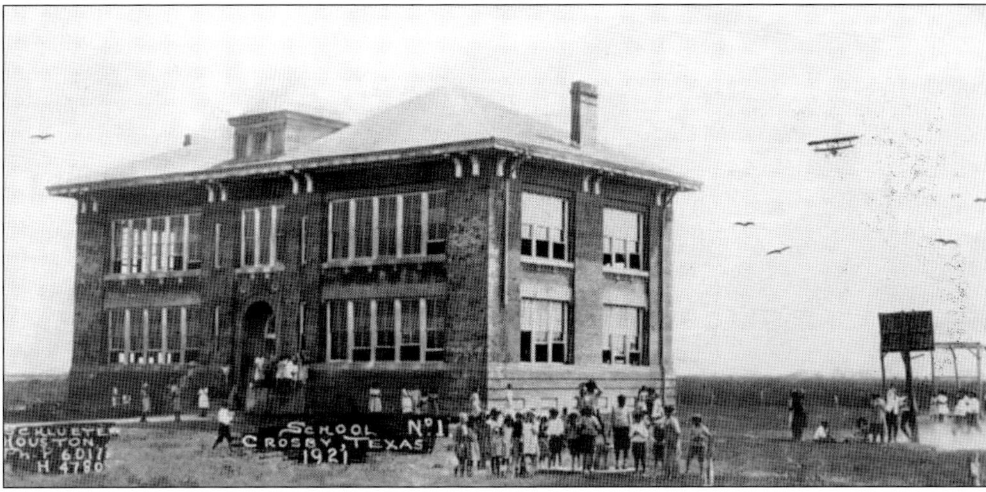

By 1916, the school had installed some fancy new playground equipment, seen to the right above and up close below. This was during the lead-up to World War I, so physical fitness was important to potential young soldiers. Above, a biplane has just taken off from the Crosby airstrip. The Nelson Addition prairie was used as a landing and refueling station for training pilots starting around 1918. The Ellington Air Base used the Fleming barn as a landmark for mock bombing missions and to mark the furthest point of trips. (Both, courtesy of the Reidland family.)

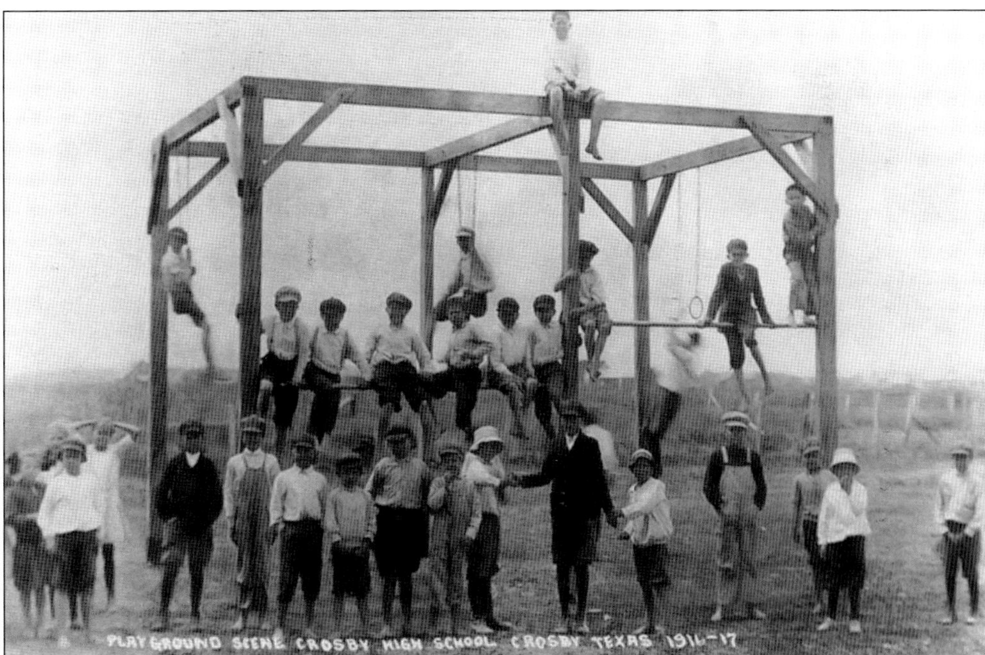

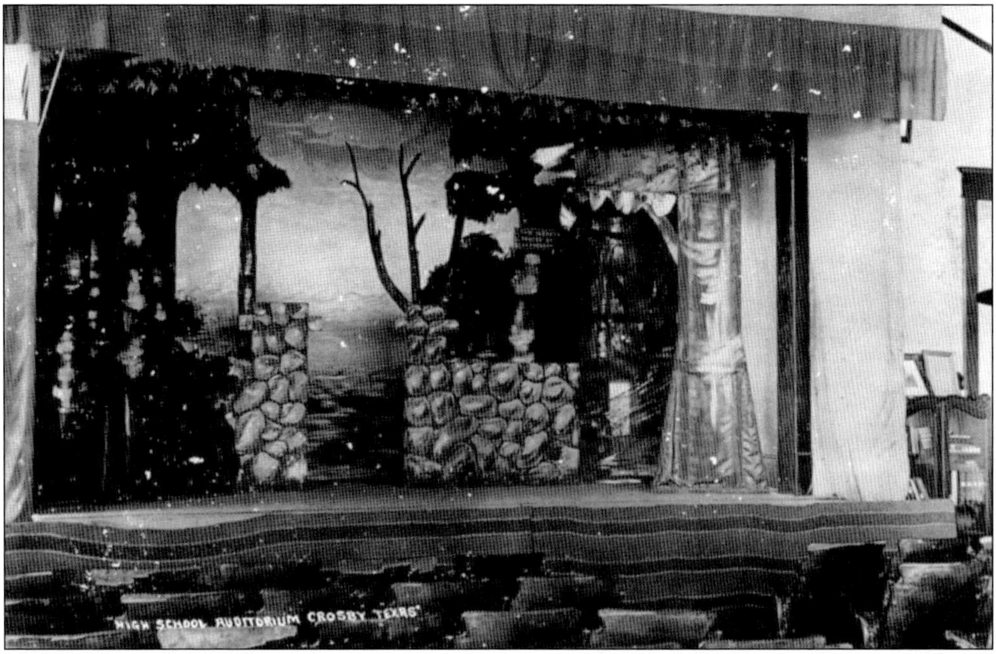

The Crosby School auditorium is pictured above around 1916–1917. The auditorium was used any time the community needed a large space. Both the Swedish community and the Czech congregations held church services in the space. It was also used for community theater productions, political events, and chamber of commerce and community meetings, as well as other types of get-togethers, not to mention school graduations. Crosby had a number of residents who played the piano and various other instruments. Their talents were put to use at the various events at the school, church, and theater, or at picnics. The photograph below is the 1923–1924 seventh-grade class.

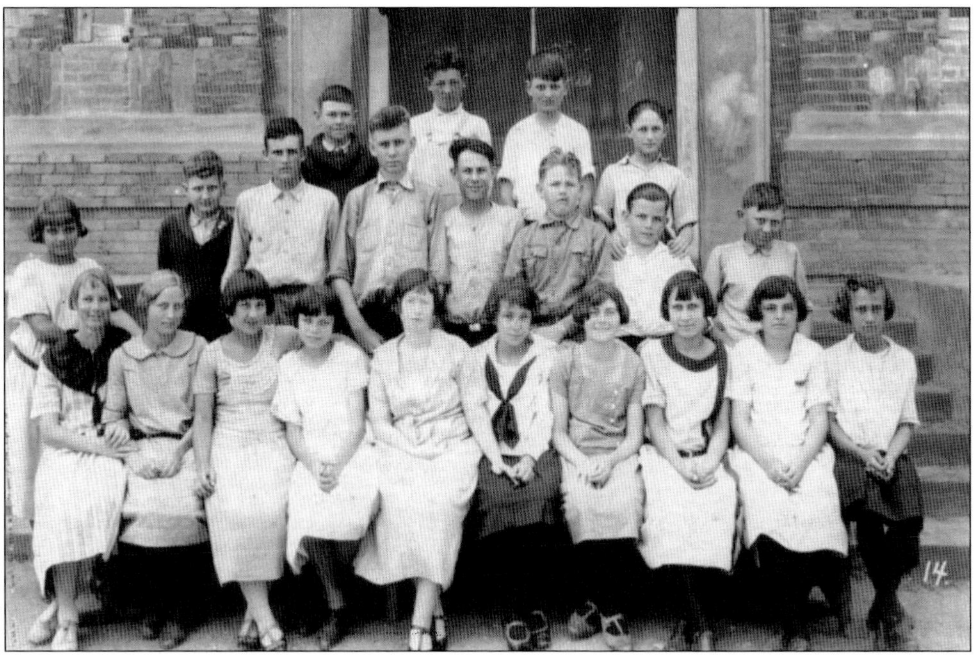

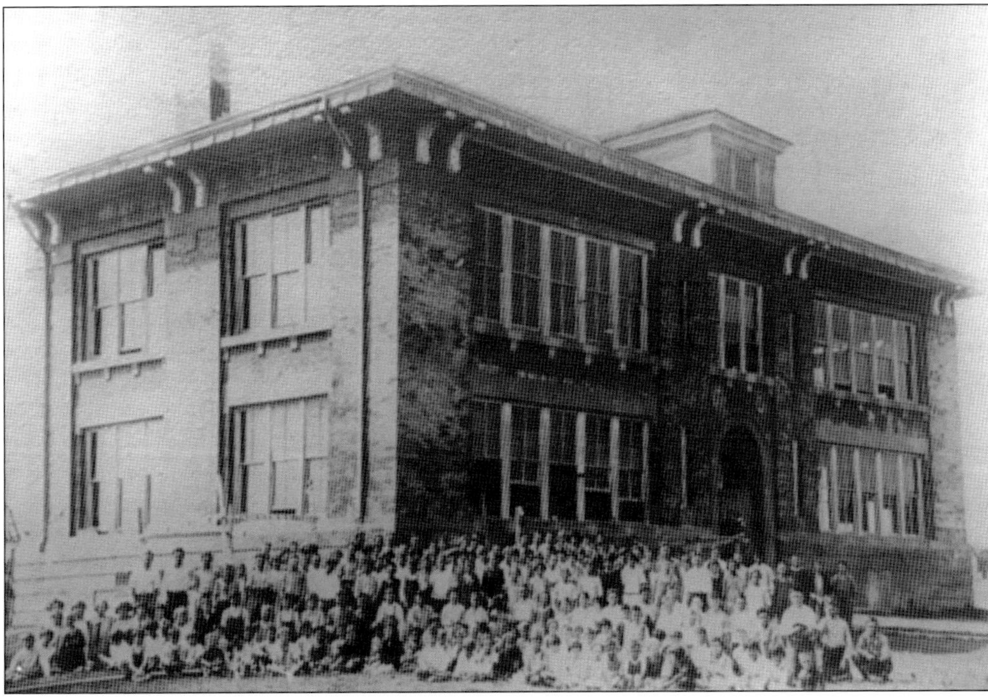

In 1929, the schoolhouse (above) was renovated to look as it appears below. The makeover converted the building into a Spanish Mission–style structure that was popular at the time, which led to its "Alamo" nickname. They removed the pitched roof, added stucco to the brick exterior, and installed a second-floor fire escape slide. In addition, a rear wing was added to the building that housed restrooms with indoor plumbing. Previously, the school used an outhouse behind the building that sat on the banks of Jackson Bayou. Playground equipment (seesaws and swings) were added to the front lawn of the school. (Above, courtesy of the Welch family; below, courtesy of the Swanson family.)

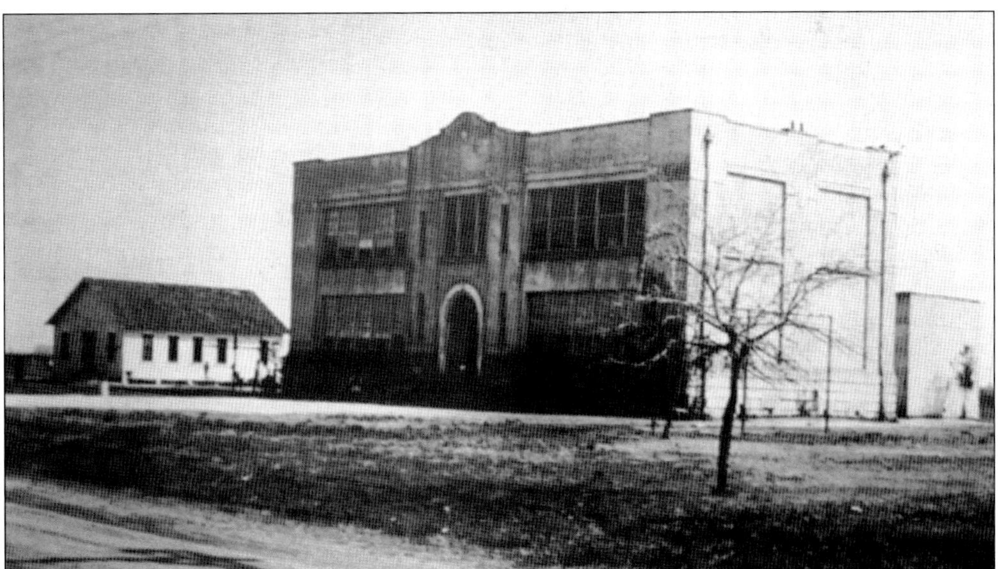

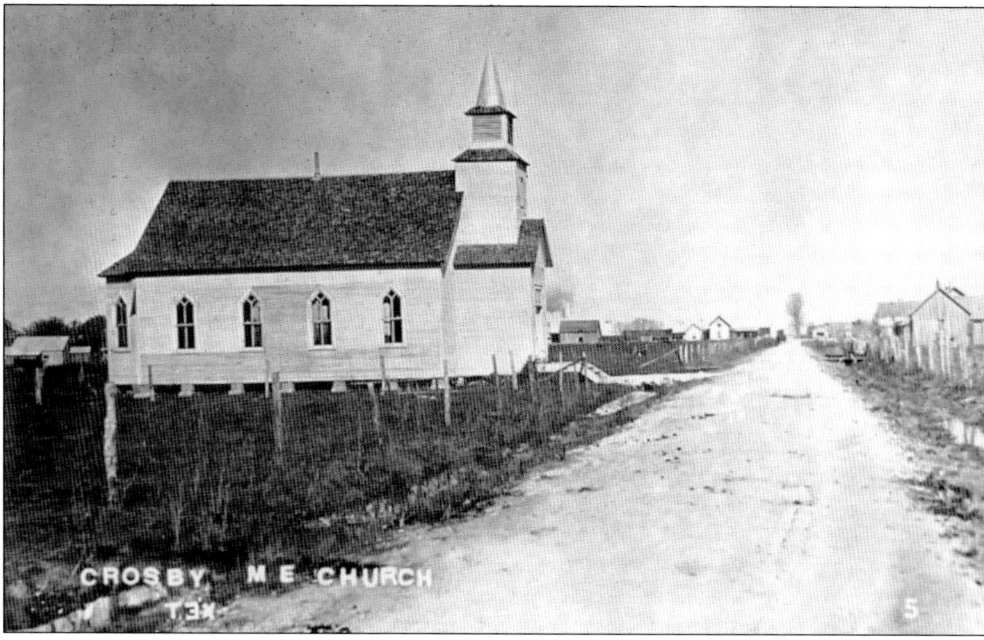

In 1897, several denominations held services at the Township School. The Methodists, Baptists, Mormons, Church of Christ, Presbyterians, and Swedish Mission Friends held services there. The Catholics held Mass in the Martin family home. In 1909, C.A. Gustafson donated land and later loaned money to build the first church building in Crosby, an interdenominational church known as the Union Community Church. The photograph above is from 1911. It was built that same year at what would eventually be the corner of First Street and Reidland Road. Along with the land, Gustafson also donated the pews. Several of the various denominations used the church for services, although some still used the school. The first wedding held in the church was that of Emma Lynch in 1912. (Above, courtesy of the Anderson family; below, courtesy of the Rook family.)

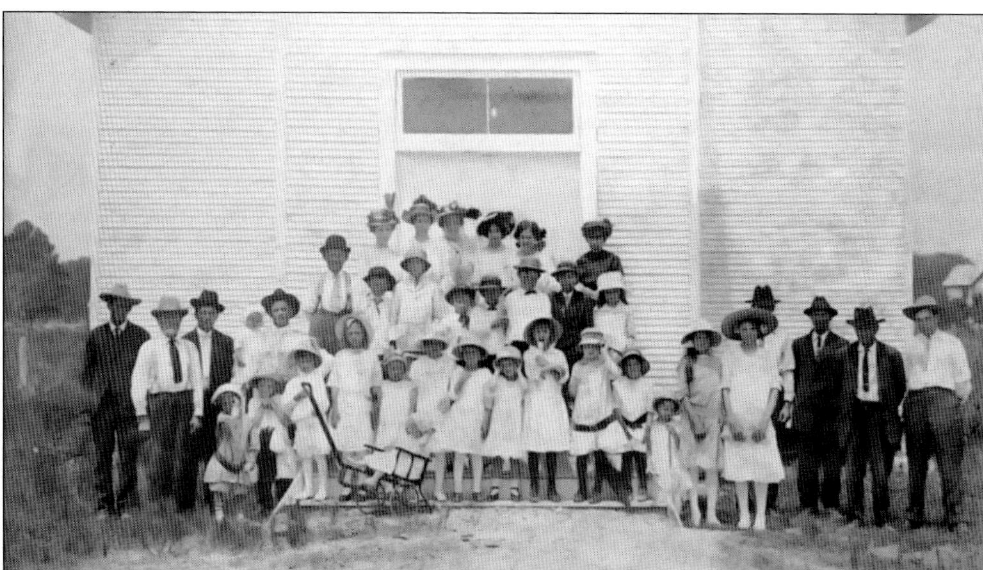

At right is the first church bell in Crosby. It was installed in the Union Community Church in 1913. The women of the church formed the Women's Missionary Society, a very active fundraising group. They helped pay the pastor's salary and furnished the parsonage. They also made money to help equip the church by making quilts and having ice-cream picnics, box suppers, and church bazaars. Today, the bell is at the Crosby Church of Christ. In 1904, residents in the Elias Carson and the Black Hope subdivision of Crosby built the Antioch Baptist Church, pictured below. It was the first building in Crosby erected exclusively for church services. Alex Washington was one of the residents who helped build it. (Right, author photograph; below, courtesy of the Mitchell family.)

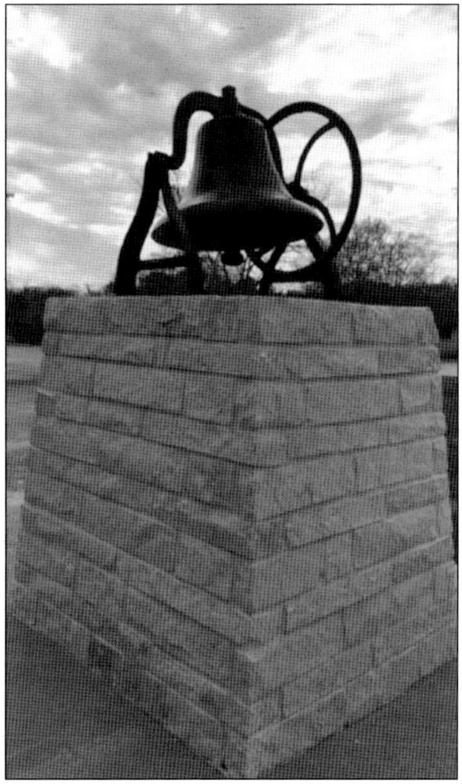

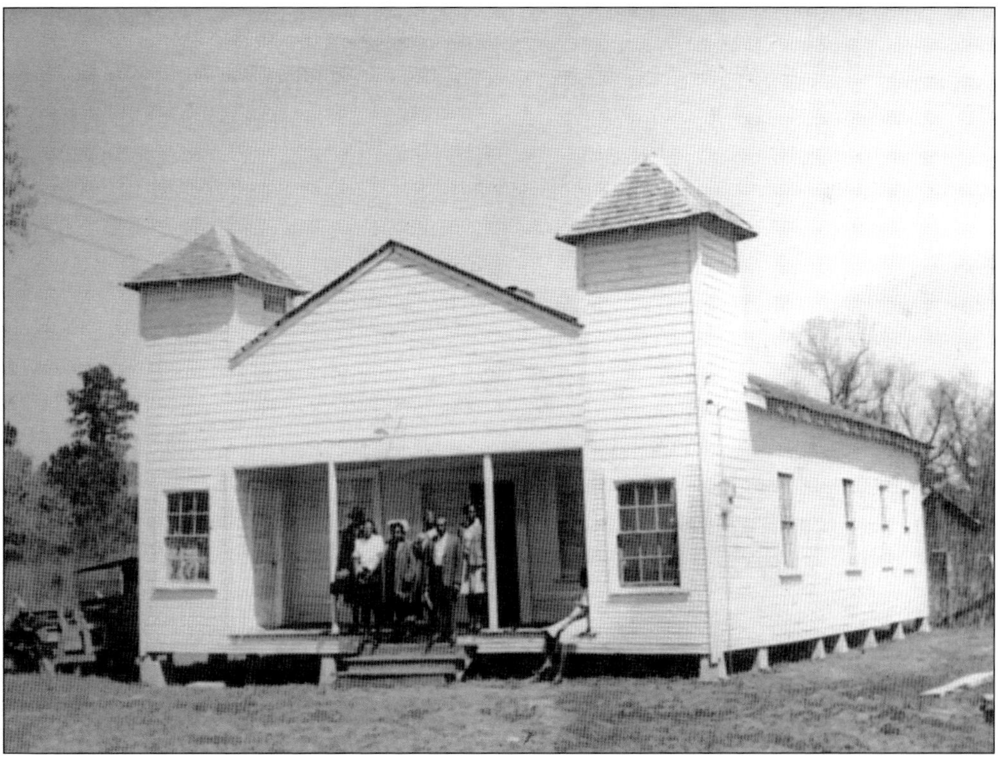

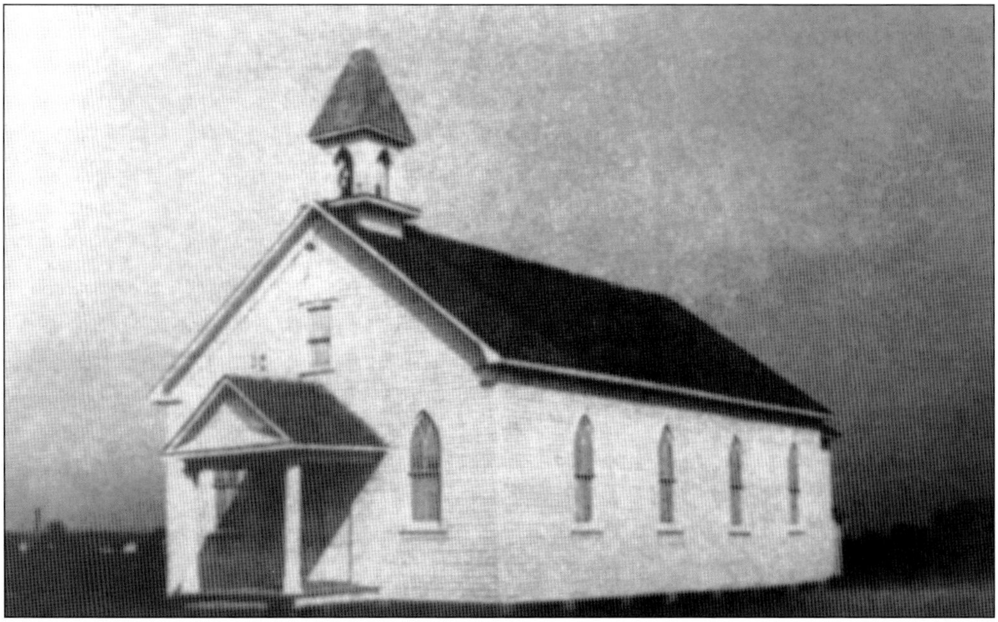

In 1913, Catholic members of the community started construction on a church (above) with the $1,100 that they had raised. Rudolph Lostak was the architect. Other families helped with the construction of the 30- by 60-foot wooden structure. The building was finished in 1914. However, on August 16–17, 1915, a hurricane destroyed it. The church was rebuilt by Joseph Malchar, again with the help of the parishioners. In 1917, the First Baptist Church began with the purchase of the former Joe Harvey garage building in the 600 block of Runneburg Road. In 1923, funds were raised with the help of Dave Reidland to build the First Baptist Church. It is pictured below, with the Catholic church in the background. (Above, courtesy of the Plocheck family; below, courtesy of the Peterson family.)

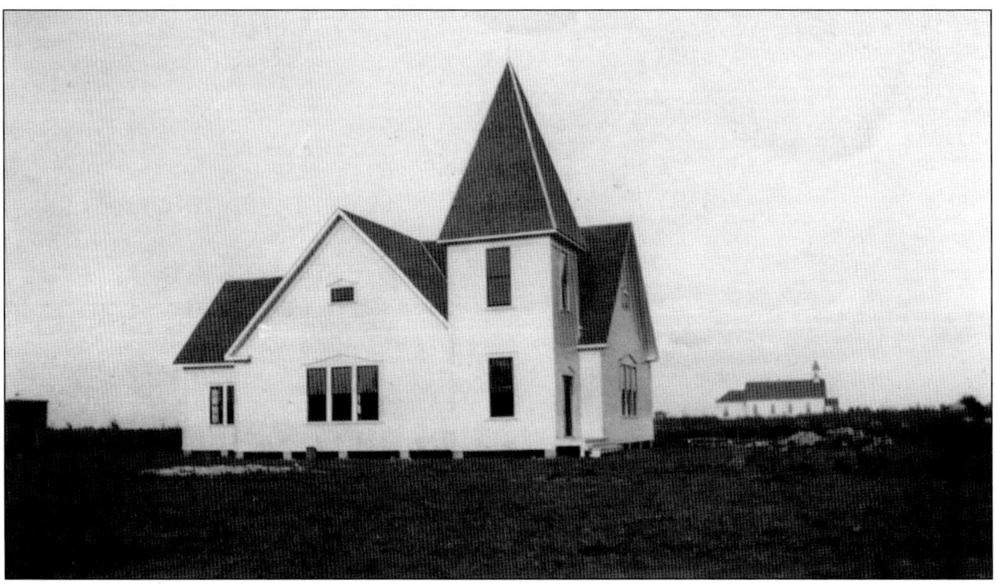

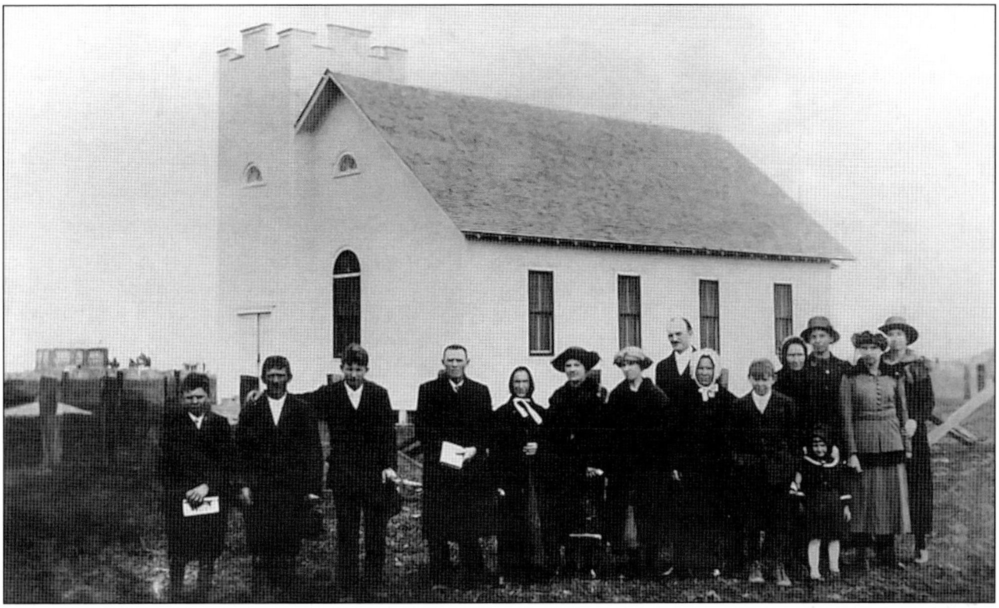

The Bohemian Brethren–Presbyterian Church pictured above was built in November 1921. It was also designed by local architect Rudolph Lostak. The land for the church was purchased in 1917. Some of the land was sold to help pay for the construction. There is some confusion on how the Brethren and Presbyterian congregations were intertwined, but evidently, the two groups joined forces to build the church. The Svoboda, Hlavaty, Danek, and Korinek families were involved in its early development. At some point between 1931 and 1939, the building was remodeled to how it appears below.

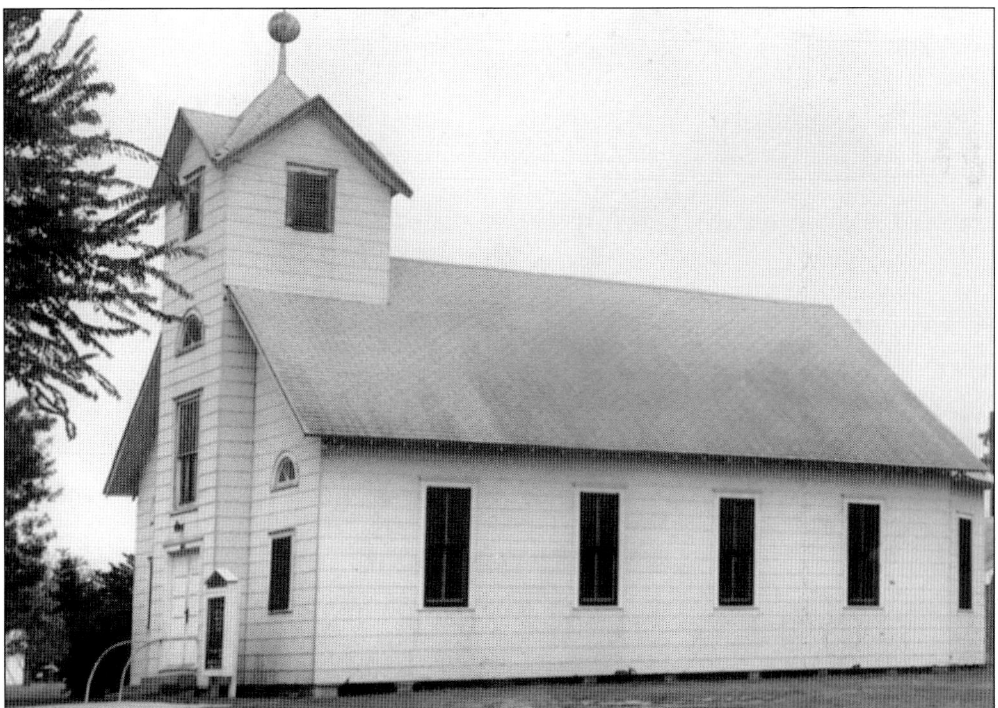